GW00693572

MEMORIES

The Autobiography of Nahum Goldmann

MEMORIES

The Autobiography of Nahum Goldmann

THE STORY OF A LIFELONG BATTLE
BY WORLD JEWRY'S AMBASSADOR AT LARGE

TRANSLATED BY HELEN SEBBA

WEIDENFELD AND NICOLSON
5 Winsley Street London W1

Contents

Sixteen pages of black and white photographs follow page 182

Preface

These memoirs are both more and less than an autobiography —less because they touch only lightly upon my personal life since my public career began, and more because they attempt to analyze and present, in the perspective of that career, the central problems my Jewish generation had to face.

Thanks either to fate or to my own character, I have been actively involved in most of the crucial questions of Jewish life of the last few decades. In this I differ from such Jewish leaders as Chaim Weizmann, David Ben-Gurion, and Moshe Sharett, who concentrated their activity almost exclusively on Zionist and Israeli problems. Therefore, any account of my contribution to the solution of the problems of my generation cannot be separated from an analysis of those problems as I saw them, and for this reason these memoirs make no claim to objectivity. The man who is actively engaged can never be entirely objective. Events and personalities are presented here, to the best of my recollection, as I saw and interpreted them, and the same is true of judgments, which obviously reflect only my own position. This book does not pretend to be an exhaustive treatment of the great Jewish problems of the last fifty years; it is, as I have said, simply an account of my share in their solution.

The reader will find that I cite only the most necessary dates and not too much documentation. I rarely made notes of important conversations, and my accounts of them are drawn largely from memory and may contain their quota of inaccuracies. Having cooperated or fought with most of the leaders and spokesmen of the various Jewish populations of the world, it would have been impossible for me to do justice to, or even to name, them all. Those I mention represent a selection dictated by the course of my narrative. Those I do not mention—and they include some of my oldest, closest, and most intimate colleagues—should not take their omission as an indication of my ingratitude.

In the concluding chapters I turn away from my own activities to talk about my views on some unsolved Jewish and Israeli problems of our time and the solutions I see for them. All these views are personal, some of them are controversial. Perhaps one of the modest achievements of these memoirs may be to encourage a continuing serious discussion of these unsolved problems.

For their work and advice on the manuscript I wish to express my heartfelt thanks to Professor Egon Schwarz of Washington University in St. Louis, my son Guido Goldman, my editor Steven Kroll, my secretary Miss Hella Moritz, and Mrs. Helen Sebba.

NAHUM GOLDMANN

Jerusalem, March 1969

MEMORIES

The Autobiography of Nahum Goldmann

1

Visznevo. Childhood in the Shtetl

Along with many other Jewish leaders, I belong to a generation, the last of its kind, that has played a unique role in Jewish life of the last three decades, a generation rooted in Eastern Europe but educated in the West and combining many features of European culture, Eastern and Western, Jewish and non-Jewish. The most eminent and in a sense the most typical representative of this generation was Chaim Weizmann. It is no accident that its leading members have played a major role in modern Zionism, for one of the characteristics of that movement is that it was based on a synthesis of East and West.

As far as I can tell (the archives of my *shtetl*, or little town, were destroyed in the First World War), I was born on July 10, 1895, in Visznevo, Lithuania. Although I spent no more than my first six years there, I vividly remember those early experiences and have always been aware that the most important influences on the development of my mind and character came from Eastern European Judaism. My parents had left for Germany soon after I was born to start a new life, and I remained in the care of my paternal grandparents. My father studied in Königsberg and Heidelberg but was unable to complete his studies for lack of money. He and my mother finally moved to Frankfurt, and when they were settled, I came to live with them. But those crucial six years of early childhood were dominated by the intimacy of my grandparents' home and by the cultural atmosphere of the Visznevo *shtetl*.

I

My grandfather was a country doctor. He had many children, and since most of the girls were still unmarried when I was a child, they, as aunts, played an important role in my early education. He himself was a robust and simple man, full of sound common sense. My intellectual heritage, however, came from my mother's family. Her father was a rabbi and a *dayyan*, or rabbinical judge, of Vilna, in Lithuania, the most respected Jewish community in the Russian Empire. He was an imposing representative of the great rabbinical tradition who throughout his life had studied nothing but Talmudic literature, while my grandmother provided their livelihood by keeping a little shop.

I remember many family stories about my Vilna grandfather, who, as a *dayyan*, was one of the most respected men in the community. As a mark of reverence for the great eighteenth-century *gaon* of Vilna, no chief rabbi was appointed to succeed him, and in his capacity as a *dayyan*, my grandfather naturally occupied a place of honor in the synagogue. It was told of him that on the high holidays, when many poor people, professional *schnorrers* (beggars), itinerant preachers, and others were relegated to the back benches because the synagogue was so crowded, my grandfather would sit on the very last bench so that no one would feel humiliated or slighted. The way he died was also typical. Having spent his life, year in and year out, in his cramped study, he contracted a lung disease and the doctors recommended a stay in the Crimea. For a long time he resisted making the journey because he would not be able to study on the train, and without the Talmud he could not live. Finally his wife and family persuaded him to undertake the trip, but he died either on the way or immediately after arriving in the Crimea. I knew this grandfather only in the last year of his life, during the few weeks I spent in Vilna on my way to Germany.

As I have said, I grew up in the home of my paternal grandfather, a man with both feet firmly on the ground, who got along splendidly with his peasant patients and was loved by them. As the only grandchild in the home I was spoiled accordingly. My memories of those early years are unclouded by a single unhappy incident, and I attribute much of my self-confidence as an adult, a quality that proved more valuable than

any other in my later political work, to the harmony and serenity of early childhood. Even as a child I showed many of my
later characteristics. I can remember organizing a gang of children and leading them into all kinds of escapades, many, it now
seems to me, not entirely innocuous. But as I recall, I toned
down our worst mischief by assuming the responsibility for it
myself. This, to be sure, involved no heroic sacrifice, because as
the grandson of the only physician in town, who had been
president of the Jewish community for years, I enjoyed a privileged position.

Although I was not a particularly unruly child, I was very
independent and took a certain delight in shocking respectable
citizens. One of my most vivid memories is riding into the
synagogue on the back of my St. Bernard dog one Sabbath
morning. This produced complete panic, when some of the en-
grossed worshipers mistook the harmless animal for a wild beast.
Women up in the gallery fainted; men rushed outside shouting.
But the uproar could not disturb the calm of my St. Bernard,
who ambled through the synagogue and delivered me to my
grandfather's seat in the front row. I survived even this desecra-
tion of the divine service without any particularly harsh
punishment.

In the *shtetl* I had the reputation of being a precocious child.
Because of ill health I rarely attended the *heder*, the elementary
school, and did not really need to because learning came easily
to me, and in a few private lessons I often mastered material that
took my friends eight to ten school lessons. I received my
earliest education from my grandfather and other teachers,
among them the rabbi of the *shtetl*. On the occasion of my bar
mitzvah this rabbi, who had meanwhile emigrated to Israel,
wrote to me of an episode from my childhood that I recount
because it seems characteristic not only of my mentality but
also of the analytical methods of Talmudic discipline. When I
was just over four years old, I took exception to the expression
olim ve-yordim ("ascending and descending") used to describe
the angels in the Biblical account of Jacob's dream. Apparently
I had asked how this could make sense, since logic demanded
that the angels, who dwelt in heaven, must descend before they

could ascend. The rabbi had been troubled by the problem himself, since Scripture can contain nothing illogical. The obvious answer never occurred to him—that *olim ve-yordim* is just an idiom of the kind that every language abounds in and could not be varied to fit the Biblical context.

Without engaging in any extensive psychological analysis, as I look back I can discern many traits in the young child that were to become significant in my more mature years. I realize that I rarely got what I wanted by crying but often by a more subtle stratagem. For instance, for months bedtime presented a serious problem. I loved the evening conversation in my grandparents' home and, like many children, hated having to go to bed long before the grown-ups. After many scenes I finally hit upon an infallible method of getting my own way. Like every religiously brought up child, I had to recite the creed, the *kriath shema*, before going to bed, and I turned this to my advantage by declaring that I would not say my evening prayer until I was actually ready to go to sleep. Furthermore, I had discovered that godliness cannot be imposed; even more important, that a prayer is meaningful only when one says it of one's own free will. The immediate result was that I was allowed to stay up until I announced that I was ready to say my evening prayer. What I had failed to accomplish through recalcitrance, I achieved, so to speak, through politics.

I had the good fortune to be surrounded, in my grandparents' home, during my most impressionable years, by kindness and love. I can hardly say who was gentlest, my grandfather, my grandmother, or the two aunts who cared for me. My trust of other people and my readiness to help them—qualities of maturer years—I attribute to that period when I felt nothing but goodness in my environment. My later self-confidence may also have something to do with the fact that my grandparents, encouraged by the rabbi of the *shtetl*, expected great things of me and devoted themselves to my development. Although the First World War and the upheaval in Russia dispersed the family and they all died before I could see them again, I have always remained aware that the serenity born of the security I enjoyed in those early years has been a blessing through all my later life.

The spiritual climate of Visznevo played no small part in the serenity I knew as a child. Much has been written about the life of Russian Jews in the typical *shtetl;* great writers have immortalized its atmosphere and way of life. It is a mistake, however, to believe, as many people do, that the Jews in the *shtetl* lived a ghetto life or felt like pariahs. This may have been true in the cities of Eastern Europe, where Jews lived as a minority, oppressed and despised, surrounded by a hostile majority. In the *shtetl* the Jew inhabited his own kingdom. He constituted the majority. All around were peasant villages, and the *shtetl* Jew quite justifiably felt superior to their inhabitants. While he was not well-off economically, he was better off than the peasants of Czarist Russia. As a buyer of the peasants' produce, he was in a stronger position than they were, both psychologically and economically (except when there was a pogrom in the making). In his *shtetl* he lived in splendid isolation, and the great non-Jewish world hardly existed for him. He did not enjoy full civil rights, but civil rights meant nothing to him. It mattered little whether he could vote in the Duma elections. To him the problems of Russian imperialism were secondary. He was immersed in his own world, endowed with all the strength and dignity of a great past and a tradition dating back thousands of years. The only problems that had any meaning were the problems of Jewish life, and these absorbed him totally. Who was to be *gabbai* (deacon), who was to be called first or second to the reading of the Torah in the synagogue service—these were the vital areas in which an individual's ambition, vanity, or desire for power and glory expressed itself.

He never doubted the rightness of his world view and possessed the inestimable blessing of religious certainty. He knew the penalty for every offense, the reward for every good deed. Not only did he know what he could expect in his earthly life; he was equally sure of his future in eternity. His seat in Paradise if he lived right, punishment in Hell if he sinned—these were unshakable certainties. He had none of the feelings of the outcast; on the contrary, he compensated for his Diaspora situation by developing an exaggerated sense of superiority. That he belonged to the Chosen People was a self-evident truth. Not only did he live on an intimate family footing with fellow Jews, who were much more to him than members of the same race or religion; he experienced a heartfelt closeness to the past of his people and to his God. When, as a child, he learned about Moses, he saw him not as a mythical figure but as an important though perhaps somewhat distant uncle. When, as a student at the rabbinical academy, the *yeshiva*, he analyzed Rabbi Akiba or Rabbi Judah, he was not an antiquarian studying history so much as a man engaging in a living discussion with an older, wiser relative. This produced an exceedingly warm, intimate atmosphere, though often a certain strained intensity too, when conflicts arose. Since everything was intimate, everything was personal. Differences of opinion were never settled objectively; they were always encumbered by personal feelings.

In all I have touched upon here, one thing is paramount; the warmth and security of my family relationships extended to the life of the *shtetl* where I grew up. I am sure that if my parents had taken me with them to Germany in my first year, I would never have acquired the self-confidence that I never lost again. In Visznevo I took it for granted that I was a Jewish child. No other possibility existed. To be sure, there were the peasant children, but no Jewish child would have wanted in his wildest dreams to be a peasant child. Being Jewish was something one took for granted, like breathing, eating, or saying your prayers. I remember once, when I was playing ball in the street a few weeks after I went to live in Frankfurt, my ball rolled between the wheels of a bicycle. The rider fell off and cursed me, calling me a "dirty Jew." I did not feel the least bit offended and just shouted back: "*Goy!*" To feel insulted at being called a Jew, which would certainly have been the reaction of a German-Jewish child, was totally foreign to me, and at the time I could not understand why this story was told and retold with such astonishment. Today I realize that my reaction was an expression of the sureness of a Jewish consciousness that can spring only from a strong living reality, never from teaching or preaching.

This, then, is what I owe to my childhood years in the *shtetl*. All the disadvantages of such a life—the narrowness, the isolation, the provincialism—I was able to overcome later when I was transplanted into the great world of Western Europe. But I took with me into that world the decisive consciousness of a complete Jewish reality such as only the *shtetl*, never Jewish life in the big cities, could bestow. Lasting as were the impressions of my later years and richly varied as my encounters have been, the primary formative factor in my life was the absence of a Jewish inferiority complex. My parents' decision to leave me with my grandparents in Visznevo was one of the most important things they did for me.

When I was almost six, my father and mother had established themselves in Frankfurt and decided that it was time for me to join them and take advantage of wider educational opportunities. My mother came to Visznevo to take me back. The journey was long. To start with, we traveled by horse-drawn cart to Smorgon, where I saw my first railroad. It was evening, and the locomotive, with its great lights, rolling to a stop, created an impression I have always remembered. It was not frightening; I have dreamed of it often since but never as a nightmare. I was glad to see it coming and felt that it was going to take me into the world.

It seems worth noting that something that frightens many children was for me a good, almost blissful, experience. Since I have been able to shape my own life, the one thing I have striven for above all has been to seek out the positive element in every experience. The effect an event or a fact produces on us is at least partly determined by our own reaction. The capacity to react positively is one of the decisive prerequisites for a happy, constructive life. We cannot always succeed in transforming negative facts, but an unremitting, ever intensified attempt to do so should be a guideline for anybody who wants to shape life rather than merely to accept it.

From Smorgon my mother took me to Vilna for a few weeks. I recall little of this spiritual and intellectual center of Lithuanian Jewry and have only vague memories of my grandparents, the frail, but extraordinarily impressive figure of my grandfather, the Talmudist, and his very down-to-earth, practical wife. Much later, at a more mature age, I was able to appreciate the architecture of the city, of which I received only a rather blurred first impression. Far more vivid in my memory is the jump-rope a friend of my mother's gave me. I romped through the park with it for hours.

In Warsaw, our next stop, we also spent several weeks. There I got to know the family of my uncle Szalkowitz, my father's brother, an eminent Hebrew publisher and a gifted writer. They, and another related family named Gordon, whose head was also a Hebrew writer and educator, are the only relatives I have remained in touch with all my life and who for me embody the essence of family. In many ways the children of these two families, who now live in Israel, have been to me what brothers and sisters are to other people.

In the spring or early summer of 1900 I arrived in Frankfurt and a world completely new to me. Yet I cannot recall that being transplanted into this utterly different environment produced any feeling of shock or strangeness. I always had a natural faculty for settling down quickly; in a way I am at home everywhere. If it had not been for this trait I could never have endured, without severe physical and mental strain, the life I was later forced to lead, with its endless traveling and commitments in many different countries and continents. I think this adaptability is also chiefly responsible for my basic feeling of security as a human being and as a Jew, of which I have already spoken. Only the man who has no firm roots is easily uprooted by a change of circumstances. The man who possesses such roots and takes them with him wherever he goes can always sink them into new ground.

It was easy for me to take root quickly in Frankfurt, partly because I found in my parents' home the same warm atmosphere I had known at my grandparents' (although the family was much smaller) and also because my parents had a circle of friends, who were mostly Russian Jews. Somehow I recaptured something of the world I had left. I very soon realized, though with more curiosity than shock, that outside my parents' home there was a foreign world inhabited by other kinds of Jews and—preponderantly—by non-Jews.

I have never been subject to the Jewish fear of the dominance of the non-Jewish world. In later years I had dealings with eminent leaders of non-Jewish peoples and countries. Often I confronted these men, who represented great powers, as the spokesman of a powerless people. Although I was always conscious of the power discrepancy, I cannot remember any encounter, whether with Mussolini or Prince Regent Paul, with General Gamelin, the French Chief of Staff, or with American presidents or British foreign ministers, when I had the least feeling of inferiority. I recognized that they were different, and in most cases more powerful, but never that they were superior.

I suppose this is why I escaped the kind of psychological crisis that a sudden change of environment can produce in a sensitive child. My strongest feeling, if I remember correctly, was the desire for knowledge. I saw strange new people, strange buildings, strange ways of life, and I wanted to get to know and understand them. During those years and later I often thought of Visznevo with pleasure and affection but never with any distressing homesickness. I had been happy there, but from the very first I felt quite at home in Frankfurt, the city where I spent my first school years.

2

Home and School Life in Frankfurt

Frankfurt became my second home. I lived there from the time I was six until I was eighteen and returned frequently as long as my parents were alive. There I completed *Gymnasium* and laid the foundations of my general education. There too I made my first attempts at writing, delivered my first speeches, and began to participate in Jewish public life. It was no less my home town than Visznevo—and as far as my conscious response to intellectual stimuli was concerned, it played an even more important role.

The center of my life was, of course, our home. In addition to the blessing of a harmonious childhood I was granted a serene boyhood. I can scarcely remember relations between my parents and myself being seriously strained. From them I inherited important traditions and attitudes to life that I adapted but carried on in all their essentials. As long as they lived, my parents were gratified by what I was doing and by my career as it took shape, and the higher expectations inevitably attached to an only child were in no way disappointed.

They were very different from one another. My father, a yielding, kindhearted, idealistic man, was imposing in appearance—what used to be called "a fine figure of a man." As a teacher and writer, he was always dedicated to a cause, to an ideal, to any opportunity of helping, and earning a living and practicing a profession were for him unavoidable but by no means agreeable necessities. Although we were not badly off he rarely earned more than we needed at any particular time. It was a great satisfaction to me to be able to relieve him of all material responsibilities in his later years, after my mother's death.

Born in Russia into a family of Hebrew educators and teachers, my father attended the Talmud Torah briefly before going on to the universities of Königsberg and Heidelberg. All his life he taught Hebrew in Frankfurt (for many years at a training college for Hebrew teachers for the colonies maintained by the Jewish Colonization Association in Palestine and Argentina), but he was also a writer and editor of the *Israelitisches Familienblatt*. He had been a Zionist from the start and belonged to the small circle around Ahad Ha-Am, who founded the Bnei Mosheh group famous in the early history of Zionism. He was active in the movement as long as he lived and was a delegate to several of the early Zionist congresses. In addition to writing, he devoted much of his time to welfare work and to helping others. When I was a boy, the Jewish community of Frankfurt included many very rich philanthropists to whom Jewish students from Eastern Europe wanting to study in Germany or Switzerland would apply for assistance. Many of these philanthropists had come to have confidence in my father and allowed him to award their stipends. As a result, our house was always full of young Jewish students. Among them were many who later became famous in Jewish life, such as Jacob Klatzkin, Mosheh Glickson, and S. M. Melamed.

My father observed the traditional Jewish way of life, less out of religious conviction than out of a wish to preserve Jewishness as something distinct. He used to say that *kashruth*, the dietary laws, would no longer be necessary once the Jews had attained their own state in Palestine; in the Diaspora, Jews were forced to observe the old customs to guard against the danger of assimilation. But on this and many other questions he was tolerant and never tried to force me to observe rites I rejected. He was a gifted stylist and a competent writer, as much at home in Hebrew as in German and combining a great wealth of Jewish knowledge with a great familiarity with Western European, especially German, philosophy. He was greatly beloved and radiated generosity, always helping other people, raising money for them, securing fair treatment from the police, and so on. He played a respected role in the Jewish life of Frankfurt, and although he was not cut out to be a leader and disliked being involved in conflict, he was unshakable in his convictions, which often forced him to take a journalistic stand against ideas and trends he thought harmful and dangerous. He had a strong influence on my development, not so much through what he said as through his personality. His example taught me that however indispensable ideas and convictions may be, human relationships are just as important, that the elementary virtues of kindness and helpfulness are more creative than fanaticism and ideological aggressiveness. To him more than anybody else I owe my introduction to the world of Judaism. I can hardly say, for instance, when I became a Zionist. Even as a child I was a Zionist without knowing it, inasmuch as I took over my father's concepts and his positive attitude to everything Jewish as axioms of my heritage.

My mother's personality was quite different. By inclination she was an intellectual who lacked sufficient opportunity to satisfy an unquenchable thirst for knowledge. She told me that when she was growing up in her father's home in Vilna, where modern literature was banned as irreligious and non-Jewish, she used to stay awake most of the night in her room reading German and Russian literature. She learned Hebrew, which was unusual in those days, when the girls in Orthodox families received hardly any education. Her outstanding characteristic was her tremendous will power; she was one of the strongest-willed people I have ever encountered.

While love bound me to my father, my relationship to my mother was based chiefly on respect and admiration. Although she rarely punished me, I was always in awe of her, an awe that sometimes became fear. There were a lot of things I could have confessed to my father but never to my mother. She was extremely puritanical, set up very rigorous standards in everything, and insisted they be maintained. Knowledge and ideas were more important to her than people. She used every free hour to attend lectures, and since we lived modestly and had little help, it was often very hard for her to combine her house-holds duties with her irregular but continuing studies.

To me at least she seemed very ambitious, not so much ma-terially as intellectually. She would never have entertained for a moment the idea of my going into business and took it for granted that I would become a scholar, a professor, or a public figure. She supervised my education very carefully, and since as a child I was completely unambitious, getting on the honor roll at school seemed to me mainly an obligation I owed to her. Physically she was frail, and her relatively early death may have had something to do with the fact that her approach to life was often in conflict with her own nature. An atmosphere of tension surrounded her constantly; she hardly ever relaxed. Everything had to serve a purpose; life consisted exclusively of responsibili-ties and challenges. I had always hoped that in old age she would begin to enjoy life more, but my wish to make things easier for her was not fulfilled. She died before I was able to do anything.

Two such dissimilar characters were bound to clash at times, but conflicts were rare, since my mother's stronger will always enabled her to get her way. I owe much to both my parents, and even after I left home I kept close ties with both of them, never marred by misunderstandings.

Although we were a small family, the house was always full. Young men, distant relatives, or the children of Russian friends, used to board with us, so I did not grow up as isolated as most only children. The students who received their scholarships through my father would regularly come to Frankfurt during the university vacations and more or less move in with us, partly to save money, partly out of affection for my father. Our house became the natural center for Eastern European Jews in Frankfurt. In addition, my father was at that time one of the most active workers in the Frankfurt Zionist movement. Some-times I even resented the constant presence of people because they interfered with my voracious reading, but, of course, my mother always saw to it that I had a room where I could be alone.

Among my parents' friends I made contacts and friendships that lasted for many years, and several of them played a significant part in my intellectual development. The most important was with Jacob Klatzkin, who was several years my senior. When I first made his acquaintance I was a child and he a first-year university student, so our real intellectual exchange did not begin until much later. Nonetheless, even as a child I belonged in a way to his circle of friends. When I was only ten or twelve, I participated in their debates with all the vehemence and self-confidence of immaturity, and they never talked down to me. In conversation they took me seriously, particularly later when I began to speak in public.

Of all the friends I have had in my life, Klatzkin probably influenced me most profoundly. He was a fascinating man, a most unusual mixture of Eastern European Jewish intellect and Western European thought. Except for one or two great Jewish scholars, I have never known anyone with such an extraordinary memory, yet this faculty for remembering everything he had ever read or experienced was combined with an analytical sharpness that was the product of centuries of intellectual breeding and undoubtedly would have made him a foremost rabbinical authority had he stayed in Eastern Europe and remained an Orthodox Jew. (His father had been a great Talmudic scholar in Poland.) These brilliant qualities were complemented, as very rarely happens, by great artistic sensitivity, and Klatzkin was undoubtedly the greatest enricher of the Hebrew language in the field of philosophy in the past hundred years. He is responsible for much of the philosophical terminology in modern Hebrew. Bialik often used to say that Jacob Klatzkin was one of the three greatest Hebraists of our time. His talent for stylization and formulation, as strong in Hebrew as in German, was fascinating, although, like all great gifts, it was not without its dangers. He was such a stylist that he often tended to be carried away by language.

Klatzkin was one of the ideologists of the Zionist movement. Although I could never accept his ideas—my dispute with him lasted thirty years and ended only with his death—I was always deeply impressed, especially during my early years, by his way of looking at problems, his extraordinary intellectual honesty, his delight in paradox, his contempt for public opinion, and his courage in living his own life. He also had a strong influence on my practical career. It was his initiative, far more than mine, that led to the founding of the *Encyclopaedia Judaica* and the Eschkol publishing company, with which I was connected for so many years.

I would like to mention briefly several other men I got to know in my parents' home. I was much impressed by Mosheh Glickson, later chief editor of the Israeli newspaper *Ha-Aretz* and one of the ideological leaders of General Zionism in Palestine, a quiet, kindly man of moral integrity whom everyone admired. He too was a great connoisseur of Jewish literature and modern philosophy and I often collaborated with him in later years.

Unquestionably one of the most curious and picturesque figures of the previous generation in Jewish arts and letters was S. M. Melamed. This half-starved son of a brutal Jewish butcher ran away at the age of fifteen and came to Frankfurt, where he became one of my father's protégés. If we can define a journalist as somebody who grasps things quickly though perhaps superficially, then Melamed was the most brilliant journalist I have ever known. In a manner I have never encountered in anyone else, he applied his journalistic technique to the most abstruse philosophical problems and wrote prize-winning philosophical books without ever having studied philosophy properly. He possessed the uncanny gift of leafing through a difficult philosophical work in a few hours and then writing a stimulating article on its thesis. He studied Hermann Cohen's difficult Neo-Kantian philosophy in this way, and his brilliant articles induced Cohen, who was a merciless critic, to express his admiration in a letter to Melamed's editor. Later Melamed admitted to me that he had never read any of Cohen's books through; his series of articles was based on a study of their table of contents and a hasty scanning of the text.

Melamed was a man of explosive temperament and considerable vitality. He could fast for weeks and then, given the opportunity, eat enough for five or ten people. I shall never forget how he once dropped in on a Jewish holiday just as we were sitting down to the festive meal. He had already been a guest at somebody else's house, where he had eaten a huge dinner, but this did not prevent him from sharing ours. A friend who was staying with us expressed her surprise at this, whereupon Melamed volunteered to eat a four-pound loaf of bread on top of the two dinners in return for a contribution to the Jewish National Fund. He was a born fighter, and it was unwise to pick a quarrel with him. Ruthless in polemics, he possessed the abstract philosopher's sovereign contempt for facts, and his basic convictions were indestructible. His literary talent later took him to America, where he worked for many years for the English-language Jewish press and for American Zionism. Melamed was a self-made man in the best sense. Among all the young students who frequented our house (most of whom were studying in Bern and belonged to the so-called Bern group, which played a very special role in Jewish life), it was his personality that most interested me as a child.

In addition to our circle of Eastern Jewish friends we also had a German-Jewish one. My father's Zionist activities brought him into friendly contact with members of the old-established Jewish community of Frankfurt, so that, unlike many East European Jews, I did not grow up in a kind of self-imposed ghetto. At school I mixed with Jewish and gentile children and at home I grew up in a milieu which, though it was predominantly composed of East European Jews, included many German Jews as well.

The Jewish community of Frankfurt had a character of its own, unique in Germany and even in Western Europe. It shared the patrician heritage of the former imperial free city that had played a significant role in the Middle Ages and again in modern times—during the meeting of the National Assembly in 1848, for example. This city where the emperors were crowned, the city of Goethe, was in the twentieth century one of the great international centers of finance. Incorporated relatively late into Prussia—something its inhabitants never completely accepted—Frankfurt was quite un-Prussian and proud of its liberal tradition. The *Frankfurter Zeitung*, one of Germany's most esteemed liberal newspapers in those days, set the city's intellectual tone. Jews represented a considerable proportion of Frankfurt's population, and they too could look back with pride on an ancient heritage. The house of Rothschild originated in Frankfurt, and the Rothschilds played an essential part in its economic and intellectual life. Many of Frankfurt's important private banks were in Jewish hands. The founder and, in my time, the chief editor of the *Frankfurter Zeitung* were Jews. It was therefore not surprising that Frankfurt's Jews should share with the city's other inhabitants a certain patrician sense of superiority, not to say snobbishness. Few cities inspired as much local pride in which Jews and gentiles shared as Frankfurt. As Friedrich Stoltze expressed it in his dialect verse: *Es will merr net in mein Kopp enei: wie kann nor e Mensch net von Frankfort sei!* ("I just can't get it through my head how anybody can't be from Frankfurt").

Frankfurt's Jews were also aware of their special history. Emancipated during the Napoleonic era, they had retained strong communal ties, in so far as this was possible during the period of assimilation. Like most German-Jewish communities of that time, they were divided into various religious groups. On the one side were the liberal, or Reform, Jews, on the other the conservatives. For the former, Judaism was a religion that found expression in specific articles of faith and the observance of certain customs, especially the high holidays and the Sabbath. For the conservatives all the old traditions remained sacred and affected daily life much more radically (through daily prayers, kosher food, and so on). In addition to these two groups, which existed in all German-Jewish communities, there was a third that had its parallel only in a few other cities: the so-called Neo-Orthodox.

Neo-Orthodoxy originated in a remarkable attempt to combine the whole tradition of rabbinic Judaism with the achievements of modern emancipation. The overwhelming and, in its way, splendid power of Jewish Orthodoxy was not confined to theory or dogma but permeated the life of all its adherents from early morning until late at night, dictating in minute detail how they were to act in any situation in life. It had evolved out of centuries of Jewish life, in isolation from surrounding intellectual currents. If it had not been for this all-embracing system, there would no longer be any such thing as a Jewish people. Its creation was perhaps the greatest achievement of the Jewish genius for self-preservation, and its significance is not merely religious. Orthodoxy meant national tradition and race, literature and art, collective and individual life; it kept Jews separate from foreign cultures and prevented assimilation. No matter where a Jew lived, he carried his homeland with him in this boundless religious reality.

The Orthodox system was organically linked with a separate Jewish existence. The ghetto was by no means a way of life imposed by non-Jews but, as history proves, a private world voluntarily created by the Jews themselves. By the time the medieval rulers made the ghetto the norm, it was already a long-established fact. The survival of this form of religion was, of course, connected with living conditions in the ghetto, in the *shtetl*, in the separate Jewish quarter.

Modern emancipation had destroyed the basis of this separate existence, causing either a gradual or a more rapid erosion of the unbroken Jewish tradition. Some of it survived—very little among the Reform Jews, more among the conservatives. Neo-Orthodoxy made a heroic and paradoxical attempt to combine time-honored values with the way of life of emancipated Jewry, to participate fully in the modern world while retaining all traditional forms.

The founder of this movement was a man of great intellectual stature with an innate talent for leadership, Samson Raphael Hirsch. He formulated his synthesis as Torah in *Derekh Eretz*, or the Law in accordance with the way of the land. The attempt, heroic as it was, somehow contravened natural developments; it stemmed from a tremendous effort of will rather than the realities of the historical moment. The inevitable consequence was that the group became rigid and fanatical. Its leaders had to be constantly on the alert because as soon as they relaxed the process of assimilation began again. The group had to segregate itself because only in isolation could it hope to realize its difficult goal. Not only did it build its own synagogue and introduce its own rite; it was so strongly separatist that it refused to allow members to be buried in the already existing Jewish cemetery and established its own instead. Like all splinter groups, it developed a strong sense of its own superiority and was sure that it alone represented true Judaism. It saw Jewish problems only from its own point of view and cut itself off from the momentous Jewish questions of our time. Neo-Orthodoxy deliberately opposed all other Jewish organizations, which it called heretical and atheistic. Its spirit was somewhat sectarian, and although the self-sacrificing devotion with which its members accepted personal inconvenience and the contribution it made to the survival of Judaism are to be highly esteemed, it was ultimately no more than an anachronistic venture on the part of a little band of determined but fanatical people, a venture that was bound to prove ineffectual in the long run.

In a Jewish community like Frankfurt's, Zionism played a negligible role in those days. It was the movement of a tiny minority consisting chiefly of Eastern Jews and including very few old-time residents of the city. But all in all and despite its inner diversity, antagonisms, and inner conflicts, the Jewish community of Frankfurt had substance and character. To grow up in its midst was a further guarantee against an inferiority complex. This was the environment of a secure Jewish community that felt itself firmly rooted and never thought of denying its Jewishness. My boyhood in Frankfurt did nothing to shake the original self-confidence I had brought with me from my *shtetl*.

When I arrived there, in my sixth year, it was time to think about school. It was decided that I should attend one of the two Jewish schools in Frankfurt, either the strictly Orthodox Israelitische Realschule or the Philantropin. My parents decided first on the Orthodox school, probably because they found its atmosphere more positively Jewish, although it was anti-Zionist. For a time I had private lessons in German, and after a few months I was admitted to the first class of the Israelitische Realschule, so that in fact I never went to elementary school and passed my final high school examination at the age of seventeen and a half.

I attended the Orthodox school for three years. Although I was a good student, I had some trouble there, and strange as it may sound for such an early age, it was trouble of an ideological nature. Even in those days I was strongly pro-Zionist, but the teachers, like all representatives of Neo-Orthodoxy, were passionately anti-Zionist. I used to carry on a kind of Zionist propaganda among my schoolmates and was often reprimanded for this, but I would get my revenge in my own way. My worst conflicts were with the Hebrew teacher. Unlike him, I spoke Hebrew quite fluently and when he asked me a question in class I would answer in Hebrew. He usually failed to understand me, particularly because I used the Sephardic pronunciation, and this did not exactly increase his authority over the class. Moreover, I did not really belong to the Orthodox community; I was an outsider and from time to time was made to feel it. I remember that at the end of my second or third year I was not awarded a prize, while one of my schoolmates, the son of the president of the congregation, received one. He returned the prize, however, in front of the whole school, saying that I deserved it more than he did. This produced quite a scandal and it was soon followed by another when I was caught at school selling *shekalim* (membership certificates in the Zionist Organization, named after the ancient Judaic coin, the *shekel*). My father then decided to remove me from this school and enroll me in the experimental Realgymnasium called Musterschule.

I felt much more at home in my new school and completed my secondary education there. It was a good, very progressive, and unusual school, and its principal, Geheimrat Walter, was an educator of international reputation. It was one of the first German schools to introduce student government. The teachers confined themselves to teaching; administration, supervision, and discipline were left to a student committee—a revolutionary phenomenon in turn-of-the-century Prussia, when most schools had adopted military discipline. Two nephews of Wilhelm II attended while I was a student, and since they were neither gifted nor hard-working, the principal suggested to their mother, the Kaiser's sister, that they transfer to a less demanding school. This caused a tremendous sensation in Frankfurt, but such was the spirit of the Realgymnasium.

I was lucky to be in a class of bright, intellectually lively boys, about half of whom were Jewish. Since I learned easily

and quickly and was active in many outside activities, I fell into the habit of not attending school two or three days a week during my last few years. I worked out a system for this. I got my father to write me three separate excuses, which I would get back and present again in turn, until one day my teacher told me not to bother any more, thus sanctioning my frequent absences, at least unofficially. I was already making public speeches in those days, and because several of my teachers used to attend, I was granted a somewhat privileged position.

Under the German *gymnasium* system final qualifying examinations for a diploma consisted of two parts, oral and written. Candidates who distinguished themselves in the written portion were exempted from the oral and merely had to be present to answer to their names. This suited me very well, because preparing for the oral, which demanded much work, such as learning poems by heart, was a great effort. I have always had a poor memory for routine things and still quickly forget numbers, addresses, and so forth. My memory is much more apt to retain ideas, books, experiences, or people, whose names I may not remember although I know quite well who they are and where I met them. Having been told that I had done well enough in the written examination to be exempted from the oral one, I devoted the intervening weeks before the day of the oral to making pro-Zionist speeches.

The evening before the examination I spoke in Giessen, about an hour's journey from Frankfurt, where I got into a heated debate with some anti-Zionists that lasted so long that I missed the last train back to Frankfurt. The first train next morning would get me back half an hour after the beginning of the oral. I was terribly worried because the examination was usually opened by an official representative of the Ministry of Education, a pedantic man everyone was afraid of. A few days earlier he had told a candidate from another school who had arrived a few minutes late to present himself again in six months' time. Since I was eager to enter the university as soon as possible, I was afraid that my lateness would cost me half a year too. This school superintendent had already lowered my German grade of "very good" on the grounds that my essay was too independent for a *Gymnasiast*. My German teacher had protested, the matter had been submitted to the teachers' council, and my grade raised again. I was therefore afraid he bore me a grudge. Fortunately my fears turned out to be unfounded. The principal and my own teacher, noticing that I was not present at the beginning of the examination, arranged for me not to be called until the superintendent had left.

A second episode that caused a lot of talk at the time was also connected with this final examination. Traditionally every graduating class held a banquet that parents and teachers attended. During our final year my class was constantly at odds with our teacher, a good scholar but a somewhat odd bachelor whom the students teased and ridiculed. To demonstrate their disapproval, all the teachers had decided not to attend the class banquet. My fellow-students were very upset, and since I had been chosen to give the valedictory address, I was asked to try to straighten things out. The school's graduation ceremony was a Frankfurt event; the auditorium was always crammed with city dignitaries and parents. The subject of my speech was Hebbel. When I had delivered it, instead of sitting down I added a few words spontaneously. Opting for complete frankness, I told the audience of the conflict between the teachers and ourselves—which produced considerable astonishment. Finally I turned to the principal and our teacher and said that while we had admittedly been undisciplined and rebellious, this was attributable to our age rather than to bad will. I asked their sympathy for our behavior, especially now that we had had the courage to apologize for it openly. Our teacher, who was a kindhearted man even if he was a crank, was so deeply affected that he began to sob, came up to me on the platform, and embraced me. Then the principal announced that the teachers, won over by the manly and truly German way in which I had acknowledged our mistakes, would now be happy to come to our banquet. The incident helped prove to me the effectiveness of well chosen words at the right moment.

I think back to my school days, especially those at the experimental Realgymnasium, with great pleasure. I never felt restricted by school regulations and learned a great deal; above all, I laid the foundation for my study of foreign languages, which was to be very valuable to me later. The school allowed me plenty of time for my own reading, and during those years I went through a great deal of German and French literature. German philosophy, history, and the history of Judaism were my favorite subjects.

I was not quite fourteen when I delivered my first speech for the Zionist Organization. The occasion was a Hannukah celebration attended by several hundred people. Because I was a boy and still in short trousers, most people assumed that I would deliver a short memorized talk. My mother was even more excited than I was, although I remember being a bit tense as I mounted the steps to the platform. But as soon as I was standing there, the audience in front of me, I felt quite calm. This relaxed attitude to public speaking, the complete freedom from stage fright, has never deserted me. Later, at debates of crucial importance, when I had to push through proposals that could have changed the course of my life, I was often tense but never nervous.

On this occasion the subject of my talk, I remember, was Judah and Hellas, the struggle between Judaism and Hellenism— an appropriate topic for the Maccabean holiday. One detail of this venture stands out. At that time I was very friendly with a girl of my own age who was impressed that I was going to speak in public and who asked me again and again how anyone could possibly speak extemporaneously. I tried to explain something of the technique to her and, showing off a bit, promised to perform a trick. The fifth time that I would use the word "Hellas" I would take out my handkerchief to demonstrate my self-assurance. She promised me a gift if I could carry it off. As I pronounced the word "Hellas" for the fifth time, and it is difficult to keep count while speaking, I took my handkerchief out of my pocket, held it in my hand, and glanced at her. She returned my look with such intense admiration that I lost the thread of my speech. This experience has often haunted me in my dreams; I felt as if I was struggling in vain against the waves of a raging ocean. The whole thing probably lasted a few seconds. I pulled myself together and recaptured my train of thought. The talk was a tremendous success, no doubt because of my age rather than because of its content. I was anxious to find out whether anybody had noticed my slip. Nobody had except my mother, who pointed out when we got home that I had become upset for a moment and lost my place.

I vividly remember another talk I gave while I was still at school, because this one caused some excitement and might easily have led to unfortunate consequences. At that time Protestant missionaries used to proselytize in Frankfurt, promising material rewards to poor immigrant Jews if they would allow themselves to be baptized. One evening some friends urged me to go to one of their meetings and speak out against them. I complied and made an aggressive and in places brash speech, typical of a young man. Some of the missionaries charged me with slandering Christianity and, when things threatened to get out of hand, the police were called. This public appearance might have ended badly for me, not only because attacks on a Christian church were not looked upon very kindly in imperial Prussia, but because as a schoolboy I had no right delivering public speeches at all. (For this reason I had not given my real name when I asked for the floor.) Just as the police were entering the hall, however, my friends smuggled me out by a rear staircase. For the rest of my time at school I confined myself to pro-Zionist speeches in the Frankfurt area.

Looking back on my speaking activities, which began at such an early age, I realize that throughout all these years, in the course of which I have made thousands of speeches in many languages, I have always felt essentially the same about public speaking. Fundamentally, I never really enjoyed it. On the other hand, I never had any trouble drafting or delivering a talk, and apart from a few important speeches in which I had to make far-reaching statements, I never spent much time preparing one. An hour beforehand is usually all I need. Whenever I have taken more time, the right tone or inspiration has eluded me. It is sufficient for me to think through what I want to say and make a few notes on one or two small cards, which I hardly ever refer to. The few times I have dictated in advance and read a speech have proven far less effective.

What interests me primarily is the clear presentation of ideas. I have always detested speeches that are not logically constructed to pursue a specific idea cogently to its end. Mere rhetoric repels me. The second essential for me is contact with the audience, and I believe I have always had a reliable sense of this. The art of oratory lies in controlling the audience, not in the speaker's ideas, which depend upon his general intellectual capacity and which he could express equally well in writing. Rhetoric stands and falls by the impression it makes on the audience; it bears a certain relationship to acting. I remember a long discussion with Werner Krauss on whether it is more difficult for an actor to play the same role or for a speaker to make the same speech thirty times. Just as a good actor feels his role afresh every evening and gives it a new shading, a good speaker, especially if he speaks extemporaneously, ought to keep varying his speech.

I believe I have never delivered exactly the same speech twice, although I have known great orators (Vladimir Jabotinsky was probably the greatest) who work a talk out carefully, learn it by heart, and are able to repeat it again and again with feeling, using the same words, the same inflections, the same jokes and rhetorical effects. For me speeches always depend very much on the general atmosphere, so that the hall, for instance, may be as important as the audience. But again, the decisive thing must be control of the audience; that is what true eloquence consists of and ultimately it can never be learned. One can learn to draft a speech and one can learn diction and intonation, yet it is the natural mastery of the audience that determines the extent of a speaker's confidence. All my life I have felt so sure of myself in this respect that when I was younger, at an age when one enjoys tricks of this kind, I would sometimes take a bet that I would get applause after a certain number of minutes or conclude a well constructed speech after exactly forty-five and a half minutes.

Perhaps the ability to control an audience, which inevitably implies a certain skepticism, explains my reservations about oratory. The longer I remain in public life, the less respect I have for the so-called masses. Mass psychology presents a central problem of our time, the threat of destruction through standardization. Anyone who has dealt much—and successfully—with large groups and does not overestimate himself will harbor serious doubts about mass reaction and about what might be called the "good sense" (or rather, non-sense) of the masses. Masses of people are irresponsible entities swayed by emotions. Someone who can play upon emotions—and rhetoric is a most effective method—can do almost anything he pleases. Anyone who possesses this gift and recognizes it is bound to be full of inner reservations. For many years I was troubled by the conflict involved in having to deal with large bodies of people (to whom, after all, my public activity addressed itself) while at the same time holding such a negative attitude toward them and feeling utterly unsure of the legitimacy of oratory as a means.

In some way everything about rhetoric is false. A practiced speaker does not need to tell untruths, yet he can hardly ever tell full truths either, not only because the public arena can never be the place for ultimate truths and it would be indecent to appear naked in public, but because you nearly always have to select what you are going to say with a view to what you hope to achieve. A speech is rarely a work of art. It lives by virtue of its effect on the listeners, of the relationship between speaker and audience. Apart from this it scarcely exists and even the most outstanding speeches of the past, that still fill us with admiration when we read them, have only a fraction of the impact they must have had when they were delivered. Oratory is essentially virtuosity, except that the orator is his own composer and performs the composition only once.

That is why speeches are never completely satisfying for the speaker, even when they are tremendously effective, produce thunderous applause, and achieve the desired results. At least I have always felt that way. You quickly get used to the applause; the more skeptically you regard the good sense of the masses and the more critically you regard yourself, the less will it seduce you. My distasteful reaction to applause was never a pose. I have been often irritated by such an interruption during a speech and have signaled to the audience to cut it short. Applause at the end is not disturbing, but it is not particularly important to me either. Personal compliments are sometimes even harder to put up with—and this is the worst thing about public speaking in America. One's most intimate thoughts and feelings are in any case hard to transmit, hardest of all through the medium of a public address, which originates in and is meant for mass communication.

Anybody who is skeptical enough about oratory can utilize its techniques without risk; otherwise it can constitute an intellectual and moral danger both to the speaker and the listeners. Our time has seen ghastly examples of the dehumanizing effects of demagoguery. Hitler would have been inconceivable without his speeches and millions paid dearly for this misuse of oratory. In an age of growing standardization the public speech is becoming an increasingly serious problem that calls for investigation in the light of history and mass psychology. In my own career, in which public speaking has been one of my most effective tools, I have been reminded again and again of its questionable aspect.

My high school days also saw the beginning of my literary activities. Like many precocious and not entirely untalented children, I wrote a lot: lyric and epic poetry and plays in iambic and trochaic meter, and tragedies in the Greek manner that I hardly ever showed to anybody. They were all lost when the Nazis destroyed my library. I realized soon enough, however, that I was not born to be a writer and gave up this hobby at the age of fifteen or sixteen.

My journalistic activities had more important consequences. The Jewish weekly my father edited, the *Frankfurter Israelitisches Familienblatt*, a paper of much higher standing than its name suggests, played a role in German-Jewish life. Conservative in religion and strongly pro-Zionist, it attracted through my father a group of unusual contributors. Partly out of esteem for my father, partly for the modest fees, Klatzkin, Melamed, Glickson, and many other brilliant Russian-Jewish students contributed to the *Familienblatt*, which thanks to them maintained an intellectual level far above the average Jewish communal newspaper. It was constantly taking issue with Neo-Orthodoxy, with pro-assimilation Reform Judaism, with God, and with the world. The intelligent, witty, uninhibited, aggressive young students and writers who appeared in its pages never failed to interest Jewish middle-class readers, though they sometimes shocked them.

I was accepted as a contributor when I was fourteen. At first I did book reviews (the main incentive being the free books), but very soon I began writing articles. Since *gymnasium* students in imperial Prussia were not allowed to publish articles, I adopted a pseudonym, Ben Kohelet, the son of Kohelet. (My father's name was Solomon, and according to Jewish tradition Solomon wrote the Book of Kohelet, or Ecclesiastes.) Many of these articles attracted attention and sometimes even aroused controversies. There was speculation about who their author might be, but my father and the proprietor of the paper kept my identity secret for many years.

When I was sixteen my parents took me to Paris and London and then to Brussels, where the world exhibition was being held. In Paris friends of my father's talked a lot about the vice president of the Alliance Israélite Universelle, Professor Salomon Reinach, the famous archaeologist who, like his brother Théodore, was one of the outstanding personalities of French Jewry and indeed of France itself. (The Reinachs originally came from Frankfurt, where they were among the leading financiers.) Reinach and the whole Alliance were strongly anti-Zionist and pro-assimilation. My father's friends went on to tell us of an incident that incensed me. The Jewish anthropologist Jacques Faitlovitch had been studying the Falasha Jews in Abyssinia and had told Reinach about them. Faitlovitch had asked that the Alliance support his work. Salomon Reinach is said to have turned him down, saying: "What you have done is unfortunate. There are too many Jews in the world already. We don't need the new problems new Jews will bring." My youthful impetuosity flared into indignation, and when I got back to Frankfurt I wrote two articles entitled "Salomon Reinach—A Type." They were extremely aggressive, created a sensation, and provoked resolutions censuring Reinach from many quarters. There was even dissension inside the Alliance itself, and Reinach resigned as vice president.

Many years later in the early 1920's Professor Haffkin, the

great physician who discovered the antiplague serum, took me to visit Reinach at his beautiful villa near Neuilly. It was a Sunday afternoon. When I mentioned in the course of conversation that I had grown up in Frankfurt, Reinach aked if I could solve a mystery for him. He told me how, many years before, two very presumptuous articles published in Frankfurt under a pseudonym had attacked him and led to his resignation as vice president of the Alliance. For months afterward he urged Frankfurt relatives to spare neither money nor effort to discover the author's name, but they never succeeded.

"Professor Reinach," I replied, "If you promise not to throw me out, I can solve the mystery for you. I wrote them myself." He gave me an astonished look and asked how it was possible, since I would have been very young at the time. I confessed I had been sixteen years old, a fact he accepted graciously, like the wise, serene, old gentleman he was.

"You know," he said, "I really ought to be ashamed that a sixteen-year-old boy could force me to resign from the Alliance, but you can be proud of it." We parted on the most friendly terms.

Two experiences from my school days particularly influenced my later life. The first, the visit to Paris, London, and Brussels that I have already mentioned, was my first encounter with Western Europe. I had become completely immersed in my world of school, Frankfurt, and German culture, and although I read French literature (at that time mainly the Encyclopedists and epigrammatic essayists), my education and way of thinking had been shaped largely by German culture. I spent only a few days in Paris and London, but I was taken with the brilliance and charm of Paris and the wonderful solidity and historical dignity of London. Of course, these impressions were only vague and superficial, and since my diaries are lost I find it hard to say precisely what impressed me most.

I remember the Jewish leader Nahum Slouszch, who lived in Paris then and who talked so interestingly about the North African Jews, of whom I knew next to nothing. And I shall never forget Dr. Salkind in London, about whom one could write a novel. He was a member of the Bern student group, a fighter whose free and easy informality and physical strength seemed quite un-Jewish, and at the same time he was a scholar, courageous to the last, aggressive to the point of provocation, and an immensely popular figure among Whitechapel Jews at the time. But whatever my detailed impressions may have been, the most important thing for a sixteen-year-old was a sense of the vastness of the world, a first glimpse beyond the boundaries of a culture that, rich as it was, was still limited, an awareness that there were still quite different ways of life and many more intellectual attitudes. For the last thirty years I have been a permanent traveler; I have undertaken longer journeys, met more interesting people, and had more dramatic experiences, but if I had to say which of my travels affected me most deeply, I would without hesitation say the first.

Two things happened during that trip that taught me a great deal, and it has always seemed to me that firsthand experiences are more lasting and make a deeper impression than those that come from reading. The first was connected with my first encounter with England. We took a ship from Ostend to Dover. At the start it was stormy. I was terribly seasick and stayed in my berth, praying that the ship would sink. This was the first and last time in my life that I was seasick, and I have made many sea voyages since. Later the weather cleared, the sun came out, and I felt better and lay in a chair on deck. At that time the British customs officers used to check baggage on board ship. Shortly before we docked I saw the customs official come on deck accompanied by a well-dressed, white-haired gentleman, very distinguished though pale and embarrassed looking, who was carrying a small leather attaché case. The official motioned to some of the passengers to gather around and announced that when asked if he had anything to declare, the man said no. Yet, when the officer opened this attaché case he found a hundred cigars. According to British law, he said, he could do three things: refuse the traveler admittance to the country; impose a heavy fine; or confiscate the cigars. But, he said, he would do none of them. Then, before all the assembled passengers he declared, "Sir, you are no gentleman," and walked away.

This incident made an indelible impression on me. It was my

first encounter with the English character, and the elegance of this sensible, effective action fascinated me. That man would never again smuggle anything into England, and he would probably have preferred the official to slap a hundred pound fine on him rather than submit to such humiliation. The customs official's action reflects some of the splendid qualities of the English people.

In Brussels I had a very different experience. My father, who was not exactly an experienced traveler, lost his wallet containing all our money. To make things worse, it was a Saturday and we were supposed to leave Brussels the next day. The Frankfurt banks were closed and we could not get any money by telegraph before Monday. We did not know a soul in Brussels and I discovered, fortunately for the only time in my life, how it feels not to have a penny to your name. Our situation was not really so desperate, but my parents took a serious view of it. However, we quickly got out of our fix when it occurred to my father to ask the proprietor of the Jewish restaurant where we had been taking our meals for a loan. Father offered his watch as security, whereupon the restaurant-keeper, who had known us only since we had been eating there, gave my father a searching look and said: "Mr. Goldmann, anyone would lend a man with your face fifty pounds without any security at all."

I also attended my first Zionist congress while I was still at school, the congress of 1911 held in Basel. My father was a delegate and I missed two weeks of school in order to accompany him. Through Jacob Klatzkin, who was at that time editor of *Die Welt* and a collaborator of David Wolfsohn, president of the World Zionist Organization, I got a seat in the box of honor with all the major figures of Hebrew and Yiddish literature. Since I was not much interested then in parliamentary politics, the congress made no lasting impression on me, and I do not remember any of the speeches. The only unforgettable episode was a humorous one, and in later years I often used to tell this story when I was asked where I learned Yiddish. At that time, of course, the Zionist movement was not yet split into all its different parties, and the delegates were broadly divided into supporters of the Executive (called at that time the Small Actions Committee) and its opponents. The tradition was that soon after the opening of the debate, a motion was brought that in order to shorten the proceedings a number of major speakers should be selected from the supporters of the Executive and from the opponents. This motion was duly proposed. As it happened, however, Russian Jewry, particularly the Zionists, was engaged at that time in a fierce language battle between the advocates of Hebrew and Yiddish. The extreme Hebraists took the line that Yiddish was a *galut* tongue, that is, a language of the Diaspora, and therefore not acceptable at Zionist meetings. Their slogan was "Russian or Hebrew but on no account Yiddish." On the other hand, the supporters of Yiddish regarded it as the second national language.

After the motion concerning major speakers had been translated into various languages, a pro-Yiddish delegate demanded that it be translated into Yiddish. The supporters of Hebrew objected as a matter of principle. This produced an uproar. The chairman was David Wolfsohn, a wealthy merchant and self-made man who possessed plenty of sound common sense and instinctive intelligence. He tried to calm things down by stating that the proposal of a Yiddish translation was a purely technical matter that had nothing to do with principle. Every delegate must be in a position to understand what he was required to vote on. Since no certified Yiddish interpreter was present and since he himself came from Shavli in Lithuania, he would translate the motion himself. "I shall first read the motion in High German," he said. "It reads: 'It is proposed that eight principal speakers be elected.' Now I shall translate it into Yiddish," and he repeated the same German statement, reversing the order of "eight principal speakers" and "be elected"—the only actual difference. Everybody burst out laughing, and that was the end of the motion for translating the agenda into Yiddish.

I have a vivid recollection of the occupants of that box of honor. There I first met Ahad Ha-Am, whose aristocratic reserve and sober-mindedness, far from attracting me, repelled the impetuous, romantic boy I was then. On the other hand, I was irresistibly drawn to Scholem Aleichem, who kept up a witty commentary on the proceedings, sharply critical at times but always full of a delightful humanity. My interest in the congress' parliamentary proceedings and the internal politics of the Zionist movement did not develop until much later, and even then Zionism was for me primarily ideological. I was much more concerned with the idea than with how it was to be realized. The questions that particular congress had to deal with were very limited ideologically and therefore held little interest for me. As far as I could see, they were purely personal or factional conflicts whose bearing on public life I did not grasp until later.

Soon after I returned from the congress my *gymnasium* career came to its close. Trying to visualize myself before I entered the university—no easy task since all my personal papers from that period no longer exist—I see a lanky youth with neurotic tendencies, precocious and excessively intellectual. In fact I felt much younger at the age of twenty-five or thirty than I did when I was sixteen or eighteen, and in my experience this is characteristic of many intellectual young Jews. Their real youth is postponed because they develop too fast mentally. Moreover, my home, mainly on account of my mother, encouraged my tendency toward a somewhat one-sided intellectuality. I took things very hard in those days and showed no sign of the facility I was later to acquire for disposing of problems quickly and easily, meeting critical situations with equanimity, and maintaining a certain irony in the face of apparently insoluble difficulties—qualities I slowly developed in later years.

I had a typically German attitude toward philosophy, my chief interest in those days, and thought that everything outside metaphysics was of secondary importance. Schopenhauer and Nietzsche, Kant and Spinoza, were my mentors, but even then I was beginning to take an interest in mysticism, a subject to which I still return whenever I have time. In literature my favorite writer was Goethe. Not only did I read his works over and over again; I never tired of reading the literature about him. I sensed his tremendous uniqueness, the balance of his mind, his ability to absorb so much and fuse it into a synthesis, his incomparable ability to stand in the midst of things and at the same time above them, to be passionate and yet cool-headed. It seemed to me that Goethe's life as well as his work exemplified the apparently paradoxical stance of the true artist.

I should also mention my delight in music. One of the great shortcomings of my life is that I did not study music in my early youth; in this respect my parents were nonartistic. Later I took up the violin for a year or two, but the mobile life and frequent traveling, which for me began so early, made regular study impossible. Nevertheless, music meant a great deal to me in those days and has remained a source of intense pleasure ever since.

Notwithstanding all my public speaking, I was not thinking of a career in public life, but rather of an academic or literary one. For a time I dreamed of dedicating myself to astronomy. In those days my parents saw in me a future lawyer, partly because of my talent for oratory, partly because I was almost engaged to be married to the daughter of one of Frankfurt's leading lawyers, whose practice I was supposed to take over. But I cannot say that they exerted any kind of pressure, and I was quite undecided about a career. Material considerations, so decisive in many people's choice of a vocation, played no role in mine, not because we were rich but because, for my parents as well as for myself, this was no more than a subordinate factor. Our kind of people did not choose a profession for its potential rewards but on the basis of talent and inclination. This was true of my father and of all my parents' close friends. When I left Frankfurt to attend the university, I did so not to prepare for a profession but out of the desire to study, to conquer an intellectual world and gain access to the profundities of culture. Instinctively I felt sure that I would never lack the necessities of life. Thanks to my self-confidence or irresponsibility, I have rarely worried about my material existence. For me the university was the gateway to the world of philosophy, science, and Western culture.

Heidelberg was the goal of my dreams. In the southern German cultural milieu where I had grown up, this time-honored university was held in the highest esteem. One obstacle remained to be overcome: I had finished high school unusually early. But the requirement that students be at least eighteen years old was waived, and I matriculated in the spring of 1912.

3

Student Days and a First Visit to Palestine

This is not the place to describe German university life before the First World War, a period still untouched by all the tragic problems mankind encountered in 1914. Nevertheless, it is important to remember that the German universities of that time were radically different from those in the English-speaking world. Academic and student freedom were complete realities, and there was almost no supervision of study. No one checked whether a student attended lectures or not; the only thing required of him was a certain amount of knowledge at examination time. Of course, students of the natural sciences were compelled, by the nature of their discipline, to attend lectures and practical classes regularly, the chemists in their laboratory, the medical students in anatomy or physiology demonstration rooms and later in clinics. But those studying the humanities—law, history, literature, art history, or philosophy—hardly needed to attend a lecture, provided they could make a satisfactory showing in the final examination.

I made good use of this academic freedom. Officially I was studying law, but I cannot remember attending regularly a single course of lectures in that subject. I once arrived ten minutes late for Professor Gradenwitz's class in Roman law, and when some of the students expressed their displeasure at this disturbance in the usual way, by stamping their feet, the professor remarked: "Gentlemen, when Mr. Goldmann gives us the honor of his company once a semester, you should welcome him more graciously."

I never found law very absorbing. Acute legal analysis, with which I was somewhat familiar from my Talmudic studies—and the Talmud, I believe, contains at least as much legal wisdom as the great Roman law—occasionally attracted me as a purely intellectual game but never very seriously. I did not want to be a lawyer because devoting my life to other people's litigation did not seem to me any kind of ideal. What might have challenged me was a career as a criminal lawyer, but even that attraction was not strong. I did in fact get my law degree, although I never knew much about jurisprudence, and if anyone holds an unearned Doctor of Law, it is I.

My real fields of interest at Heidelberg were philosophy, which I studied under Heinrich Rickert and later under Karl Jaspers; sociology, which gave me the chance to hear the brilliant Max Weber, and literature, in which I attended the lectures of one of the most original and cultivated literary historians, Friedrich Gundolf. But I derived most of my education from reading. Lectures were for me a guide and a stimulus to my own reading and thinking rather than a substitute for them. I would often leave Heidelberg to spend a few days in one of the many charming towns and villages of the enchanting Neckar Valley, where in summer I would lie on the grass, reading literature or philosophy and getting much more out of it than out of the best lectures.

I took no very active part in student life. I did join the Zionist fraternity of the Jewish student organization, but I never put much heart into it. This somewhat slipshod combination of German-Jewish ways and Zionist ideas, unruffled by any precise knowledge of Jewish history or Zionist ideology, was not particularly attractive to me. I do remember one passionate controversy within the fraternity (which over the years played quite an important role in German Zionism because it produced many of its outstanding leaders) over the question of "unconditional satisfaction." Today problems of this kind are incomprehensible even to those who knew prewar Germany; for a non-German reader they must border on the absurd. As everybody knows, the pernicious institution of dueling was entrenched in the German universities. There was also a great deal of anti-Semitism among German students and the question at issue was whether a member of the Zionist fraternity was obliged to react to anti-Semitic abuse with a challenge. I regarded the whole thing as an attempt to mimic German student traditions and this seemed to me particularly ridiculous on the part of a group of students who were insisting on being Jewish and even Zionist. The dispute was settled at a Zionist student congress, the so-called *Kartelltag* held in Königsberg. I was one of the few delegates who vehemently opposed the motion—quite unsuccessfully, of course. I was outvoted by an overwhelming majority, but since the war broke out in 1914 and dueling fell into disrepute in the universities after the German revolution, this senseless decision of the Königsberg congress had no lasting consequences.

During the academic year I continued my speaking activities to a limited extent, partly to propagandize for Zionism but also to supplement the modest monthly allowance from my parents by speaking to non-Zionist groups. On one of those non-Zionist occasions I met Theodor Heuss, the future president of the German Federal Republic. For a fee of a hundred marks per lecture I had agreed to give a series of talks on the contemporary Jewish question, in Heilbronn, where there was a small but active Jewish community. Theodor Heuss was at that time editor of the *Heilbronner Neckarzeitung*, a provincial but very influential paper highly respected for its courageous liberalism. He was interested in Jewish affairs even then and attended my lectures. A few hours before the second or third of them I met a fascinating Polish girl, also a student in Heidelberg, and took a walk with her to the castle. On the way we got into such a deeply personal conversation that I completely forgot that my train for Heilbronn left at six o'clock. When I finally remembered, it was too late. The lecture committee had gone to the station to meet me but returned without a speaker. A large audience was assembled, and it had paid admission. Nobody knew what to do. Suddenly Dr. Heuss, who was well known in Heilbronn, stood up and announced that he would speak in my place, not on the Jewish question but on Germany's Near Eastern policy. He made only one condition—that the fee be paid to me. I was told of this when I arrived for my next lecture and, as a result, got to know Theodor Heuss. Our friendship lasted for a long time, was later broken, but was renewed when, after he became president in 1952, I was negotiating the restitution agreement between Germany and Israel.

As I have said, I was not a very diligent student and spent a lot of time during the academic year with my parents in Frankfurt and in excursions to the Odenwald or the Neckar Valley. All in all my relationship to the university was not very close, and when the chance of going to Palestine was offered to me in 1913, I jumped at it. A group of students was going there on a visit organized and led by Theodor Zlocisti, one of the oldest German Zionists in Berlin, a physician by profession and a man of literary interests. I was asked if I would like to go along; my expenses would be paid by a wealthy friend of the family. The trip was supposed to last four weeks, but I stayed five months and skipped a whole semester at Heidelberg.

Since I was the only Hebrew-speaking member of the group, I involuntarily became its spokesman in Palestine. This soon became very trying. The trip had been organized in typically German fashion. For example, it was taken for granted that we had to go everywhere on foot, which was very difficult in that hot climate. In those days there were no comfortable accommodations and we walked cross-country for six to eight hours every day. In the evening we would reach some kind of settlement where there would be a big reception, because ours was the first student group from Western Europe to come to Palestine and naturally we caused some excitement. A feature of these receptions was two to three hours of welcoming speeches in Hebrew, which none of our group understood. After the speeches I had to respond in Hebrew and the sensational novelty of a Hebrew-speaking German-Jewish student never failed to arouse terrific applause. Only then could my poor fellow students, dog-tired, make their way to their primitive sleeping quarters, where the best they could hope for was to get through the night without being devoured by bedbugs.

To me, however, it seemed more important to get to know

the country than to sweat through an eight-hour march every day, so before long I rented a donkey and rode comfortably along as the only mounted member of the expedition. This involved me in violent arguments with the very strict and correct student leader, who scathingly admonished me for this infraction of order and team spirit. But as I was the only Hebrew-speaking member of the group, which was looked at askance for speaking German, he had to put up with me. Nonetheless, the evening receptions and my own guilty conscience were too much for me, despite the favored treatment. I left the group, which was returning to Germany shortly in any case, and decided really to get to know the country. Although I have been in Palestine probably more than a hundred times since then, I have never again had the opportunity to discover it at such a leisurely yet intensive pace. Free of the group's daily hikes, receptions, and ceremonies and having decided to stay several months, I could dispose of my time as I pleased.

I spent several weeks in Tel Aviv, which then consisted of only a few streets, several more in Rishon le-Zion and Rehovot, and a week in Rosh Pina in Galilee. But most of my time I spent in Jerusalem, where I rented, in what was then the Russian apartment-house complex, a romantic attic with a balcony. I used to sleep on the balcony when the weather got warm.

A detailed account of colonization in those days is beyond the scope of this book, but it was all in quite a primitive stage, except for a few old-established settlements such as Petah Tiqva, Rishon le-Zion, and one or two others. I was especially impressed by kibbutzim, such as Deganyah and Kinneret, and by the type of young *halutz*, or pioneer, Zionists I encountered for the first time. In Jerusalem I tried to get to know the old *yishuv*, the pre-Zionist Orthodox Jewish community, as well as the new one and had some very impressive encounters with kabbalists and mystics in the Meah Shearim quarter of Jerusalem. For a time I visited with Bokharan Jews, in those days the richest in Jerusalem. Their leader, an extremely wealthy carpet merchant, tried hard to persuade me to marry his fifteen-year-old daughter, the only condition being that I was not to take another wife for five years. I became a close friend of Brose, the famous settler in Motza, in whose garden Theodor Herzl had planted a tree. He gave me permission to bring my friends to see him and to drink his wine, no matter how late at night.

I often used to take long moonlight rides with friends and once, on our way back, we were surrounded by a Bedouin band. They would certainly have robbed us and left us naked on the road if one of my companions, who was familiar with the country, had not advised us to act naturally, to sing and occasionally pat our hip pockets as if we were carrying guns. Apparently this produced the desired effect. After riding along with us for about ten minutes, the Bedouin suddenly scattered. Another time I found myself in a precarious situation when my Arab guide in Jericho arranged for me to be a hidden spectator at an Arab wedding and at the bride's dancing—something forbidden to foreigners under Bedouin law. I had already watched several dances, unforgettable in their wild passion, when my guide rushed up to me, pale with fear, and said that one of the bride's relatives had noticed something and was looking for me. We disappeared as fast as we could and got back to the hotel before it was too late.

I got to know many of the leaders of the *yishuv*, several of whom were to remain my friends, though a number of them are no longer alive. There was the imposing patriarchal figure Mordecai ben Hillel Ha-Cohen, one of the patricians of old-time Tel Aviv, a Hebrew writer who was active in many fields. He was a friend of my father's and I stayed at his house on Herzl St., *the* street to live on in those days. One of his sons is David Ha-Cohen, chairman of the Committee for Foreign Affairs in the Israeli parliament, and his daughter married Dr. Arthur Ruppin. I saw a lot of Dr. Ruppin, the greatest pioneer in the history of Jewish colonization, whose achievements cannot be overestimated. Of all the Zionist leaders I have known he was the most unbiased and the one who identified most completely with the work he had undertaken. He was a man of unusual sincerity, objective in his judgment of people and his analysis of problems, and he possessed a genuine modesty that is much rarer than is commonly supposed. For all his sobriety and dryness, he was an idealist and romantic of the first order and had an adventurous streak that came out in his decision, while an assistant judge of the state of Prussia, to go to Palestine as a pioneer. I also met David Yellin, director of the Hebrew Teachers College, a scholar and a leader of the Jerusalem *yishuv*, who founded one of the most important families of Palestine at that time. I was close to Dr. Nissan Turow, too, one of the leading educators of Palestine, a friend of my mother's and a true aristocrat, both in appearance and cast of mind. He later left Palestine and died in America.

Naturally I often came in contact with men from the Hebrew *gymnasium*, which was, in a manner of speaking, the cultural center of the country. Among them were Dr. Ben-Zion Mossenson, Dr. Hayyim Bogratschof, Dr. Metman Cohen and Hayyim Harari. E. L. Sukenik, future professor of archaeology at the Hebrew University and father of Yigael Yadin, and Dov Kimche, the Hebrew writer and translator, were among my closest friends. Both were engaged to be married at the time, and I used to go with them and their fiancées on excursions lasting several days. In Rehovot I met Mosheh Smilansky, a most impressive man, a pioneer in independent colonization and a highly esteemed writer from whom I learned a great deal, even in those early days, about the problem of co-existence between Jews and Arabs.

But even more than the people and the early achievements of Jewish colonization, the country itself impressed me. Never again was Palestine to have such an impact upon me. For one thing I was younger and more sensitive to such impressions and less distracted by other responsibilities than I was during later visits. The exceptional quality of this curious little territory, which has acquired a unique significance in human history not to be explained by its natural resources or geopolitical situation— what I would like to call its mystical meaning—was brought home to me then as never again. Later it became much more difficult to sense that special aura; one was too distracted by what was happening in and to the country. But at that time Palestine was still untouched. You felt the presence of the mountains without having to think about the settlements that would be established on them. You rode across the plains unmarred by buildings and highways. You traveled very slowly; there were no cars and only a few trains; you usually rode on horseback or in a cart. It took two days to get from Haifa to Jerusalem. One saw the country clearly as if emerging from thousands of years of enchantment. The clearness of the air, the brilliance of the starry sky, the mystery of the austere mountains, made it seem as though its history had grown out of the landscape. In those days it was an extraordinarily peaceful, idealistic country, absorbed in a reverie of its own unique past. In the atmosphere lingered something of the prophets and the great Talmudists, of Jesus and the Apostles, of the Safed kabbalists, and the singers of bygone centuries.

Later, when I saw Palestine in the tempo of Zionist development, with all the noise of our tireless activity, I felt we had done the country a wrong. Nowhere have I realized more clearly the original sin inherent in all development—the violation of the world of nature. And even here it would not have struck me so forcefully if I had not experienced the country so intensely in its early years. Much of what moved me most deeply during those months had no connection with things Jewish. In the garden of the Protestant monastery at Tapcha or the Italian monastery of Kubeba or on the hill of Ein Karem, where there was then no Jewish settlement, I received some of my most memorable impressions of Palestine and its landscape. Modern Zionism and all it brought inevitably destroyed this dreamlike feeling of the untouched.

I have often wondered whether the Jewish people, now that it has returned to its land, will ever succeed in restoring, on any high level, the harmonious wholeness of the country and its aura of history. In a sense this is the crux of the fateful question of Israel's future and the historic meaning of Zionism. It is plain to me that the first or second generation of returning Jews can never achieve this. We have been forced to introduce ways of life and values that did not stem from the country's original character and history but which came from the many countries where the various branches of the Jewish people had been scattered. From an esthetic and human viewpoint this has often had distressing results: an architecture foreign to the land, a working tempo that is European rather than Oriental, ways of life rooted in quite different civilizations. But shocking as it may be, this was unavoidable. The great question is whether those Jews who have returned will ever succeed in fusing the new with the old, in becoming a Palestinian nation in the fullest sense, instead of merely politically and geographically, and establishing a culture that will express, in its creations and its forms, the grandiose character of the country. No one can give the answer to this question and our generation will never learn it in any case. But it is essential to realize that the question exists and that, historically speaking and disregarding all the prosaic political and economic problems of the present, this must be the supreme question for the Israel of tomorrow and the day after.

Of course, I did not realize all this so clearly at the time, but experiences never just disappear. If they are fruitful, they change and grow within a person. One constantly sees people, landscapes, and cultures in a new light, but often this happens when they are no longer physically visible and exist only as memories. Today Palestine means something quite different to me from what it did in those days, but the essentials of my present feeling for it, which are closely bound up with my memories, date back to those months. In this sense my first encounter was a decisive event for me, an event that linked my future with that country. Since then I have established many other ties of a political, organizational, and personal nature with individuals, collaborators, and colleagues in Palestine, but my decisive, mystical experience of the country dates back to that first visit.

My immediate reaction was different from the one I have described looking back over the years. I was full of youthful enthusiasm and sentimental emotions. Almost every week I wrote an account of what I had seen and experienced. These were published in the *Israelitisches Familienblatt* and later, unrevised and in the original, slightly naïve form in which I wrote them down as they occurred to me, in a book entitled *Eretz Israel, Reisebriefe aus Palästina*, that was published in 1913. Because I was still a minor when the book appeared, I was never consulted on it. My father arranged everything with the publisher, and perhaps it was better that I did not try to rewrite those impressions. When I left Palestine my Zionism had been enriched by a momentous factor, the country itself. Until then Zionism had been an abstract idea to me, and I had no real conception of what the return of the Jews meant in any concrete sense. My visit gave me that feeling for the soil without which Zionism is bound to remain quite unsubstantial. From then on I began to understand what it means, not merely negatively in terms of leaving the Diaspora behind, but also positively, as a new beginning in a Jewish homeland.

From Palestine I took a slow route home, spending several days in Egypt to see the Pyramids and the Nile and going to Italy for my first sight of the fairy-tale city of Venice. Then I went on to the Eleventh Zionist Congress in Vienna, where I met my parents and returned with them to Frankfurt. I remember just as little of the Vienna congress as I do of the one at Basel in 1911, and this proves to me that even then I had little inclination for the real business of politics. My memories of Vienna, of its theaters, its women, and its landscape, are more vivid than those of the congress, and I attended very few sessions.

In Vienna I met some of my Russian relatives, for the congress provided an occasion for a family reunion. The world war had dispersed our family beyond recall, and those two weeks, when its various branches were together for the last time, are a particularly treasured memory.

4

Pro-Jewish Activities During the First World War

When I returned to Germany I resumed my studies at Heidelberg but stayed there only one semester, from 1913 to 1914. My interest in law had not increased. On the other hand, I enriched my knowledge of Judaism through my acquaintance with an extraordinary man named Rabinkow, one of the most brilliant people I have ever met. Rabinkow was of Russian origin and had studied at a yeshiva in Russia. Although he was an ordained rabbi, he did not practice his profession. Despite—or perhaps because of—his religious convictions, he felt an aversion to living off his religion, so to speak. His tremendous store of rabbinical learning was supplemented by a wide-ranging Western European education. His conversation sparkled with perspicacity and wit, profound philosophical thought, and revealing flashes of insight, in many fields, including history, the philosophy of religion, and jurisprudence. Rabinkow was a most impressive teacher and conversationalist, but he had absolutely no talent for writing. After spending a few hours with him I always regretted that he had no Eckermann to record his sayings that, written down, would have had lasting value. Undemanding as a saint or ascetic, he refused to accept any fee from his numerous pupils in Talmud and theology, who included professors at the University of Heidelberg. His generosity and tolerance were touching; what he hated was any kind of religious fanaticism.

Rabinkow was a bitter opponent of Neo-Orthodoxy then under discussion in Frankfurt, and I remember a wonderful remark of his on that subject. Among his pupils was the son of the rabbi of the Frankfurt Neo-Orthodox, a young fanatic who was continually in conflict with Rabinkow because he could neither understand nor approve the latter's tolerance. This young man once admonished his teacher for not wearing a beard, as Jewish tradition demands. Rabinkow reproved him first by explaining in a trenchant Talmudic argument that from the standpoint of Jewish tradition the wearing of a beard is quite unessential. Then he went on: "But let us assume that you are right. Suppose I live out my life without a beard. When I die and come before God's throne in the next and better world, the worst that can happen is that He will say to me, 'Jew Rabinkow, where is your beard?' To which I shall have to reply, 'Lord, here is a Jew without a beard.' But when *you* appear before God, He'll ask, 'Beard, where is your Jew?' " I owe to him deep insights into the world of true Jewish tradition and religious concepts. If I have ever in my life found intellectual pleasure in exposition of the Law, it was while I was studying Talmud with Rabinkow and following his splendid analysis of Talmudic law.

Rabinkow was also a convinced socialist and revolutionary. For him the teachings of the prophets were not abstract phrases but were to be applied to reality. Poor as he was, he helped other people and spent half his time procuring support for poor Jewish students from Eastern Europe. We became close friends. He was an ardent Zionist and—characteristically—surrounded himself with freethinkers and revolutionists rather than representatives of rigid Jewish Orthodoxy, although he scrupulously observed Jewish customs.

I was always urging him to dictate his thoughts to a secretary or a friend, but his modesty made him refuse. He distributed his intellectual largesse with the generosity of a millionaire of the mind and despised the type of intellectual who thinks every trifling remark so important that it should be written down and handed on to posterity. In my life he stood for the most marvelous embodiment of teacher and master. I think the ancient incarnations of the founders of religions must have been much like Rabinkow, selflessly and unsparingly disseminating knowledge and spiritual riches among their disciples. Rabinkow died rather young; he was constitutionally delicate and, as one might expect, never took care of his health.

Early in 1914 I decided to transfer from Heidelberg to Marburg. At that time Marburg was a center of the Neo-Kantian school founded by Hermann Cohen and continued by Paul Natorp and others. I was very preoccupied with the problems of Kantian philosophy; the boldness of Kant's critique of knowledge and his recognition of the subjectivity of all knowledge stirred and attracted me. This was the beginning of my conviction that no knowledge, at any rate no rational knowledge, can convey absolute truths. What fascinated me so strongly in the "Copernican" method of the Kantian critique of knowledge was its intellectual integrity and honesty, its courage in admitting limits to knowledge, and its refusal to make claims the human intellect could not fulfill, as other philosophical systems did almost to the point of fraud.

I spent a fruitful summer in Marburg, interrupted by occasional speaking engagements and many excursions into the beautiful surrounding countryside. I was not much interested in politics then and read the newspapers only cursorily, if at all. I was therefore totally unprepared when I came back to my room after playing tennis one afternoon and found that war had broken out. My parents happened to be on vacation on the Dutch coast, where I was supposed to join them a few days later. Instead, we all returned to Frankfurt.

I was not a German citizen at that time. The old Prussia was never eager to naturalize Jews from Eastern Europe, and since in those days being an alien entailed few disadvantages apart from not being able to vote, which mattered little to me or my parents, and since no passports or visas were required for traveling, we had never applied for citizenship. We did not hold Russian passports either, because the Russian consulate charged rather high annual fees for issuing them to citizens living abroad. From the German standpoint, however, we were unquestionably Russians, that is, enemy aliens.

Nevertheless, I was then a German patriot. Educated in German schools, I had a natural feeling of gratitude toward Germany. Like everybody else who lived in Germany and derived his notions of political developments from German newspapers, I was convinced that the Allies had attacked Germany unjustly. There was no disputing the fact too—and it was a decisive one—that the Western powers were allies of Czarist Russia, the Russia of the pogroms, the Russia that had deprived Jews of rights and herded its Jewish population into the infamous settlement districts. Russia was the archenemy. I volunteered for military service but—fortunately, as I now realize—was not accepted, because the German authorities expected victory within a few weeks. It was not worthwhile for them to pay the price of German citizenship for a few weeks of army service.

However, the war had an unpleasant consequence for me; I was barred from the university as an enemy alien. Like everybody else, I was certain that the war could not last long, so I looked around for a way of spending the interlude usefully. Since I had already begun to publish articles in the *Frankfurter Zeitung*, I volunteered to work full-time for this paper, whose owner, Dr. Heinrich Simon, I knew well. My plan was frustrated by an unforeseen development. In the early weeks of the war the military authorities ordered all enemy aliens who had lived in Frankfurt for less than ten years to leave the city (Frankfurt was of some strategic importance because it contained zeppelin hangars). My parents and I, having lived there over ten years, were not affected by this regulation, but a number of our close friends were, and for them it was upsetting personally.

I went to see the deputy chief of the Frankfurt police, who knew me from my speeches, to try to persuade him to rescind the order. After a fierce argument he refused on the grounds that, harsh as it was, the order was necessary for victory. To this I replied with youthful brashness: "If you can't win the war except through measures like this, it would be better if you lost it." This ended the conversation, but the next morning I received a deportation order for me personally, though not for my parents. I went to my friend Heinrich Simon, whose position as chief editor of the *Frankfurter Zeitung* made him very influential. We got into a car and went to see the commanding general, Baron von Eichhorn (who was murdered by Russian terrorists in Kiev after the war). This friendly gentleman naturally had the authority, as commander-in-chief, to cancel the deportation order, and he was willing to do so. However, he advised me against this step, which would only antagonize the deputy chief of police, and suggested that I leave Frankfurt briefly—for he too was convinced that the war would not last long, especially since German troops were already in Belgium and France—and return, with his permission, as soon as the incident had been forgotten.

This advice seemed sound and I decided to go for a time to Bad Nauheim, where hundreds of Eastern European Jews, who had been spending the summer at German spas, were stranded. They were allowed to live in the hotels, and since most of them had plenty of money, they were very comfortably situated. (Later, arrangements were made for them to return to Russia by the way of Sweden.) I was very happy at Bad Nauheim. I founded a Zionist club, learned Russian in my spare time, and got to know several families whose friendship I enjoyed for many years. My parents and Frankfurt friends could visit me as often as they liked because Bad Nauheim was only three-quarters of an hour away. Since the Eastern European Jews considered me to all intents and purposes a German and, moreover, a man trained in the law, I became their spokesman with the authorities. The police commissioner was a good-natured man, and I often managed to obtain facilities for the Russian-Jewish colony.

One more amusing case bears retelling. Among the internees were several dozen Orthodox Jews, including a few rabbis, who complained to me that for the first time in their lives they would have to celebrate the new year, which was about to begin, without a *mikvah*, or ritual bath. Jewish custom demands not only that brides attend the *mikvah* before marriage but that devout Jews go before celebrating New Year and the Day of Atonement. Bad Nauheim had no ritual bath, but there was one fifteen minutes away in Friedberg, the seat of a very old Jewish community. I was asked to get permission from the police commissioner for the rabbis to go to Friedberg, accompanied by the police. However, my interview with the chief of police was fruitless because he either could not or would not understand what a *mikvah* was. "I don't understand you," he said. "In the past year, forty thousand people have come to Nauheim especially to take baths and you're trying to tell me that your rabbis have to be sent to Friedberg for one. Tell your rabbinical friends that I'll be happy if they take a bath of any kind, even if it's only in Nauheim."

This decision was heartbreaking to the Orthodox group; some of them had tears in their eyes at the thought of the sin they were going to be compelled to commit. In my desire to help I remembered my acquaintance with the commanding general in Frankfurt. My plan took into account the deep-rooted respect the old Prussia had for all religions. I got the rabbis to show me the paragraph stipulating the *mikvah* ritual in the Jewish legal code, the *Shulhan Arukh,* and sent General von Eichhorn a telegram on behalf of these devout people asking for the required permission on the basis of section so-and-so. Next morning the police commissioner received a telegram ordering him to send the whole group to Friedberg with a police escort. Today such treatment of so-called enemies seems almost inconceivably humanitarian.

I liked Bad Nauheim so well that instead of availing myself of General von Eichhorn's permission to return to Frankfurt, I stayed there eight or nine months, still keeping up my contributions to the *Frankfurter Zeitung*. I wrote a series of articles justifying Germany's position toward its enemies from a philosophical and historical viewpoint. I attempted to uphold the German authoritarian system, accompanied by social legislation, through which imperial Germany had made considerable progress, against the Western system of individualistic liberalism. When I reread these articles today, they seem contrived and immature, but when one is young he is given to constructing systems and dividing the world into categories; later, he discovers the many facets of reality and the difficulty in forcing it into a Procrustean bed of abstract patterns. Partly as an intellectual joke, partly to give the series journalistic timelessness, I entitled it "The Spirit of Militarism," an allusion to the First World War's great battle cry against German militarism. Even before the war was over I learned that the Western world rightly considered German militarism dangerous and threatening. And later I turned radically against it. Like everybody else I have made my share of misjudgments, but even today I am not ashamed of my emotional ties to the country and the culture in which I grew up.

I sent my articles to Dr. Simon, who was so impressed with them that he passed them on to the editor of a series of brochures entitled "The German War." These presented fairly sophisticated German propaganda and were written by such men as Bernhard von Bülow, the former German chancellor, Albert Ballin, the head of the Hapag shipping line, and many leading writers. The editor, Ernst Jäckh, later director of the *Hochschule für Politik* in Berlin and subsequently professor at Columbia University, and Paul Rohrbach, a well-known writer, published my articles in this series, an unusual distinction for an unknown young man who was not even a German citizen. The brochures were distributed by the tens of thousands, and as a result, my name came to the attention of the propaganda division of the Ministry of Foreign Affairs.

In the meantime most of the alien Jews in Bad Nauheim had returned to Russia, and there was no longer any reason for me to remain there. Since I could still not re-enter the university, I decided to apply for permission to live in Berlin. I wrote to Dr. Jäckh and received an invitation to join the propaganda division of the Ministry of Foreign Affairs, which I accepted. I remained in Berlin until the end of the war in the somewhat anomalous position of having to report to the police twice a week as an enemy alien while working in the Foreign Ministry and traveling on a German diplomatic passport. This paradoxical situation arose because it never occurred to anyone in the legal division, where the contracts for new employees were written, that any candidate for the Foreign Ministry might not be a German citizen. I felt no obligation to mention my Russian citizenship and so the contract was signed.

My new position opened a new world to me. I was assigned to
the news division but was later transferred to Jewish affairs. In
the First World War Germany had the most pressing Jewish
problem of all the great powers. Poland and Lithuania, with
their millions of Jews, were occupied by the German army.
Palestine, being Turkish, was in the hands of one of Germany's
allies, so the problems that most concerned me, namely, the
rights of Eastern European Jewry and the colonization of Palestine, lay within the German sphere of influence. I brought this
to the attention of my superiors and suggested that a permanent
division for Jewish affairs be established. This was finally done
at the end of the war, after I had left the Ministry, and the
department remained the only one of its kind in the world until
Hitler became chancellor.

In the news division I had worked at first under a remarkable
man, Baron Buri, an aristocrat of Austrian descent, a cultivated
grand seigneur and slightly cynical roué, who was always telling me that Siamese dancing girls (whom he had come to appreciate when he was minister to Siam) were the highest expression of human culture. At bottom, he was anti-German, having
something of the decadent old Austrian aristocracy's contempt
for modern Prussia. I often told him that he had still not got
over the battle of Königgrätz. When there was no danger of
our being overheard, he used to speak French with me—in the
Foreign Ministry in the middle of the war—because he maintained that German was a barbarian language. On my first day
there, when he was assigning me my duties—reading sixty or
seventy newspapers and writing short résumés—he laid down
the following guidelines: When I read a news item, I was to
discount half of it because it appeared in a newspaper. Then I
was to discount the other half because it appeared in this particular newspaper. If I believed only half of what was left, he said,
I would never be taken in.

It did not take me long to discover the clumsiness and inepti-
tude of German diplomacy. I could cite unbelievable examples
of its lack of finesse and political subtlety, but for the sake of
brevity I shall confine myself to one that will also show the
hostility the lack of political acumen aroused, thus contributing

to defeat. For a time I worked chiefly with the neutralist correspondents of the Scandinavian press, but I was able nevertheless to establish contact with an influential pro-German journalist who was a distant relative of the Norwegian writer Björnstjerne Björnson. He explained to me why most of the Scandinavian correspondents were anti-German. Many of them were in the pay of the British, but in a subtle, not a crass way. For instance, the chief editor of one paper had been paid a high fee for an article in the *Encyclopaedia Britannica* he was never required to write; another had been invited to England, and the check for his trip had been enough for him to live on for a year. What the Foreign Ministry must do, this journalist said, is outbid the British in certain appropriate cases. He named names in all these charges, and I was terribly shocked. Young and naïve as I was, I thought of journalism as a sacred calling, dedicated to communicating ideas and beliefs. My acquaintance only smiled and accused me of being a child. "Journalism is a profession like any other. If I manufacture shoes, I sell them to the highest bidder. If I write articles, I do the same."

I reported what he had told me to my chief and suggested that his advice be followed. He suggested that I go to Scandinavia and see what could be done, but since I had no civil service rating, an old-line attaché was sent instead. He went to Copenhagen, where he wrote to a lot of people that he was authorized to offer them better terms than the British. I must admit that I never saw the actual letters, but that must have been their gist because the result was that an important Danish newspaper published a protest against attempts by German propagandists to corrupt the press, and the well-meaning attaché had to leave Copenhagen in a hurry.

After I had watched these goings-on for a year, it was clear to me that Germany was going to lose the war. Besides, reading the Western European press had given me a new insight into the war's causes, and I was no longer convinced that Germany was absolutely in the right. I might say in passing that the basic defect of German diplomats was that they were exactly like other civil servants: hard-working, dedicated, honorable, but bureaucrats through and through. I remember that even then a reform of the diplomatic service was under discussion and a high Foreign Ministry official who knew me and regularly read my reports asked me to write a memorandum containing my suggestions for its improvement. I refused on the grounds that my premises would be unacceptable a priori. The biggest mistake, I said, is that officials spend twelve to fourteen hours a day on paper work, which is all right for people in the Ministry of Finance, but diplomacy requires ideas that can be gotten only if one has time to take a walk with a girl, read a book, or lie on his back in the woods. You never get ideas from reading files. In my opinion, I said, the first reform should be to give the top officials of the Foreign Ministry very little work and a lot of free time. The diplomat made a hopeless gesture and said, "That's out of the question in our department."

After a year of this work which, though interesting at first, was not really in my line, I was able to concern myself more with the Jewish questions I've already mentioned. What interested me most was the legal status of Polish and Lithuanian Jewry. At that time Germany was planning to establish a Polish republic or grand duchy and intended to separate Lithuania and the Baltic provinces from Russia, and I hoped to work toward a guarantee of civil and minority rights for the millions of Jews who had hitherto been deprived of them, a guarantee designed to give them not merely equality as individual citizens but something approaching national and cultural autonomy. These questions being studied by the German-Jewish Committee for the East, to which Franz Oppenheimer, Adolf Friedmann, Moritz Sobernheim, and other eminent German Jews belonged. I was in touch with this committee, and although as a young man I had no influence to speak of in the Foreign Ministry, I did what I could. I visited Warsaw several times, made my first acquaintance with Polish Jewry, and wrote reports for the Foreign Ministry recommending cultural autonomy to promote a distinct Jewish way of life.

Many of the most respected leaders of German Jewry who favored assimilation categorically rejected this idea. They regarded Yiddish as a heritage of the ghetto, and a Jewish people conceived of in national terms was anathema to them. To many of them my presence in the Foreign Ministry was a thorn in the flesh, for it must not be forgotten that in imperial Germany Jews were generally not admitted to the civil service, and the Foreign Ministry, the most prestigious of the ministries, was closed altogether to Jews. They took it as an affront that an Eastern Jew, and a Zionist radical to boot, had gained a foothold there.

One day Baron Buri called me in and said with a smile that he had something curious to tell me. A deputation of three eminent Jews had just been to see him, though he would not tell me their names. They had expressed surprise at my appointment to the Foreign Ministry and asked whether he knew that I was not a German. He replied that if the imperial government was satisfied with Herr Goldmann's patriotism, they could be too. Forced to drop this argument, they then asked whether the ministry was aware that I was a Zionist, while the overwhelming majority of German Jews was anti-Zionist. My chief replied that although he knew very little about internal Jewish problems and controversies, he had known since his youth that German Jews constantly complained that the government asked every janitor whether he was a Jew or a Christian. "And now they're demanding," he said, "that when we do employ a Jew we ask what kind of Jew he is. That's going entirely too far!"

Of course, my attempts to secure civil rights and autonomy for the Polish and Lithuanian Jews came to nothing; Germany lost the war and had no voice in their future. In my line of duty I also tried to concern myself with the question of Palestine, but I was no more successful there because my position was a subordinate one and I could intervene only as a representative of the propaganda division. Nevertheless, I was able to accomplish a few things that were beyond private individuals or even the German Zionist organization, since channels for promulgating news in other countries were open to me. I was in touch with the leaders of the Zionist movement in Berlin, including Dr. Victor Jacobson, Dr. Arthur Hantke, and Kurt Blumenfeld, and was familiar with their demands and plans, which I was occasionally able to further.

I remember one particular instance in connection with Kemal

Pasha's retaliation for Vladimir Jabotinsky's establishment of the Jewish Legion: the brutal order to evacuate all the Jewish colonies, which would certainly have led to their destruction. The Turkish expulsion and massacre of hundreds of thousands of Armenians was all too fresh in everyone's memory. The only means of preventing a catastrophe was through drastic intervention by Germany, and this would require the mobilization of public opinion throughout the world. The most difficult thing was to get news items into the international press, since there was strict censorship both in Turkey and Germany. However, I succeeded in placing a good deal of material that aroused Jewish and subsequently non-Jewish opinion so that I could point out to the Foreign Ministry the propagandistic dangers in allowing the Turks to carry out their plans. Several interventions in Constantinople proved fruitless because of the autocratic, obstinate nature of Kemal Pasha himself, but finally Wilhelm II was persuaded to make a personal request for the cancellation of the order.

I also played a small part in getting the German government to issue a declaration of sympathy for Zionist aims, though it could never have amounted to anything since it was already clear that Germany had lost the war and that the fate of Palestine would be determined by the Western powers.

Toward the end I did not enjoy my work at the Foreign Ministry very much. The atmosphere had never been exactly *gemütlich;* the place was swarming with barons, titles, and monocles, and while I was never overawed by that sort of thing, I can't say that I could ever have felt at home with it. As the war drew to a close, I had to decide whether I wanted to stay in the foreign service, which would have meant taking an examination. Since Germany would have little say in the world, and since I had by then almost made up my mind to devote my life to Jewish affairs, I decided to give up this career. In the meantime the German revolution had broken out and I received the tempting offer to become a high official in the German Chancellory. The proposition did not attract me. I made sure that the office of Jewish affairs would remain in existence and took my leave, bringing to an end the somewhat remarkable three-year period of my life when I was, in a manner of speaking, a German diplomat.

As a result of my work in the Foreign Ministry, I had established active contacts with various German-Jewish groups, especially with the members of the Committee for the East. One of these was the eminent sociologist, Franz Oppenheimer. Far from being a dry scholar, Oppenheimer was a spirited man who lived life to the full, an impressive speaker and conversationalist of great wit, and a courageous upholder of his liberal political views and unconventional sociological theories. Another member of the same group was Dr. Adolf Friedmann, one of the first German Zionists. Among the active Zionist leaders I often met Dr. Alfred Klee, a professional yet very effective speaker and a popular leader who was also a successful attorney and well-known spokesman for German Zionism. He was later to play an important role in internal German-Jewish politics. Heinrich Loewe, a scholar and librarian, in whose house I was a frequent visitor in those days, was quite a different type. He had lived in Palestine for a time and while there had been elected a delegate to the First Zionist Congress. He had a thorough knowledge of the Hebrew language and was a passionate champion of the Zionist idea. Eventually he settled in Palestine and died in Tel Aviv at an advanced age.

In those years I had only slight contact with the official representatives of German Zionism, such as Dr. Hantke, Kurt Blumenfeld, and Richard Lichtheim. My collaboration with these men dates from a later period. But at this time I did get to know Professor Moritz Sobernheim; when the Foreign Ministry's office of Jewish affairs, which I had founded, was turned into a regular section, he was appointed head of it. The son of a wealthy family, he belonged to the German-Jewish upper bourgeoisie and possessed all its characteristics. He was something of a scholar, but looked upon scholarship as a hobby. He was kind, helpful, vitally interested in Jewish matters, but here again in a somewhat superficial, lordly manner. In short, those years brought me into contact, distant though it was at first, with the leading minds of German Jewry, more especially its representatives in Berlin.

German Jewry, whose existence came to an end in the Nazi period, was one of the most interesting branches of European Jewry and one of the most influential in modern Jewish history. It had experienced an enormous development during the era of emancipation, that is, during the nineteenth and the early twentieth century. It combined the talents developed in a large section of the Jewish people by centuries of embittered struggle for existence with many of the characteristic qualities, both good and bad, of the Germans. It had participated fully in the rapid economic rise of modern Germany, had contributed richly to it, and secured a place for itself in the German economy. The economic position of the German Jew compared to the Jews in other countries, including America, was unequaled. Jews were represented on the boards of the big banks— something that had been unparalleled elsewhere—and they had also made their way into industry. They controlled a significant proportion of wholesale trade and even participated in branches of the economy like shipping or the electrical industry; they played a leading role, as names such as Ballin or Rathenau prove.

I know of no emancipated Jewish population, in Europe or America, as firmly rooted in the general economy of its country as that of Germany was. Contemporary American Jews are richer, both absolutely and relatively, but even in America, with its unlimited opportunities, they have never succeeded in penetrating the central core of the economy—heavy industry, high finance, shipping, and railroads—as they did to a high degree in Germany. Their position in the intellectual life of the country was almost unique too. Brilliant names represented them in literature. The theater was, to a considerable extent, in their hands. The daily press, especially the sector of it that had international influence, was substantially Jewish-owned or edited. I would confidently assert, paradoxical as this may sound after the Hitler period, that no other branch of the Jewish people was able to make such use of the opportunities offered by nineteenth-century emancipation. The history of the Jews in Germany from 1870 to 1930 represents the most spectacular rise any branch of Jewry has ever achieved.

Yet we must not forget that even before Hitler the emancipation of the German Jews was not complete. Social anti-Semitism was almost a matter of course among the upper classes, though not in the insulting forms found in the United States, where residential areas, apartment houses, and hotels that exclude Jews are common. In a certain sense the Jews were always second-class citizens politically. A Jewish cabinet minister would have been unthinkable in imperial Germany; careers in the higher grades of the civil service or the military were mostly closed to Jews, and in a country where these professions played an incomparably more important role than in any Western democracy, this was of great importance.

There must then be good reasons to account for the German Jews having made such extraordinary strides despite the anti-Semitism always endemic in Germany, and it would be worth investigating those reasons even now, when it is all part of history. I have always felt that in many areas a certain affinity existed between the German and the Jewish mind: the tendency to analyze and formulate everything, the great dialectical talent, the propensity for systematizing. These, it seems to me, are traits as German as they are Jewish, though of course they all have their individual variations. The Jewish intellect, trained by centuries of ghetto life, was more akin to the German spirit than to the *esprit* and elegant logic of the French or to the Englishman's powerful practical sense and brilliant subtlety in matters of politics and international relations. The fact that in the transition period, when the Jews were moving out of the isolation of ghetto life into the full light of Europe, Western Europe was for them almost synonymous with German culture is not explained by geography alone. It was from Lessing, Schiller, and Heine that thousands of Eastern European Jewish intellectuals learned what modern literature is; for decades philosophy meant German philosophy to them. Of course, the closeness of Yiddish to German helped a great deal, but whatever the reasons, the phenomenal rise of the Jews in Germany was a fact not only during the Weimar Republic, which abolished the last restrictions on Jews' civil rights, but already in imperial Germany.

It was hardly surprising that German Jews should feel some gratitude for all this. They knew what they owed to the opportunities this emancipation had afforded them; to most of them the last two or three generations of their own families offered living proof of the strides that had been made. The reaction of the vast majority was an unconditional willingness to adapt to German ways and become an integral part of the German fatherland. They went about this with more vigor than patience, fascinated and dazzled by the invitation to become part of the new Germany and failing to realize that processes of this kind, even when they are accepted ideologically, take time, natural evolution, and tact. With characteristic energy and absolutely fanatical determination, they threw themselves into the arms of the new Germany, hoping in one or two generations to eradicate a separatism that had existed for centuries. For this reason the assimilation of Jews seemed more contrived, more obstinate, in Germany than it did elsewhere during the nineteenth century. There was also the Jewish tendency to find an ideological justification for everything, and this was intensified by the essentially similar German mania for presenting everything as a matter of principle.

So it is not surprising that the whole theory of modern Jewish assimilation was developed by German Jews. Jews in other countries were assimilated too but in a more natural way. They assimilated *de facto*, while the German Jews had to do it out of a profound *Weltanschauung*. Not content with being assimilated, the German Jews insisted on proving to themselves and the world that assimilation was something sacred, an ethical imperative, Jewry's historic mission, somehow attempting in this way to soothe their Jewish conscience. German Jewry had arisen out of a great tradition that had preserved its continuity for years. The geographic closeness of Eastern European Jewry, with its great creative religious and cultural centers, had kept mutual intellectual influence alive. German Jews began subconsciously to have qualms about their rapid and successful assimilation and in a typically German-Jewish way they tried to alleviate them with ideologies and theories, claiming that assimilation was not merely an organic process but a moral imperative and arguing that they were submitting to it not simply to participate in German advantages but to fulfill a sacred mission. It was a frantic attempt to eat their cake and have it too, to escape the fundamental, paradoxical, and often tragic question, "Jew or German?"

Enormous intellectual energy went into building up this case. When we read the literature today, after Hitler, it sounds prehistoric and at best arouses ironic sympathy, but in its time it was sincere. Most German Jews shrank from examining the problem and coming to grips with it courageously and uncompromisingly, which would quickly have revealed its absurdity. The only exception was the small minority of intellectual Zionists who broke with assimilation and created what Kurt Blumenfeld, one of its most gifted representatives, called post-assimilation Zionism.

Despite the intense desire for assimilation and its sound theoretical basis, any outsider—I myself, for instance—who had never been through a process of this kind and had therefore maintained an ironic detachment, could see that in the last analysis it was a failure. It was never harmonious or spontaneous but always self-conscious. Even the baptized Jews who had not been deterred by the final step were somehow uneasy. The well-known German-Jewish joke about the Jew who has himself baptized first Protestant and then Catholic so that if anyone asks what he used to be he can say "Protestant" is a reflection of this lack of confidence.

This resulted in the remarkable social and psychological structure of German Jewry, with its very capable, gifted, hard-working people, whose Jewish qualities were reinforced by German ones but whose unusually intense intellectual liveliness and responsiveness to all trends never made it immune to a deep-seated discord that all its success could not alleviate. There is hardly a German-Jewish writer or musician in whom this lack of harmony is not to be found. The tragic irony of Heine, who was honest enough to admit it, was in a way the hallmark of nearly all German-Jewish literature and stemmed from this very discord. The literature was always in some way self-conscious and competent, but it was rarely the product of organic growth. German-Jewish literature has never produced a Stifter, a Goethe, or even a Rilke. Although the Jewish contribution is an essential element in the intellectual life of nineteenth-century Germany and played a leading part in enriching, refining, diversifying, and, if I may use the term, administering German culture, a list of the ten most important exponents of that culture would include no Jewish name—if we except the economic and scientific spheres, which require different qualities.

The enforced adaptation was accomplished so rapidly that important Jewish elements were left intact. The bulk of German Jews was never totally assimilated. Compared with the Jewish populations of other Western European countries, they were much more Jewish. Even their deliberate stressing of assimilation, their loud, often embarrassing reminder "See how German we are!", arose from their ultimate certainty that they were still Jewish. People tried to prove to themselves that it was their duty as Jews to assimilate, not merely because they wanted to justify assimilation but because at the same time they wanted to remain Jewish. The whole thing was a true compromise, unsatisfactory in human terms and a great strain psychologically. From the Jewish point of view it had the advantage that a good deal of Jewishness was able to survive. It would be equally unjust and historically false to attempt to deny the role German Jewry played in the recent history of the Jewish people, despite its tendency to assimilate. Moses Hess and Theodor Herzl, Abraham Geiger and Wilhelm Grätz, Samson Raphael Hirsch and Nathan Birnbaum, among many others, wrote in German and were products of German culture. A majority of the ideas that today still motivate and enrich Jewish life and by which British and especially American Jewry live originated in German Jewry. In the history of modern Zionism the German Jews deserve a place of honor; their efforts, whether voluntary or as a result of constraint, have made an essential contribution to the development of Israel.

During the First World War I did not realize all this as clearly as I did after having been active for a long time within German Jewry and after many opportunities to compare German Jews

with Jewish minorities in other countries, but I sensed it intuitively even then. All my lectures centered on the German-
Jewish experience to some extent, particularly one on Heine,
Rathenau, and Weininger, representatives of three types of
modern German-Jewish assimilation, that I repeated several
times. The great problem of assimilation was a recurrent theme
in my thinking, and I believe it was more easily accessible to me
because I had never consciously been through the process of
assimilation myself. My Jewishness was entirely organic and
spontaneous. Perhaps I was able to understand and appreciate
post-assimilation Zionism better because I was basically a pre-
assimilation Zionist.

My work during those years was essentially propagandistic. I
was too young and unknown to play a role in the leadership of
German Zionism, not to speak of world Zionism, which was
partly directed from Berlin. Besides, my interest in the organizational and political side of the movement had not yet been
awakened. What interested me was ideology and propaganda. I
fought assimilation, tried to propagate theoretical Zionism, and
addressed myself to the questions I worked on professionally in
the Ministry of Foreign Affairs. Berlin offered me excellent
opportunities for deepening my education. I was enrolled at the
University of Berlin, and although my work left me little spare
time, I attended a number of courses—though not the ones
intended for students of law. The lectures I remember best are
Eduard Meyer's on history, Ernst Troeltsch's on the philosophy
of religion, and some of Wilamowitz-Moellendorff's.

During a lecture by the great historian of antiquity Eduard
Meyer, an incident occurred that made a great impression on
me. Notoriously something of an anti-Semite, Professor Meyer
was giving a course on Biblical antiquity, and on this particular
occasion he was discussing the patriarchs. He closed with the
following words, declaimed with great emotion: "The ancient
Israelites pronounced the name Ja-acob. The modern Jews have
turned it into Yankel. The difference between Ja-acob and
Yankel exemplifies the total decadence of this race." I was indignant at this malicious remark, yet at the same time overcome
by its partial truth.

During those war years I read much more than ever before,

attended the concerts Berlin offered in such rich variety and
also the theater. Twice a week for two whole winters I sat
through the rehearsals of the St. Matthew's and St. John's Passions by the Ochs Choir whose German-Jewish director has
probably never been surpassed as an interpreter of Bach's choral
works. I lived in the city of Berlin only for the first year and
then moved to Zehlendorf and later to Schlachtensee. At that
time I was very friendly with Arnold Zweig's wife and sister-in-
law (Zweig himself was away on military service), and I owe
much to both of them. They belonged to a literary milieu, and
partly through them, partly through friends they introduced me
to, the world of art and music was opened to me—a blessed
antidote to the very real danger of exclusive intellectuality to
which young Jews of my background always tended.

My work in the Foreign Ministry was no burden, since I was
not a regular civil servant. I went to the ministry only three
times a week and used the remainder of my time for reading or
walking in the romantic country around the lake at Schlachtensee. My bachelor apartment had no telephone, so if a meeting
requiring my presence was called at the ministry, the police
commissioner would come and fetch me. For him the term
Reich Chancellor covered everything connected with the government and Wilhelmstrasse, and often when I was lying reading in my garden or by the lake—for he knew all my favorite
places—this corpulent little man would come panting up, calling: Herr Goldmann, you're wanted in town at once. The
"Chancellor" needs you.

And it was during those years that I made my first contacts,
tenuous as they still were, with the world of German politics. I
had already met some diplomats in the Foreign Ministry (I shall
have more to say about some of them later) and at the end of
the war, when the German revolution broke out, I established
contact with the leaders of the Social Democratic Party. I got to
know Friedrich Ebert, future president of the Weimar Republic, Philipp Scheidemann, its first chancellor, and Carl Severing.
Internal German politics left me cold, but I was passionately
interested in the German revolution, which I experienced at
first hand in Berlin. I cannot say that I was very impressed by

any of the spokesmen for German socialism; they were all good, decent men, totally lacking in imagination and vision, typical representatives of the petty bourgeoisie, with a strong sense of order and discipline and imbued with respect for authority even in the midst of revolution.

One experience I had at that time revealed the nature of the German "revolutionaries" more tellingly than any book. I liked to wander freely about Berlin, sometimes in districts where fighting or shooting was taking place. One day I was passing the Lustgarten on Unter den Linden just as a big demonstration by the left-wing socialists was beginning. I waited to listen to the speakers, who were vehement and sometimes inflammatory, but while they were roaring their revolutionary slogans and the audience was yelling its enthusiasm, policemen were going around collecting five pfennigs each from the people sitting on park chairs. Everyone paid up. It's all right to overthrow a government, but you mustn't overlook the regular charge for seats. I went home and told my friends we couldn't expect much from the German revolution. It seemed to me impossible to do both things at the same time: carry on a revolution and collect chair money. From the behavior of that audience it was obvious to me which alternative the German revolutionists would choose if they had to.

There was little reason for me to stay on in Berlin. I had to get my degree and to do so I needed a more peaceful atmosphere. Only by doing this could I decide what I really wanted to do in the future. I had rejected the possibility of a diplomatic career. I had long been sure that I did not want to be a lawyer and the personal reasons for pursuing that profession no longer existed. More and more often I found myself thinking of Jewish or Zionist public service, which could, of course, be combined with an academic career. I had the happiest memories of my days in Heidelberg and the thought of its atmosphere and landscape stimulated me. Homesick for the world of professors and lecturers after years of bureaucratic and ultimately unrewarding work in official propaganda, I decided to return to Heidelberg.

I said good-by to Berlin with a fairly confident feeling that I would return. This was the center of Germany—from a Jewish point of view too. One sensed that the end of the Empire was going to provide new opportunities. Besides, I had personal ties with close friends in Berlin, and it was my intention to return to Heidelberg for no more than one or two semesters, just long enough to get my degree. I did not know that several years would elapse before my work would take me back to Berlin.

5

Law Degree and a Career in Journalism

I completed my study of law at Heidelberg in a couple of semesters without attending lectures any more regularly than I had before. I left the real preparation for the final examination to what was called in Germany a *repetitor*, a tutor who crammed three years' subject matter into your head in eight weeks and whose greatest asset was his familiarity with the questions each individual professor was most likely to ask. I crammed with him for a few weeks because I felt I ought to complete the course of study I had begun, although it was already clear to me that law would never be my field. After I had passed the oral examination, the question of a dissertation arose. Naturally I did not want to waste several more months writing a dissertation on a subject that held neither theoretical nor practical interest for me, so I conceived the idea of basing it on a series of articles on "The Concept of *Bürger* and Gentleman" that I had published in *Die Tat*, a most reputable periodical. I added some legal material on the concept of civil rights and submitted this dissertation to a famous professor who was about to retire and was accepting doctoral candidates freely before doing so. I was lucky enough to get it back from this benevolent old gentleman with the notation "satisfactory."

What really enthralled me at the university was the study of sociology, philosophy, and literature. I attended the lectures and seminars of the foremost existentialist philosopher, Karl Jaspers, still creative in his old age, who introduced me to the philoso-

phy of Kierkegaard, which I found deeply moving. In Jaspers'
seminar I read a paper on Spengler, whose *Decline of the West*
had made a tremendous impression on the whole intellectual
world. I also had some contact with the group around Max and
Alfred Weber. Without doubt Max Weber was at that time the
most brilliant thinker at the university of Heidelberg and one of
the boldest sociologists in Europe, no less significant as a man
than as author. He was no longer lecturing, but privileged students could visit him at his house, where he held a kind of
seminar, talking and passing out stimulating ideas as only an
intellectual giant can afford to do. I was not fortunate enough to
know him intimately, but even my slight acquaintance was
something to cherish forever. He was a true genius and like
most geniuses, he did not care whether he was essentially right
or not. Geniuses are usually much too one-sided to be right.
Their great achievement is to discover new points of view, to
sound unplumbed depths, to draw back curtains hiding whole
new worlds, to scatter flashes of intellect, each of which can
illuminate a whole area of darkness. Whatever Max Weber
touched—the problems of capital, the relationship of Puritanism
to modern society, the sociology of theology, the burning questions of contemporary post-revolutionary Germany that interested him passionately, questions of the recent and future
development of mankind—it was all new, fascinating and
thought-provoking and it compelled further reflection. I also
attended some of the lectures of Alfred Weber who, although
less brilliant than his brother, was extremely instructive and
possessed encyclopedic knowledge.

I also enjoyed Friedrich Gundolf's lectures and my acquaintance with him, and through him I came into contact with the
Stefan George Circle. Although Gundolf was known to be of
Jewish extraction, he was totally indifferent to everything Jewish and represented the acme of German-Jewish assimilation. He
had the intellectual and emotional sensitivity of the heir to an
ancient, highly refined culture. In addition to an extraordinary
memory, he had the gift of making everything he knew cre-
atively alive. He gave me my first intimate glimpse into the
writer's workshop and taught me to analyze a poem. To him, as

to the whole George Circle, language was a sacral force. That words can work magic—the primeval magic idea behind everything that has to do with poetry—was absolutely axiomatic to Gundolf and his school. At the same time, like most outstanding men, he was even more interesting for his personality than for his books. Every lecture, every conversation with him, was a work of art, and for me, with my somewhat unartistic Jewish background, to know him was a formative, enriching experience.

For a time I studied with Heinrich Rickert but did not particularly enjoy him. I thought he did not compare with the great German philosophers, even those of modern times. He was more a historian of philosophy than the theoretician he prided himself on being. My studies with him ended rather abruptly after a brief but violent clash. He used to hold his seminar at his house, since in those days he was subject to attacks of anxiety and preferred not to come to the university. One day about fifteen of us were sitting in his living room. The name of Hermann Cohen had come up, and I began to interpret a problem according to Cohen's ideas. Rickert stopped me irritably, saying that Cohen's philosophy is "more race than philosophy." I was annoyed and replied: "Herr Geheimrat, in the first place your remark isn't true and in the second place it too is certainly more race than philosophy." At this the somewhat neurotic old gentleman took offense and left the room. Since we were in his home, we did not quite know what we should do. We waited a few minutes and then left the house. I never went back.

During those months in Heidelberg I had been considering an academic career. With my speaking ability, I could count on becoming a popular lecturer. I finally dropped the idea after discussing it with my friends on the faculty, not so much on account of the limited material recompense and the obstacles in the way of a university career for an Eastern Jew as because of an overwhelming dislike for academic life. I do not know from firsthand experience what it is like at other universities, but I have reason to assume that it was more or less the same everywhere. In those days I naïvely thought that a university, dedicated entirely to study, must produce an atmosphere of intellectuality, of honest human relations, in which only knowledge and thought matter. Instead, I observed at Heidelberg, especially after I became friendly with a number of professors, a web of jealousies and vanities, rivalry and envy, that entangled all aspects of life in a very circumscribed world. This made the intellectual climate much more stifling than that of, say, the world of politics. In later life I got to know many politicians, and from very personal experience I know a lot about political fights. I think I can say that political conflicts, while not always conducted in an objective, gentlemanly fashion, are often less shabby than their counterparts among scholars and men of learning. Compared to the scholar, the politician always has something of the man of the world about him, a certain insouciance. He does not take his problems with such deadly seriousness as the man of learning. He is more ironical or more cynical. He forgets yesterday's tensions more easily. The sphere he moves in extends, after all, to a whole nation or several nations. When academics quarrel, they throw all their scholarly prestige into the fight. They methodically lay the groundwork for their fights and then build theories upon it, and the harder they pretend that what is at stake is concrete problems and not personal ambition, professional careers, power, and vanity, the more false and dishonest the controversy becomes.

I sensed this fairly strongly at Heidelberg and it was not exactly an inducement to spend my life in such an atmosphere. Also, the idea of settling in a small town, even one as picturesque and rich in tradition as Heidelberg, repelled me. I wanted to see other countries, travel, get to know a lot of people. And even if I made a success of it, the prospect of getting stuck in a provincial town, under pressure to publish, and of being tied to a fixed lecture schedule, was not alluring, whatever compensations the profession might otherwise offer.

The appeal of Zionist work was growing steadily stronger. I gave a lot of talks, many of them to non-Jewish audiences. This was the time when, in fighting the results of the German revolution, the reactionary nationalistic forces were becoming active again. The best known group was the Deutsch-Völkischer Schutz- und Trutz-Bund (German Nationalist League for Defense and Defiance). Although they did not yet represent a serious danger, they were all obstreperous, and I was eager to take a crack at them. I had prepared a lecture entitled "The Jews and the Nations," that, now that I look at it from a more mature viewpoint, I have to admit was pretty provocative—what you might call anti-Semitism in reverse, a sharp indictment in which the nations of the world were presented with the bill for their treatment of the Jews throughout the centuries. Well received in many quarters, this lecture was naturally a challenge to the opposition and there were several violent episodes. In Stuttgart one of them turned into a big fight with the anti-Semitic students of the Hohenheim agricultural college, and several members of the audience wound up in the hospital.

The worst disorder occurred in Heidelberg. My lecture, widely publicized by the Jewish student organization, attracted hundreds of students, Zionists, anti-Zionists, non-Jewish democrats, and anti-Semites. The chairman was my lifelong friend and former fellow student, Dr. Yeshayahu Foerder, who later went to Palestine, was for many years a prominent member of the Knesset and is today president of the Bank Leumi, the largest bank in Israel. I delivered my lecture, interrupted several times by applause and boos, and a very heated discussion developed. Members of the Kartell Convent, an anti-Zionist Jewish organization, attacked me for my Zionism, as others began to spout their rabble-rousing anti-Semitism. Well to the fore was a private docent in philosophy at the university of Heidelberg, a Dr. Rugge, who later became a well-known Nazi. (Before this, however, he had been dropped from the university as a result of anti-Semitic incidents.) The meeting ended in a tremendous uproar and the police had to intervene.

My activities as a lecturer and writer of newspaper articles however, were only incidental to my commitment to Zionism. My main interest was the development of Zionist policy. I was young, radical in my views, and very aggressive. By nature I was more at home with the opposition than with the Establishment, and the years I spent as a member of Zionist groups, often very small ones, opposing the dominant party, were in many ways more rewarding than the later years after I came to power, so to speak, and had to fight the opposition.

In those days a place among the leaders of Zionism held very little attraction for me. What fascinated me was the main line of Zionist evolution and the dangers already threatening the movement as a result of its early successes. Those were the years following the Balfour Declaration, heady years of naïve illusions, when the Jewish people, so inexperienced politically, believed that the British were going to provide them with a Jewish state, free, gratis, for nothing. It was the time when every British diplomat who appeared at a Zionist meeting was welcomed with enthusiastic applause. I was afraid that the movement might flatten out into a purely political affair or get detoured into diplomatic channels. I was alarmed by the mistaken belief that we would achieve a Jewish state through the benevolence of ministers and generals and by the danger of failing to recognize the truly great problems of Zionism: on the one hand, relations with the Arab world, on the other, the decisive importance of our own efforts. I was afraid that a cheap and easy form of Zionism might emerge, consisting of resolutions and cheering, diplomatic exercises and promises, all at the expense of the revolutionary, idealistic character of the movement.

My friend Jacob Klatzkin shared these fears. He had spent the war years in Switzerland, but we got in touch again after the war and discovered that our views were much alike. He was older than I and his name was better known, but we both felt a strong desire to work together and decided to found a Zionist periodical in Heidelberg, without official support, without money, and without backing from a publishing house. We named it *Freie Zionistische Blätter* and, as we said in our preliminary announcement, the stress was on the word *frei*. We wanted to be free from party discipline and from any kind of dependence on the Establishment, free too as far as publication dates were concerned. We were determined to present our ideas and beliefs and those of a small group of like-minded writers to the Zionist public, without regard for the consequences. Not many issues of this journal appeared, but I think it had a certain influence. Among our contributors were Hans Kohn (who unfortunately turned his back on Zionism later), Eugen Höflich, and Felix Weltsch. Klatzkin and I wrote most of the articles, and in that respect it was a typical independent journal. All the authorities either resented us or refused to take us seriously. But thirty-three years later, when I reread many of the articles we published, I am surprised at their foresight and at how little the Zionist situation has fundamentally changed.

Like everybody who grows, I have made shifts in my Zionist political position. Only stubborn minds stick to all their opinions for life. I have changed my mind many times on practical and administrative matters and on questions of party affiliation, and I am not ashamed of it. When all is said and done, these are only means to an end. A party is not an end in itself, an organizational structure is not an ultimate goal, and anyone who lacks the flexibility for tactical politics should keep out of politics altogether. When it comes to principles, however, my conception of Zionism as a great historical, moral and spiritual movement is essentially the same today as it was then.

6

Years of Contemplation in Murnau

The *Freie Zionistische Blätter* did not survive long because we lacked funds. Since we had no organization behind us, and Klatzkin and I had to be responsible for running and financing the paper, as well as editing it, and since the venture was in any case too independent and critical for the official Zionists, we had to give it up. Once I had received my degree, there was really no reason for me to stay in Heidelberg. On the other hand, I was in no hurry to accept a position that would chain me to an office and regular hours, especially since I felt a need to continue my education and follow my own bent.

My uncle, a Hebrew publisher from Warsaw, happened to be in America just at that time and at my request arranged for me to write two or three light articles a month for the New York Yiddish newspaper *The Day*. For these I received twenty to twenty-five dollars apiece. The inflation overwhelming Germany in those years meant sudden poverty and real need for many people, but to me it brought the chance of devoting myself exclusively to my studies and inclinations for a while, free of the necessity of earning my bread by daily work.

Within a brief time the dollar was worth millions and then billions of marks. Once, on my way to the bank to cash a dollar check, I was detained by a friend, with the result that I got several times the sum I would have received an hour earlier. Others might have used my dollar payments to buy real estate or other tangible assets, but I wanted to take advantage of this unusual chance to live for my studies alone. Klatzkin had similar intentions and we began to look for a place where we could live pleasantly for as long as our means allowed. I learned from my good friend Fritz Sternberg, who later became a well-known economist and sociologist, that he had rented a house in Murnau but was not able to occupy it. I went to see it, liked it, and took it over. Klatzkin soon joined me and established himself in a neighboring cottage. I spent just under two years in Murnau and they were among the most enjoyable and fruitful of my life.

A little town in Bavaria, Murnau is a few minutes from Garmisch-Partenkirchen and about an hour from Munich, one of the liveliest centers of art and music, famous for its Schwabing bohemian colony, its carnival, its theater, and its gay, carefree atmosphere. Many painters lived in Murnau in those days. Situated on the charming Lake Staffelsee, Murnau was remote enough to permit complete concentration but near enough to the Bavarian capital to make good theater and music available whenever one felt the desire for them. Rich as I was, thanks to my American dollars, I could live by myself. I lived the good life and did not lack company. Klatzkin was close by. Half an hour away in Starnberg lived my friend Arnold Zweig and his wife, and I received frequent visits from acquaintances and friends whom I could easily entertain in my house. My permanent house guest was a German shepherd dog I named Adin, which in Hebrew means "the gentle one." Every day I used to take long walks with him, which I recorded in a never-finished manuscript entitled "Conversations with Adin" that was later destroyed, with all my other writings, by the Nazis. Like many, I always did my best thinking while walking and I fell into the habit of formulating my thoughts in a kind of peripatetic conversation with myself.

My thinking on Jewish issues was greatly stimulated by my daily contact with Klatzkin, who was then working on his definitive book on Zionist theory, published as *Probleme des modernen Judentums* (*Problems of Modern Judaism*) but later (at my suggestion) called *Krisis und Entscheidung* (*Crisis and Decision*). Klatzkin was probably the most acute theoretician of contemporary Jewish questions; his radically logical mind never flinched from even the most extreme conclusions. In a sense he delighted in radicalism, because he had a great gift for paradox and liked to play the intellectual outsider. He was the most Zionist of all the thinkers in the movement, the only really hundred percent Zionist, who uncompromisingly pursued the basic concept to its conclusion as nobody else did.

The Zionist outlook was of course based on the thesis that the survival of the Jewish people was threatened by its geographical dispersion and that only its concentration in the ancient homeland of Palestine could save the millions of persecuted, homeless Jews and guarantee their survival as a people. All the theoreticians agreed on this. Klatzkin's radical and original development of this theory denied that any part of the people that remained in the Diaspora after the establishment of a Jewish state in Palestine could survive. In penetrating analyses backed by his comprehensive knowledge of Jewish history and culture, he tried to show that the unnatural existence of a Jewish community possessing no territorial center depended on one factor alone: the religious life that had dominated ghetto life throughout the centuries. Now that religion had lost its control over the Jew's daily life as a result of modern emancipation, the Jewish minorities within other nations could no longer maintain their distinctive character. Moreover, he predicted, after a few generations of normal life in its own country the Palestinian nation would have no common language and no connection with the minority in the Diaspora. While the Palestinian Jews would acquire all the characteristics of a normal nation—their own language, way of life, interests, and goals—he thought that the Diaspora communities, out of their fear of identifying themselves with the established nation in Palestine, were inevitably fated to lose their own culture and become an amorphous group, retaining only quite superficial and meaningless symbols of the ancient Jewish religion and losing their own creative vitality. They would become like gypsies, and no one would know for certain what they were or why they existed, until finally they disappeared altogether. Klatzkin pursued to its conclusion this negation of the Diaspora, which every Zionist theory contains to some extent, supporting his case with an extraordinary wealth of arguments from philosophy, psychology, and the history of ideas.

In Murnau I discussed these opinions with him in an endless dialogue, a dialogue terminated many years later only by his death because each of us stuck to his own position. At that time, when it was still too early for empirical, after-the-event wisdom, I used to cite the Jewish past as an argument against his logically irrefutable statements. I said that logically the Jewish people ought to have vanished long ago, that its Diaspora existence contravened all the so-called laws of history. I already doubted the validity of those laws and was to grow even more skeptical of them every year as I observed history in the making. To say that everything that has happened in history was bound to happen—that splendid but grotesque crux of Hegel's philosophy—seemed slightly absurd to me even then and seems to me today absolutely ludicrous. The more you study history, especially if you have close, firsthand experience of great events, the less likely you are to arrive at the untenable conclusion that everything that is, must be—that is, unless you take a religious approach to world history, holding that a good, evil, or indifferent god directs everything according to what is, to him at least, a meaningful plan. To cite just one example, perhaps the most ghastly in world history. To assume that Hitler and the Nazi era were inevitable and therefore meaningful is a logical and moral somersault that no reasonable, decent man can attempt.

Since I could not believe in the lawfulness of historic events and even doubted the absolute truth of the apparently unassailable lawfulness of natural events, I rejected Klatzkin's thesis that the Jewish communities of the Diaspora had no future because peoples lacking a territorial home cannot survive. I reminded him that in contrast to other peoples the history of the Jews is unique, that they have survived not one but several diasporas. Jewish history actually began with a Diaspora, the Egyptian one, and the distinctive rhythm of this history is its alternate shifts between concentration and dispersal. It seems to me that the Jewish character shows an instinct for dispersal at least as strong as for the land of Israel and territorial consolidation.

According to everything I know about Jewish history, it is

naïve and false to believe that the gentile world imposed these various dispersals upon the Jews through coercion and superior strength. In the long run, a people cannot be coerced, and despotism is never more than episodic. Ultimately a people lives as it wants to live and in some way deserves its fate. One people is never exterminated by another; the crime of genocide does not exist in history. Millions of one race may be annihilated, as we Jews were in Hitler's Reich, but a people as a whole never perishes unless it gives up its struggle to survive. If a nation's impotence causes it to despair so that it can no longer muster the revolutionary spirit it needs to resist the enemy's apparently invincible superiority, it perishes, but this is a case of suicide, not murder.

As a result, I held and still hold the opinion that the Diaspora fulfills some deep need of the Jewish spirit or of the collective Jewish soul. We went into the Diaspora of our own free will, just as we voluntarily created the ghetto in order to survive in the Diaspora. Somehow we have at one and the same time the roving, adventurous spirit of a world people and a yearning for the homeland, a longing to be left alone with God and our culture. Jewish history has always shifted back and forth between these two poles and this led me to the conclusion that our situation cannot really be normalized by assembling a small portion of the people in Palestine and writing off the rest. I cannot accept the desirability of our becoming just a nation like all the rest, relinquishing the openness to the world and the global breadth of outlook that characterize us today. If the Diaspora could survive along with the Jewish center, this would make our little country, which is destined to remain forever small, distinctive and unique.

Klatzkin would ask how the Jewish communities in the Diaspora could possibly maintain their link with the Jewish state and their distinctive spiritual life, after emancipation and the collapse of ghetto existence. In reply I would again rely on the lessons of history rather than logical analysis. I would remind him that the Jews' survival throughout the Diaspora represents a unique achievement of the national instinct for self-preservation and the national genius—perhaps its most impressive achievement of all time. I remember often saying to him, "Suppose a Jacob Klatzkin had been living after the destruction of the Second Temple and the so-called expulsion of the Jews from Palestine. He would have proved, with all your logical brilliance, that there was no hope of their surviving as a people after the loss of their national and religious center." Perhaps such a Klatzkin did once exist and perhaps he wrote a book as brilliant in its way as *Krisis und Entscheidung*. But if so, the Jewish people has lost all memory of him. And indeed what a people preserves out of its whole intellectual creation is very characteristic of it. Anything detrimental to its existence is often forgotten, just as an individual's memory usually obliterates what might be hurtful to him. In individuals, as in nations, memory is, after all, an instrument of self-preservation. Whether or not that earlier Klatzkin ever existed, the fact remains that the Jewish people has survived in defiance of any logical negation of the Diaspora (which theoretically would have been just as tenable then as it is today). It has survived because, despite all the so-called laws of history, its invincible will to do so produced ways of life that made possible its continued existence.

Something similar, I concluded, will happen again when a Jewish state finally exists. We shall find some new way of continuing the intimate, fateful relationship between the state and the people, the center and the periphery, and thus acquire the spiritual strength necessary to guarantee the survival of the Jewish communities in the Diaspora. The situation of the Jews will never be normalized through a state alone, but only by creating a center in Palestine while at the same time retaining the great Diaspora, linked with the state in an enduring and mutually enriching relationship.

I have given this detailed account of my argument with Klatzkin because it pinpoints the central Jewish problem of our time, now that the Jewish state exists. I never convinced Klatzkin, and he never convinced me. The dilemma that preoccupied me so intensely then still worries many Zionist thinkers and many sections of the Jewish people, to whom it is as timely as it has been for me ever since those days. I have always admitted that Klatzkin was right on one point. If the Jews fail to recognize this problem and do not make every effort to solve it constructively, there is a danger that his prognosis will be fulfilled. If the State of Israel and the Diaspora communities live their separate lives, if the two branches of the people do not feel a mutual responsibility and coordinate their major decisions, then we shall pay a tragic price for the creation of the state: the disappearance of the remainder of the Jewish people.

Notwithstanding the many disturbing symptoms of this danger, I have not abandoned my faith in the Jewish national genius. From it I take hope that despite the force of habit in everyday life, despite the natural self-centeredness of Israel and the equally understandable egoism of individual Jewish communities, our generation and the ones to come will succeed in mastering the problem and in realizing that the question of Jewish survival has by no means been solved by the founding of the State of Israel. There still lies ahead the great task of forging between Israel and the Jewish people outside it a bond that will guarantee the survival of both, in keeping with the unique character of their past.

Besides deepening my understanding of the modern Jewish problem, my almost daily contact with Jacob Klatzkin greatly enriched my general Jewish knowledge. Klatzkin was an expert in Jewish philosophy and Hebrew literature. He had an admirable memory and his insatiable interest in ancient literature had led him to build up a remarkable library of medieval and modern Hebrew texts. It was he, in the main, who introduced me to medieval philosophy of religion, Kabbalah and Hasidism. My conversations with him and the reading he recommended laid the foundation for the knowledge of these subjects I was later able to acquire.

Apart from my interest in things Jewish, I used the leisure of my Murnau period to study philosophy. In Heidelberg, under the direction of Rickert and Jaspers, I had gained some knowledge of modern philosophy. In Murnau I tried to supplement this general philosophical education by a more searching investigation of mysticism. I had always been skeptical of the possibility of discovering absolute truth by purely logical and epistemological means, and all my life I had been fascinated by other sources of experience and knowing, especially mystical apperception. If the absolute can be experienced anywhere, I felt, it is in mysticism. On the other hand, during those years I came to understand the paradox of mystical instruction expressed in the well-known words of one of the greatest mystics, Meister Eckhart, that the true mystic must keep silent. The words of rational speech are not capable of adequately rendering the experience of a great mystic, and for this reason all mystical writings are ultimately only inarticulate stammering. They speak in similes and symbols, and in this lies their fascination and their difficulty. During those years I read the great mystics of antiquity and spent a while at the monastery at Beuren, where there were some eminent experts in medieval Catholic mysticism. I began a paper on the antinomy of mystical knowledge and have retained my interest in this problem until the present day, sometimes to the astonishment of my friends. Even today it is hard for me to say for sure whether this propensity for mysticism may not camouflage some religious need. Perhaps I am not yet old enough to know the truth about myself in this respect.

I attended the Munich theater, visited friends, gave Zionist speeches, and often went to see my Warsaw uncle, the Hebrew publisher Szalkowitz, but otherwise my idyllic Murnau existence was rudely disturbed only once—by a visit from a high Munich police official accompanied by some of his assistants. They said they had come in response to denunciations made against me. There was at that time a vigorous National Socialist group in Murnau. This group was raising a lot of dust because Adolf Hitler, after his abortive Munich putsch, was living very close by, in the Hanfstängl family house in Uffing. The denunciation contained three charges: that I was not a German citizen but only claimed to be one, that I had no doctoral degree, and that I was director of a Communist youth propaganda center for Western Europe located in Murnau. After the Munich criminal investigators had found in a desk drawer my doctoral diploma and a letter from Chancellor Bethmann-Hollweg thanking me for my work in the Foreign Ministry, and had checked through my library and assured themselves that it consisted of philosophical, mystical, and Hebrew books, they made friends with me, took me swimming in Lake Staffelsee, and warned the Murnau German Nationalists, as they called themselves in those days, that I was under the protection of the Munich police. My friendship with the high police official involved lasted for many years, and on various occasions I made use of the acquaintance-ship to get deportation orders against East European Jews living in Munich canceled or to smooth out other difficulties.

I could not prolong my stay in Murnau after the German inflation came to an end and twenty-five dollars were only one hundred marks. This took away the incentive to continue writing light articles in Yiddish, particularly since, after the stabilization of the mark, the German press began to pay much better. I was faced with the necessity of finding some occupation by which I could earn a living. Moreover, it was obvious to me that I could not indefinitely devote myself to study but would have to start doing something productive. From my association with my uncle I had acquired an interest in publishing. This uncle, a man full of ideas and initiative, had planned after the war to move his business from Poland to Berlin, because Berlin under the Weimar Republic had become a mecca for the Eastern European intelligentsia and a lot of eminent Hebrew and Yiddish writers had gone to live there. He was thinking of opening a branch of his publishing house in Berlin in partnership with me and also of reviving the old idea of a great modern Jewish encyclopedia. From the outset I included Klatzkin in these discussions. When my uncle died, leaving only young children, it was natural that his family should ask me to carry out his ambitious plans. This finally crystallized in a decision to found a publishing house in Berlin specializing in Hebrew literature, a house that would also continue the *Encyclopaedia Judaica* project. I was confronted with the necessity, now by no means unwelcome, of returning to Berlin.

7

Encyclopaedia Judaica

I worked on the *Encyclopaedia Judaica* from 1923 to 1932, and until Hitler came to power. The notion of a comprehensive Jewish encyclopedia that would make the knowledge of Judaism accessible to the Jewish and gentile world and also record the Jewish contribution to world culture had been advocated by many Jewish scholars and thinkers of the previous generation. Ahad Ha-Am in particular had devoted much effort to founding a work of this kind, but without success. In 1912 the *Jewish Encyclopaedia* had appeared in America—a welcome beginning with a number of excellent articles although, like all such first steps, it was inevitably incomplete (in this case too because America was not yet the main center of Jewish scholarship). In this respect Berlin seemed the ideal place for the next attempt, but one of the main obstacles was the geographical and linguistic fragmentation of world Jewry. If the work was to be accessible, it would have to be published in three languages: German, English, and Hebrew. When we decided to undertake the project, neither Klatzkin nor I had the least idea of the tremendous scholarly, administrative, and, above all, financial difficulties ahead. Otherwise we would probably have been deterred.

Klatzkin, who was a perfectionist in all he did, and I, who knew very little about financial matters in those days and was unimpressed by great amounts of money, decided that the encyclopedia had no point unless it could be conceived on a major scale and be exhaustive from the scholarly and technical point of view. Of course, neither of us could put up money to launch the gigantic project. Obviously it could not be presented purely as a business venture, and there was no sense in asking any existing publishers to finance a work that would cost millions of marks. Instead we decided to found a house for the purpose, to call it Eschkol (the Hebrew for "grapevine," an ancient symbol of abundance), and to raise the money with the help of Jewish Maecenases. Since it was to be a trilingual reference work, it was to be internationally financed. Committees would have to be set up in various countries, including America, to secure the scholarly and financial co-operation of the Jewish communities. What the scheme in fact amounted to was a kind of world Jewish organization dedicated solely to launching this gigantic work, which was to represent the major achievement of modern Jewish scholarship.

We had no funds at all when we started, but friends came to our help, and a time of feverish preparations, involving much traveling, began. We set up committees in most European countries. It was relatively easy to enlist the scholars; the backers gave us more trouble. The first thing we had to do was produce a specimen volume, to show interested people what such an encyclopedia would look like. After a lot of difficulty we succeeded in getting one printed, and armed with this we set off for America, hoping to find the millions of marks we needed, especially for the English edition.

This was my first visit to the New World. We had barely enough money to pay our passage, but on board ship I succeeded in interesting a South African diamond millionaire, who gave us a check that would cover our initial living expenses at least. I cannot say we got a rousing reception from American Jewry, although several prominent men, such as Stephen Wise and Cyrus Adler, head of the Jewish Theological Seminary, and of course many scholars, were very responsive. But in those days, and it is no different today, rich American Jews were far more interested in charity and relief work than in scholarship. I still remember a Jewish millionaire in a big Mid-Western city who promised me a contribution because I had been recommended by a good friend of his but who asked, with some embarrassment, that I not send him a copy of the encyclopedia. His wife thought books were dust-catchers.

Two men showed real interest and both of them could easily

have financed the encyclopedia. One was Ludwig Vogelstein, founder of the American Metal Company, brother and son of liberal rabbis in Germany, president of the organization of American Reform Jews, and a man with a genuine love of Jewish scholarship. We spent a lot of time with him. Although he was a stubborn anti-Zionist and was afraid that we might misuse the encyclopedia for Zionist propaganda, from time to time it looked as if he would contribute. In the end, however, he merely held out a prospect of future help.

The second man was Adolf Ochs, owner of *The New York Times*. He too seemed seriously interested, but as a cautious businessman he did not want to become involved in financing the English translation unless he was sure the German edition would be completed first. Although he could not then have foreseen Hitler, he was quite right. The Nazi regime prevented the completion of the German edition, and to this day it has remained a ten-volume skeleton. At one point we had the prospect of enlisting the support of the Rockefeller Foundation, but here again the real obstacle was the misgivings (quite justified, as I now see) of all these men and institutions when it came to financing such a costly undertaking that was not undertaken by any reputable publishing company or well-known Jewish organization but only under the initiative and self-confidence of two relatively unknown Jewish writers.

We went home empty-handed, having gained some knowledge of American Jews and lost a few illusions. After this failure it took a lot of courage to carry on and any moderately prudent businessman would probably have given up, but we continued our search for patrons. Albert Einstein, whom both Klatzkin and I knew well and who wanted to promote the *Encyclopaedia Judaica*, gave me an introduction to Anthony de Rothschild, head of the London firm of bankers. I had to go to London in any case for a meeting of the Zionist General Council and took the opportunity of asking Rothschild for an appointment. I was promptly invited to tea at the Rothschild bank, where I was given a most cordial reception by its two directors, Anthony and Lionel. They asked a lot of questions, and I explained the project in detail. They seemed quite taken with it, and after half an hour Anthony de Rothschild asked me to excuse him and his cousin so they could discuss their answer in an adjoining room. In my mind's eye I already saw a check for at least ten thousand pounds. After about ten minutes they returned, and Anthony de Rothschild told me, with a very serious, solemn face, that he and his cousin had discussed the project thoroughly and decided to advise me strongly to drop it. The reason they gave, set forth in very sound, astute arguments, was the international economic crisis.

I listened to them quietly and then replied that the journey to London was costing me twenty-five to thirty pounds. Luckily, I went on, I also had to attend a meeting of the Zionist General Council. But had there been no meeting even, it would have been quite sensible, with the backing of a letter from Einstein, to invest twenty-five pounds in the head of the House of Rothschild and make the journey. Do you think, I asked in conclusion, that it was smart to spend this much money just to get your judicious advice?

Rothschild did not bat an eye but replied that his advice was worth much more than twenty-five pounds and many of his business friends, to whom he had given similar counsel, had every reason to be grateful later. I rejoined that his business friends had something to lose, that such a warning may have meant money to them, but my friends and I, having nothing to lose, would scarcely accept his advice.

He then asked rather indignantly, "Where will you get the money?" I told him the old story of the bankrupt Jewish businessman who refuses to file a schedule of assets. When the judge asks him why, he replies: "As an honest man, Your Honor, I cannot swear that I have no money as long as there are other Jews who have some." The two Rothschilds were not much impressed by this method of raising money. They finally offered me a few hundred pounds, which, with the pride of the pauper, I refused. Then I proudly took my leave of them.

I had similar experiences with other Maecenases, and we often came close to giving up. But in the meantime we had engaged collaborators, and it was no longer a question of prestige only. The livelihood of good friends was now dependent on the project, and we felt that somehow we would win through.

The turning point came thanks to one of Germany's leading

Jewish financiers, Jacob Goldschmidt, managing director of the Darmstadt and National Bank, a dynamic, gifted banker of the younger generation, then at the height of his career in finance. Actually he gave us his decisive help without really intending to. I had been introduced to him by a colleague and he had given me a modest contribution. When I saw he was interested in the project, I asked him to inform the manager of the branch of his bank where our publishing firm had its account of his friendly interest, so they would treat us kindly. He agreed, and we managed to give the branch manager the impression that Mr. Goldschmidt had more or less guaranteed our account, with the result that after a few months we had a considerable overdraft (amounting to about eighty thousand marks, if I remember rightly). One day a furious Goldschmidt telephoned and demanded I come and see him immediately. He had just learned that we had persuaded the branch to allow us to overdraw on the basis of an alleged guarantee he had never given. Our conversation was not very pleasant. After he had calmed down a little, I said I would come to see him that afternoon and suggest a way to settle the problem. When I arrived, he was still quite excited, not so much over the money he had to repay but over the fact that a young man like myself had fooled him. I asked him to be patient and listen to the following story.

A Jewish *schnorrer*, or beggar, newly arrived in town, goes to the best restaurant, eats a delectable meal, and then informs the owner that he has no money. When the indignant owner threatens to call the police, the *schnorrer* replies: "What good will the police do? You'll do much better to analyze the situation logically. There are three possibilities. The first is to give me credit for a week. By then I'll have finished my begging here, and before I leave town I'll return and pay you. To this first possibility you'll probably raise the reasonable objection: Why should you give credit to a *schnorrer* you've never seen before? The second possibility is to go begging with me and get your money as it comes in. To this you'll object that a prosperous restaurant proprietor wouldn't go begging for money with a poor *schnorrer*. And you're absolutely right. So there remains only the third possibility: to go and beg for the money yourself."

This story was the source of my inspiration, and the third possibility was exactly what I proposed to Goldschmidt. I presented him with a list of prominent German-Jewish financiers and told him that with his reputation he would have no difficulty persuading them to make an annual contribution of three thousand marks for a period of eight years. And that is what actually happened, with the gratifying result that some eight hundred thousand marks were guaranteed, spread over a period of seven to eight years, and the real financial foundation of our venture was laid.

Organizing the scholarly side of the *Encyclopaedia*, however, also presented difficulties. As we were determined that the work must meet the most rigorous scholarly standards, we had to confine ourselves to a very small and select range of editors and contributors. Most of the eminent Jewish scholars were tied to their positions, and to assemble an editorial board in Berlin was not easy. The fact that in the end the *Encyclopaedia* office employed some sixty people will give some idea of the magnitude of the task. Klatzkin was chief editor and Professor Ismar Elbogen deputy chief, they were soon joined on the board by Dr. Max Soloveichik, a Biblical scholar and active Zionist leader who had been a member of the Lithuanian government at one time and who later became a member of the Zionist Executive in London. During the planning and production of the first few volumes we had the great good fortune to secure the collaboration of Dr. J. N. Simchoni, an extraordinary young scholar who was a walking encyclopedia. Without him, the preliminary work, which for a lexicon is almost as onerous as actually assembling the material, would hardly have been possible. I was in charge of all articles on contemporary Jewish subjects and had the unenviable job of deciding which contemporary Jews were "immortal" and to be included and which were not. In order to prove that the work would have no propagandistic slant, I invited Rabbi Benno Jacob of Essen, a recognized Jewish scholar but a convinced anti-Zionist, to collaborate with me in the contemporary area, and although we often took opposite sides in public life, I am happy to say that in all our years together we had practically no differences of opinion.

After the first volume had appeared in German, we began to solicit subscribers and within a short time had enrolled over three thousand. Soon we started work on the Hebrew edition, of which two volumes appeared. The English edition was postponed (pending the approval of Adolf Ochs for one thing) until the original German edition would be completed. After nine volumes of the original appeared and the tenth was in preparation, the reputation and authority of the *Encyclopaedia Judaica* were firmly established. It looked as though the fifteen-volume German edition would be completed within a few years. The Hebrew and English editions would then follow at a much more rapid rate. It even looked as though the original investment would be recovered after the publication of the English edition, possibly at a good rate of interest. Our intention was to use the profits for frequent revised and updated editions. But shortly before the tenth volume went to press, Hitler came to power. Our time in Germany was up; I was particularly endangered. Moreover, the National Socialist authorities took exception to a number of articles in the *Encyclopaedia*, and all existing copies that had not been sold, more than forty thousand in storage in Leipzig, were destroyed.

The *Encyclopaedia Judaica*, as it exists today in ten German and two Hebrew volumes, represents, as more competent experts than myself have often stated, one of the true achievements of Jewish scholarship in our generation and ranks as the most reliable reference work on Jewish matters. That it had to remain unfinished is more than a pity. In recent years I, along with others, have taken steps to complete the *Encyclopaedia Judaica* in a new edition—not in German, since German-speaking Jewry has been largely destroyed, but in English. In collaboration first with the Palestine Economic Corporation and the Israeli publishing company Massadah and later with the Rassco Rural and Suburban Settlement Company, we managed to get the preliminary work for a new encyclopedia started. Publication was then taken over by the Israel Program for Scientific Translations, a publishing house financed by the Israeli government, and the work is scheduled to appear in fifteen volumes within two to three years. In view of all that has happened lately in Jewish life, the need for a new Jewish encyclopedia is obvious. It will appear initially in English, but it will be edited and printed in Israel. Translations into other languages will follow later. The Eschkol material will be extensively used.

In my years in Berlin devoted primarily to work on the *Encyclopaedia Judaica*, I had the opportunity of getting to know many of Germany's leading Jewish personalities. But to conclude this chapter I want to record my impressions of the man who was unquestionably the foremost intellectual figure of our time: Albert Einstein.

I got to know Einstein through his interest in Zionism and resettlement work in Palestine and had many conversations with him in Berlin. Of all the outstanding personalities I have met in my life, he was without doubt the most brilliant. To me he was the incarnation of genius. I have always been convinced that the difference between talent and genius is a qualitative one. Geniuses are not just unusually talented people. A man of talent has the characteristics of a normal man, except that some of these characteristics are unusually developed. A man of genius is of another breed; his approach to things is fundamentally different from that of the man of talent. Somebody once made the witty remark that only men of talent are original; geniuses are always repeating the same eternal truths. This intentional paradox contains deep insight. The genius cuts the Gordian knot of the problems he is working on; he sees the world anew. Whether he is right in every detail is irrelevant; such criteria are for the man of talent. What men of genius give to the world is a new viewpoint that immediately becomes self-evident, so that you sometimes wonder why you didn't think of it for yourself.

In this sense Einstein personified genius. Of course, my conversations with him did not deal with his scientific theories, of which I understood little. But sometimes, when he was obsessed with an idea, he would talk about it, and what always astounded me was his simple way of tackling the most complicated problems. He would speak of basic metaphysical concepts such as time or space as matter-of-factly as others speak of sandwiches or potatoes. He had that characteristic quirk of genius, an inability to understand why others couldn't understand him. At the

time of the German inflation, when he was very badly off finan-
cially because his salary was devalued in the first few days of
every month, I found him one day absorbed in an American
magazine. He pointed in astonishment to the magazine—it was
the *Saturday Evening Post*—which was offering twenty-five
hundred dollars for a few pages explaining the theory of relativity in popular terms. "Just think," he mused, "what that amount
of money would mean to me." Then he confessed that he had
been sitting for days, thinking, trying to figure out how to
explain it in a way that readers could understand.

At the height of his fame he was invited to give a popular
lecture on the theory of relativity in the main auditorium at the
University of Berlin. Of course, the hall was crowded; the intellectual elite of Berlin was present. Before he could start, a
representative of one of the student fraternities stood up and
protested that the nonacademic public should not have been
admitted because according to paragraph so-and-so of the university rules the auditorium was reserved for academic functions. Einstein replied: "It's quite true that the paragraph you
cite does contain that rule, but where is the paragraph that
obliges us to enforce that paragraph?" After this characteristic
touch of humanity, he began his lecture with quite primitive
concepts, as though he were teaching beginning high school
students. Obviously he had been warned that his audience
would not consist of experts. But before anyone could catch his
breath he was suddenly in the upper reaches of mathematics,
where most of his listeners could not follow him.

Einstein was also a genius in character, if one can put it that
way. He had the naïveté of a child—not a child who still
knows nothing of life but of one who has gone through all the
complications, intellectual and practical, and reduced them to
their simplest terms. I always regarded him as the personification of every great quality a man can have: goodness of heart,
honesty, and boundless love for all living creatures. It would
have been almost impossible to discover a character defect in
him; but perhaps his most amazing quality was his absolute sim-
plicity. He was what he was in a perfectly natural way, without
any effort. He could not understand how one could be anything
else or realize that other people had characters unlike his. I once

spent hours explaining to him why one of his colleagues on the board of trustees of Hebrew University had done something that was not entirely according to protocol. It was impossible to get Einstein to understand. "How could he do a thing like that?" he kept asking. "How can a man do a thing like that?"

He lived in a time of great demoralization, during which the worst crimes in human history were perpetrated, but even in that world he remained to his last breath a great innocent child. He was unbelievably trusting, and people often succeeded in fooling him because he could not imagine that anyone would deliberately abuse his trust. He understood nothing of political reality but took it for granted that politics must rest on moral principles. He hated war, aggressive nationalism, and reaction. It was his profound humane impulses that made of him a conscious Jew and led him to help in the settlement of Palestine. He had no Jewish education and did not know much about Jewish culture. But he suffered because of the Jews' inequality and the injustice done to them and felt it his duty to do what he could to compensate by helping to found a homeland. It was a grievous loss to Israel that the attempt to bring Einstein to the University of Jerusalem when he left Germany failed and that later, when Weizmann died, he could not be persuaded to accept the presidency of Israel as Ben-Gurion proposed to him.

Einstein had the modesty of all truly great men, yet he made a deep impression on everybody with his appearance and manner. One Sunday I was taking a walk with him in Berlin, and he asked me for a cigar. I had none. The shops were closed, but we managed to find a little tavern where they sold cheap cigars. We entered. The owner was standing behind the counter, and when Einstein asked for a cigar, he said: "What kind? A twenty pfennig cigar?"

"Do I look as if I smoke such expensive cigars?"

The proprietor looked him over and said: "Well, you know, you don't look exactly commonplace either."

The hours I was privileged to spend with this unique personality in Berlin are among the enduring impressions of my lifetime.

8

Training in Zionist Politics

It was during my second period in Berlin, from 1925 to 1933, that I first began to engage in political and organizational work. Until then my Zionist activity had been divided between analysis of contemporary Jewish problems and efforts in the field of propaganda. I was already known in Zionist and Jewish circles and received many invitations to speak, invitations I accepted whenever I could combine them with the rather heavy demands of the *Encyclopaedia Judaica*. I made my start in Zionist politics, as so many politicians do, in the opposition.

I got into politics by way of ideology and I had the profound faith in fine ideological distinctions that is typical of young people with no political experience. Only after many years did I find out how many concessions to existing realities must be made in implementing an idea even in part, how insufficient just proclaiming it is. My background had confirmed in me the Diaspora Jew's belief that salvation is to be found only in ideas and ideologies. In centuries of ghetto life, Jews had to live in a reality created by a host nation; all their creative energies were channeled into the realm of pure theory. The escape into theory was their only compensation. This was the origin of the mistaken Jewish belief in the power of logic, of fanaticism and stubbornness in defending ideologies of any stripe, and of sovereign disdain for practical matters that led inevitably to radicalism and passionate battles over ideological formulations that, when applied to reality, were basically meaningless.

These tendencies were just as strong in me as they were in other Jewish intellectuals, and it took several years of organizational work and encounters with other nationalities and political techniques before I overcame them and learned to make concessions, to compromise and recognize that psychology is more important than ideology. The main thing is what a man, a party, or a nation wants. The rational superstructure that reinforces these wants (and which springs from regions much deeper than logic) follows of itself. It is not very difficult, particularly for a people as highly trained in logical and speculative thought as the Jews, to find a convincing ideological justification for every psychological need. When I did comprehend all this, it was thanks chiefly to my understanding of British political life that, when I survey the nations of the globe, still seems to me the most intelligent and responsible of all. But in those Berlin years I was ideologically motivated; what interested me in every question was the principle involved and the debates I participated in centered less on what was feasible and attainable than on fidelity to logical principles.

I thought of Zionism not just as a political movement that hoped to solve the Jewish question by establishing a national home, but also as a people-oriented movement destined to create something new in Palestine—an order based on moral and social principles and consistent with the great Jewish ethical values. At that time the three great problems practical Zionism had to tackle were first, the type of development to be planned in Palestine; second, co-operation with non-Zionist Jewry; and third, its attitude to the policies of the British mandatory power. (This last subject will be discussed in the next chapter.)

On the first problem, I belonged heart and soul to those who envisaged a radically new society. I was unequivocally on the side of labor and of the experiments then being made in Palestine with collective agricultural settlements, such as the kibbutz (with no private property) and the co-operative *moshav*. However, I was never formally a member of the Zionist Labor Party. Eliezer Kaplan, who was to become Israel's first minister of finance and who was then in Berlin, persuaded me to join the party's congressional delegation, but I resigned a couple of days later when it was explained to me that I should be subject to party discipline; that is, I could be compelled to vote for a resolution at the congress, against my convictions, if a majority of the delegation had decided to support it. Yet I was moderately leftist, progressive and liberal, and remained in contact with the Zionist labor movement. In this respect I was a follower of Dr. Chaim Weizmann, who throughout his life held this progressive, moderate position and whose Zionist policy hinged on the closest co-operation with labor. The vast majority of German Zionists felt the same way, so I rarely had to fight for these opinions and felt myself quite adequately represented by the official spokesmen, especially by the most outstanding of them, Kurt Blumenfeld.

Blumenfeld, whom I came to know better during those years and to whom I was always particularly close, except during short periods of political disagreement, was the most exceptional leader German Zionism produced. He was the typical representative of what he named "post-assimilation Zionism," Zionism that did not stem directly from Jewish tradition but sought to return to Jewishness out of assimilation. Blumenfeld had made the whole wealth of modern European culture, especially that of Germany, his own. He was sensitive and well informed about modern intellectual trends, and his concept of Zionism derived from Western European, no less than Jewish, roots. For him Hölderlin and Goethe, Rilke and Stefan George, Scheler and Heidegger were sources of Zionist creation as valid as Ahad Ha-Am and Herzl or the great intellectual heroes of Jewish history. He was a fascinating talker less interested in clarifying things objectively or communicating than in brilliant exposition for its own sake. He was an out-and-out propagandist, much less effective when he ventured into practical questions than when he was propagandizing. And he was unsurpassed in converting prominent personalities to Zionism: Oskar Wassermann, for instance, one of Germany's leading Jewish bankers, or Albert Einstein. He managed to give Zionism a basis of common humanity, to link it with every great cultural movement of our time and give it a tremendous openness to the world.

Blumenfeld's limitation was that he was personally so strongly tied to German culture. The curse of Jewish geography—the necessity of becoming at home in so many different linguistic and cultural worlds, a serious problem to anyone who wants to disseminate Zionism internationally—was for Blumenfeld an almost insuperable obstacle, especially after Hitler came to power. Being so firmly rooted in Germany, he had difficulty adjusting to other cultural milieus, and his later attempts to use his original methods of propagandizing among American Jews ended in failure because of his lack of understanding of Americans and their entirely different response. But through his challenge to every Jew to make Palestine part of his most personal life, he effectively "Zionized" a large part of German Jewish youth.

Blumenfeld's approach to Zionist propaganda was not essentially different from mine, although my speaking technique was quite different. In his speeches one brilliant thought followed another; the string of remarks could be broken off at any point or extended indefinitely without harming the total structure. A speech of mine is always a structured edifice of ideas; it cannot be interrupted in the middle; it has a beginning, a climax, and a conclusion. Blumenfeld's speeches were like a beautiful road along which you walk without any thought of your destination, you simply stroll along as long as you are enjoying it. My speeches are like a pyramid: you have to reach the summit before you can begin the descent. But apart from this difference, our way of drawing upon modern European ideas as well as Jewish ones for our conceptions of Zionism was identical, and I always thought very highly of his method of propaganda and learned a great deal from it.

On the two other paramount problems of contemporary Zionist politics I not only differed from Kurt Blumenfeld and the majority he represented but soon found myself at variance with the unchallenged leader of world Zionism, Chaim Weizmann. Then, as later, the Zionist movement represented a minority of world Jewry. Weizmann, whose great historical achievement—in addition to the Balfour Declaration, Zionism's first great victory—was to recognize that any political success means no more than what it accomplishes concretely, was the splendid representative of what may be called practical Zionism. His aim was not to accumulate political declarations of support from those in power but to create a Jewish reality in Palestine.

Earlier Weizmann was one of those who opposed Theodor Herzl's simplistic attitude to the Jewish question, an attitude that sought to establish a Jewish state from above, through an agreement with the Sultan or the great powers, but which showed little understanding of the much more important daily work of colonization in Palestine.

Weizmann's aim was to establish incontestable realities in Palestine and this naturally led him to ask how the maximum energies of the Jewish people could be mobilized for the work of resettlement. There were, and still are, many Jews, especially in wealthy, influential circles, who rejected the ideology of Zionism and refused to consider themselves as belonging to that part of the people which, according to the Zionist creed, is dispossessed and homeless. On the one hand, they were afraid that such an admission would harm their social and economic standing, yet at the same time they felt sufficiently Jewish to want to lend a hand in resettling the persecuted and genuinely homeless Jews of Eastern Europe in Palestine. Weizmann wanted to enlist this help and utilize it systematically.

In the British mandate for Palestine the Zionist organization had been recognized under the designation (J.A.), the Jewish Agency for Palestine, as having the right to co-operate with the mandatory power in developing the national homeland. The mandate had already anticipated the possibility that non-Zionist groups might become part of the officially recognized Jewish Agency. Weizmann tried to make this possibility a reality. Together with his closest friends he evolved a plan for an enlarged agency to consist half of Zionists and half of non-Zionists. This met with opposition within the Zionist movement from those who did not mind non-Zionists cooperating in the economic development of Palestine but who rejected political co-operation because they feared non-Zionists might water down their program. Two political objectives in particular were bound to be unacceptable to the non-Zionists: the Jewish state (which at that time was only our tacit goal, not a declared one) and resistance to the mandatory power whenever this might prove necessary. Therefore the opposition proposed to create a joint body with the non-Zionists for economic development but to leave political affairs exclusively in the hands of the Zionist Executive and the

Zionist Congress. This fight lasted for years and was not settled until 1929, when the enlarged Jewish Agency was founded.

From the start I belonged to the opposition. To divide responsibility in this way seemed to me politically and ideologically dangerous and, moreover, a surrender of inalienable principles. In this battle, which was fought out in numerous sessions of the Zionist Executive and at many congresses, Yitzhak Gruenbaum was our most beloved and respected leader. He represented not only Polish Zionism but Polish Jewry as a whole in its struggle for political rights. Besides enjoying full civil rights (at least on paper), Polish Jews were at that time constitutionally recognized as a national minority, like the White Russians, Ukrainians, and others. They had their own Jewish parties that sent delegates to the Polish parliament, and the strongest of these was the Zionist party. Year after year Gruenbaum fought with unsurpassed courage for Jewish rights in Poland. The Jews adored him; the Poles hated and feared him.

Gruenbaum was a man of unassailable integrity, frugal in his own demands, prepared to sacrifice everything for his ideas, fearless even when outmatched in power, and a stirring speaker. He was a born fighter, more interested in the fight than in victory. Lacking tactical sense, obstinate and obsessed, he was the best representative an oppressed minority could want, but he was less successful when it came to getting compromises accepted. He was happiest when he stood alone. The fiercer the opposition, the more hopeless the battle, the better he liked it. Steeped in Jewish culture, he was still a typical son of Polish Jewry. His distinction of mind and fidelity to his convictions were admired throughout world Zionism, but he was much less effective in this wider sphere than he was in Poland.

Gruenbaum was one of those tragic figures who are born to be revolutionaries, but whose effectiveness diminishes when they come to power. After participating for a while in the first government of Israel, he maneuvered himself out of one party after another and in his old age became a complete outsider—which was quite in keeping with his character. I always admired him for his moral qualities and was proud to call myself his friend. Nonetheless, after I had worked with him for a few

years I began to doubt that he possessed the necessary talent for
party leadership when it came to getting things done rather than
protesting and criticizing. Although our differences grew with
regard to political tactics, this never affected my personal liking
for him.

Yitzhak Gruenbaum was the unanimously recognized spokesman in our fight against the enlarged Jewish Agency. With us
he formed a new Zionist party, the Radicals, among whose
members were Max Soloveichik, my close collaborator on the
Encyclopaedia Judaica, Emil Margulies, a kind of Czech counterpart of Gruenbaum and a vigorous fighter for the rights of
the Czech Jewish minority, and Robert Stricker, the most interesting of the Austrian Zionist leaders, a leading parliamentarian
and a cultivated, emotionally forceful speaker who went fearlessly and proudly to his death in a Nazi concentration camp
while I was trying, without success, to get him to Palestine.

I was extremely active in the Radical Party and in the 1920's
represented it at Zionist congresses. Before long I was elected
to the Zionist General Council (the parliamentary body of the
World Zionist Organization between congresses) and took part
in the election campaigns for Zionist congresses. The Radicals
were a unique phenomenon in Zionist party life: small but
effective. Whenever Gruenbaum and I drove up in a taxi at the
Karlsbad congress of 1923, people would say: "Here comes the
Radical Party." Nevertheless, a number of the most distinctive
figures in Zionism, some of whom I have already mentioned,
belonged to the party, and even if it carried no great weight in
the voting, it was universally esteemed for its intellectual
standing.

In our resistance to the enlarged Jewish Agency we had an
ally in the Revisionist Party, founded and led by Vladimir
Jabotinsky. In later years he and I were usually to be found on
opposite sides of the barricades, but at that time we worked
together and I got to know him well. Matched against the leaders of any great nation, Jabotinsky would easily have held his
own. He was a gifted man, very Russian—more Russian than
Jewish—and one of the very few so-called post-assimilation
Zionist leaders from Russia. He had an unusual linguistic flair
and was an exciting speaker in several languages, though he

preferred Russian. In his early days he was a writer and poet, and in one sense he was the greatest Zionist orator. His speeches were elaborate works of art which he would write out down to the last word but deliver extemporaneously, so that his listeners never knew they were prepared.

I happened to meet him once years later in a Chicago hotel and talked with him at length about the art of oratory. He had just come from a student meeting, where he had spoken for over two hours. When I asked how many had been there, he said about thirty. I was surprised he could speak so long to such a small audience, but he said the audience really made no difference, that it did not matter to him whether there were five thousand people in the auditorium or twenty. His speech had its own autonomous existence. Suggesting a parallel I have never forgotten, he asked me if I thought the Mona Lisa cared whether she was looked at by one man, nobody at all, or a hundred people. She remains the same work of art, he thought, regardless of her admirers. It's the same with a speech, he went on. It exists in its own right as a work of art. It's not dependent on the number of listeners or their reaction.

Jabotinsky's speeches were monologues, I explained to him, a kind of brilliant recital, and therefore independent of the size or the character of the audience. My speeches are dialogues with the audience, even if I am the only one to speak. The auditors' part of the dialogue consists in their reaction: silence, approval, laughter, indignation, to which in turn I adjust.

Jabotinsky's political methods were similar in character to his rhetoric. They were also in a certain way monologues. He would state his position vehemently and brilliantly and expected everybody who heard it to agree with him without argument. I would say that he possessed all the characteristics of a dictator, except the quality of ruthlessness, for he was a very goodhearted man. This made it hard to work with him. You either had to admire and go along with him or else break off the friendship; to argue was impossible. To reject his proposals automatically made you his political opponent and unfit to talk to. The Revisionist Party, which worshiped him, consisted chiefly of people for whom his opinion was absolute law. Anyone who considered himself Jabotinsky's equal could never collaborate with him in the long run, as I very quickly discovered. He did not resent criticism, but he never paid any attention to it either. This made him extremist in his political attitudes.

Jabotinsky was a monologuist with regard to reality too and brooked no interference from facts. He applied Hegel's philosophical method to politics. When an astronomer once told Hegel that a theory he had evolved concerning the stars was incompatible with astronomical facts, Hegel replied, unperturbed: "So much the worse for the stars." It was no wonder that Jabotinsky soon ran afoul of Dr. Weizmann, the practical politician par excellence, as well as most of the other Zionist leaders. It did not matter to him, however, for he preferred a small dedicated party to a coalition that required constant concessions. His Revisionist Party was extreme in its slogan, "a Jewish state on both sides of the Jordan;" it was violently anti-British during the time of the mandate, and it recklessly opposed the majority parties that controlled Zionism, especially the Labor Party and the middle class elements represented by Weizmann.

The tragic thing about Jabotinsky was that he had no feeling either for empirical facts or for the time factor in politics. What the English call timing, the ability to recognize the right moment for putting forward a political idea, was something absolutely foreign to him. He and his supporters used to boast that they had invented most of the political slogans of the Zionist movement years before they were proclaimed. He was especially proud of this and did not realize that it pinpointed his political weakness. Agreeing with them or not, he invariably expressed his political ideas at the wrong moment. The rightness of a political idea is never absolute; it always has a lot to do with the propitious moment. When Jabotinsky demanded, at the exciting Seventeenth Zionist Congress in 1931, that the official Zionist program include the establishment of a Jewish state, this demand, which was rejected by the vast majority, was at that time politically absurd. If the congress had accepted this plank, continued resettlement and the peaceful conquest of Palestine would have been impossible. All of us who voted against it desired a Jewish state just as fervently as Jabotinsky did, but we knew that the time was not ripe. Not until the time seemed to have come, at the Biltmore Conference during the Second World War, did we proclaim the establishment of the Jewish state as a political demand.

Jabotinsky's genius lay elsewhere. It is no mean tribute to call a man the greatest orator of a movement as dependent upon the spoken word as Zionism. His literary talent and his personal courage also deserve mention. For all his weaknesses as a politician, he was one of the most influential Zionist figures of all time, a lovable man, and a wonderful friend. Despite the limitations I have mentioned, he formulated and helped to propagate many of the seminal ideas of Zionism, and at least one concrete political achievement will always be associated with his name: the creation of the Jewish Legion during the First World War. Indirectly he also had a strong influence on his opponents. All in all he will be remembered as a man of grandiose stature, more artist than politician, more fiery orator than diplomat. Now that he is no longer with us, even those who fought him bitterly in the early years must pay him affectionate and reverent homage.

Despite these valuable alliances and the numerous influential Zionist leaders who joined in the struggle against the enlarged Jewish Agency, we were defeated. The Weizmann program was finally adopted in Zurich in 1929, and immediately after this the first meeting of the enlarged Jewish Agency was held. This, as even we of the opposition had to admit, was the most comprehensive Jewish congress ever convened. Non-Zionists who participated included men such as Léon Blum, Oskar Wassermann, Louis Marshall, and Lord Melchett, the true elite of non-Zionist Jewry. In this sense the founding congress was a great success. I attended as a member of the Zionist delegation and it fell to me to declare, on behalf of the Radical Party, that, as good democrats we would respect the majority decision and collaborate constructively with the enlarged body, unlike other representatives, among them the Revisionist Party, who had opposed it and now refused their co-operation.

The enlarged Jewish Agency was a failure from a practical point of view, however, despite its triumphant beginnings. Our fears were fulfilled in an unexpected way. Although the non-

Zionists caused little trouble, their co-operation was very limited. None of the leading non-Zionists were prepared to serve
on the Jewish Agency Executive, which was based in London
and Jerusalem. The great non-Zionist personalities sent assistants
to represent them on the Executive—good, dedicated workers
who naturally lacked the authority and stature of Zionist members, such as Weizmann and David Ben-Gurion. The fifty-fifty
principle soon proved impracticable because the non-Zionists
simply could not find enough eminent men to maintain their
quota, and although the enlarged Jewish Agency existed formally for many years, it became more and more of a fiction. In
the end it had become so meaningless that to this day no one has
bothered to dissolve it. The project lawyers and politicians had
worked on for years and that had been so complicated to put
into practice simply evaporated.

However, it is only fair to note that it did accomplish one
thing. It made a number of leading non-Zionists, especially in
America, more aware of Palestine, induced them to contribute
more money, interest others, and promote the practical work of
resettlement. But, of course, this could probably have been done
at much less cost, without the complicated apparatus of the
enlarged Jewish Agency and without tying up the Zionist
movement for years in a fight over it.

Personally the fight over enlarging the Jewish Agency was
very meaningful, for it was the first battle over a concrete political issue in which I was involved. Our official spokesman was
Yitzhak Gruenbaum, and although I took part in the debates at
Zionist congresses, my work was done chiefly in committee and
in detailed discussions of the complicated Agency constitution. I
learned the importance of by-laws and statutes, discovered that
great speeches in the forefront of political events are much less
decisive than quiet argument in private committee rooms, came
to understand many connections between personal and concrete
matters of which I had previously been innocent, and learned
what it means to stand up against recognized authorities. It was
my first course, my first seminar, in practical day-to-day politics. This phase of Zionist history was of the utmost importance
to me, because it was then that I earned a place for myself
among the leaders of the World Zionist Organization (WZO).

9

My Introduction to Foreign Affairs

Although the fight over the enlarged Jewish Agency accounted for most of my Zionist work at the time, I was beginning to take a lively interest in the movement's foreign policy problems, which were to absorb me increasingly until in 1933 I moved to Geneva to devote myself to them almost exclusively. My attitude to foreign politics is much the same as to public speaking; I had a facility for both, and without over-estimating my achievements, I think I have accomplished something in both fields. I have already said something about my ambivalence toward public speaking and although it has always fascinated me, I am just as skeptical about the ultimate importance of foreign politics.

Only with a great many reservations can I accept the famous statement that politics is our destiny. It is true that international politics is the *arena* in which peoples' and countries' destinies are decided, but nations' destinies only *seem* to be decided there. The decisive events actually occur in quite other spheres: in cultural, social, and psychological areas, in a nation's collective mind, social structure, and intellectual and moral attitudes. In foreign politics these unseen factors become visible, processes long under way crystallize. Foreign politics does not create the facts; it merely draws the consequences from existing situations. In the final analysis its role is only secondary. Although a superficial study of world history may suggest that great statesmen and generals striding so forcefully and visibly across the stage of history shape the destinies of nations, anyone who has studied a little more closely knows this is an illusion. All these great actors in the forefront of world events are puppets. The strings are pulled by less conspicuous powers at work in the background: by thinkers and writers, religious and social leaders, by mass movements, and by that almost indefinable thing we call the soul of a nation.

The politician draws the balance of all these forces and the more successfully he does it, the more accurately he appraises his own nation and others in all their multifarious and complicated aspects, the greater he will be as a statesman. This is what makes foreign politics so fascinating—at least to me. The necessity of reckoning with innumerable factors, of standing at a vantage point that will give you the broadest possible horizon, of bringing into play elements that apparently have nothing to do with the problem at hand—this is what is so difficult but so challenging in foreign politics. The higher your vantage point, the clearer and more comprehensive your view. Nothing is more destructive than pettiness and provincialism; hence the maxim that nothing is more detrimental to foreign politics than domination by internal politics. This explains why foreign affairs are so lacking in elegance in a democratic age when governments depend upon the mood of the people. There is something undeniably right in the principle of secret diplomacy, even if it is hardly feasible today. To be successful in foreign affairs nowadays a politician must, whether he wants to or not, engage in domestic politics too, otherwise he cannot get anything done. Yet the conditions and ground rules of domestic politics are totally different. This dependence afflicts the foreign policy of many nations—and this is just as true of Zionism as of the state of Israel. The difference between a politician and a statesman is that the former considers only the wishes of his supporters, while the latter also makes allowances for the wishes of his opponents.

I like freedom of scope; nothing is more foreign to my character than exclusiveness, fanatical self-limitation to one single thing. All my life the one-way street has never been my kind of street. I try to see all aspects of a problem from the outset and I have never believed in absolute truths in either individual or national life. Obviously I did not realize until later that the viewpoint of the opposition also has its *raison d'être*, but I had always sensed this intuitively. My strong point has been the ability to keep many elements in play, to unite different points of view, to seek compromises between contending demands, and to find a formulation by which everybody gains something, most of all the feeling of having achieved something essential.

For anyone with this kind of bent, foreign policy is obviously the appropriate field. The opponents you encounter are not so fanatical as the partisan politicians at home. Even in bitter fights they are more courteous, more generous in their approach to problems, more skilled in argument than those you find in the often overheated, narrow-minded atmosphere of Jewish party politics and internal affairs. Zionism's greatest problem up until the establishment of the State of Israel was to act as a state without being one. Men like Herzl and Weizmann maintained this stance to perfection, and I tried in many years to learn from them, with, I hope, some measure of success.

Of course, the psychological satisfactions of work in foreign policy did not become apparent until later. When I first became interested, in Berlin, I did not yet possess the self-control or the necessary realism; these I had to acquire, often through painful experience. At the time my concept of foreign policy was based for the most part on ideology. Principles meant more to me than realistic possibilities; my positions were dictated by the natural radicalism of youth.

The greatest controversy at that time was over the Zionist attitude to the British policy in Palestine. Those were the years when the movement had to learn to bury one by one the illusory hopes it had attached to the Balfour Declaration of 1917, above all the naïve belief that the British Empire was about to present the Jewish people with a ready-made national home, perhaps even a Jewish state. In our centuries in the Diaspora we had learned to write books, evolve philosophical systems, compose poetry and music, and do business, but founding a state was something unknown and foreign to us. We did not realize that a state can only be created by the people themselves, that a nation cannot make another nation a present of anything essential. What a nation attains depends upon itself. Basically it was the task of modern Zionism to say to the Jews: Do not be too much afraid of your enemies, but do not put too much faith in your friends either. You yourselves must decide your fate.

This does not mean that the Zionist movement was immune to overoptimistic hopes aroused by the Balfour Declaration. Most of us were unwilling to admit that the British had an empire to govern in which the Arab peoples played an essential role and that British statesmen envisaged a key position for Britain in the Near East. With the impatience of a people oppressed for centuries and with the tremendous drive and pertinacity that characterize us, we demanded that the British behave in Palestine as if they were Jews. But the British mandatory authorities used British methods. Slowly, cautiously, hesitantly, they would take a couple of steps forward only to take one—sometimes two—backward. They would yield to Arab pressure, then to our counterpressure. Not to satisfy either party gradually became the golden rule. The fact that the Arabs and the Jews both denounce us, the British officials I dealt with later used to say, shows that Britain is acting rightly and taking a position of unbiased neutrality in the Jewish-Arab conflict.

This point of view was incomprehensible to us. We thought we held a promissory note in our hands, and we were impatient to see it honored. We took the hesitant British policy as a breach of promise and felt it to be anti-Zionist. As a result, soon after the "honeymoon" that followed the Balfour Declaration, most Jews felt a deep dissatisfaction with British policy that varied in intensity according to party and temperament, but in effect dominated everything. Young and radical, I was among the more dissatisfied. I had never overestimated the importance of the Balfour Declaration. Without rationally knowing why, I sensed that the main factor Zionism had to reckon with was not Britain but the Jewish people, and that the second factor was the Arabs. All the same, I was among the most bitter critics of British policy because I was unable or unwilling to understand the British attitude to the Palestine problem.

My gradual initiation into questions of foreign policy brought me into more intimate touch with Dr. Weizmann. Since for the next three decades my lifework was closely interwoven with his and since my relations with him were an essential factor in my political career, it seems appropriate to describe his personality. There is no doubt that after Theodor Herzl, the founder of the Zionist movement, Chaim Weizmann was its most important leader. In the last decade of his life his name was synonymous with Zionism for millions of people, especially non-Jews. Above all, he was responsible for two monumental achievements. In internal politics he made possible Zionism's change of course in favor of realistic colonization of Palestine, when it abandoned Herzl's tactics of working for a Jewish state through political agreements. In foreign policy he obtained the Balfour Declaration, the essential prerequisite for the great work of resettlement and the *de facto* establishment of a Jewish national home. All the internal controversies of the movement revolved around Weizmann personally. He was fanatically opposed and slandered by many, revered, not to say worshiped, by others. It was hardly possible for a Zionist to be indifferent toward him. You hated him or loved him, regarded him as the savior of the movement or its gravedigger.

My relations with him over almost thirty years varied at different periods. First came a short period of very close collaboration that led to some degree of personal intimacy, despite the difference in our ages. Within a few days at the Seventeenth Zionist Congress in 1931, this gave way to out-and-out antagonism that brought a complete rupture of personal relations for three years. Finally, in the last ten years of his life, our cooperation was so close that I became one of his most intimate friends and colleagues. Yet even in the years when we were closest, I tried to maintain my inner independence. Despite my admiration and my realization that I had learned much from him, I was never one of the blind, uncritical yes-men he was always surrounded by and so never a member of what might be called his royal household.

Chaim Weizmann was by no means easy to understand. There was something mercurial and contradictory about him, and his career, like his character, was compounded of the most diverse elements. As an Eastern European Jew who first came to Western Europe as a student, he was at home in the rich culture of Eastern Jewry while at the same time he had assimilated the essential values of four great European cultures: Russian, German, French, and Anglo-Saxon. His extraordinarily sympathetic insight enabled him to penetrate very deeply into the spirit of all these worlds, but ultimately he always remained the boy from Motele, the village near Pinsk where he was born, and when he was among friends his favorite language was Yiddish. This did not prevent the synthesis of East and West from being more complete in Weizmann than it was in many of his generation. He was scholar and artist in one, combining the often incompatible characteristics of both.

He had the scholar's realistic posture, his faith in empiricism and facts and figures, his dislike of hollow phrases, his refusal to believe in miracles, his cool, sober attitude, and his ever alert fear of letting himself be carried away into premature conclusions. His view of Zionism was the scholarly one. The slow, step-by-step preliminaries, the patient amassing of facts, the acceptance of what seemed unavoidable, the derisive attitude toward hotheads, and a contempt for empty political protests—all this drove many of us, including myself as a young man, to distraction, but in the end it proved remarkably beneficial and trained the movement for serious, responsible action. Weizmann abhorred emotionalism and demagoguery in any form. Yet he was a master of polemic. He lacked the verve to be a great orator, but he could be uncommonly critical and analytical in debate.

Pragmatic as he was in the concrete day-to-day work of resettling Palestine, in politics he was an artist, fascinating Jews and gentiles alike by his charm and sparkling intelligence. He could characterize a man—and dispose of him—in a single word. Like all great artists, he was extremely subjective, not to say egocentric. Without realizing it, he constructed a world of his own and placed himself at its center. When he took action he was not an intellectual making a firm distinction between subject and object, but an artist identifying himself with his medium. Zionism was an expression of Weizmann's personality. The famous sentence *"l'état c'est moi"* was applicable to him as to few other men. His own destiny and that of the movement were to him one and the same. When he had to resign from leadership of the movement in 1931, he was not so much angry as completely surprised. Ten minutes before the vote of censure he would not have thought it possible that a majority of the Zionist Congress could demand his resignation. To him it was as if, by doing so, the movement had dissolved itself.

This was what made it so difficult to oppose Weizmann. He had learned much from the British, but not their great talent for keeping political and personal relations separate. Anyone who opposed him politically was automatically his personal enemy. After I brought my successful motion of censure against him at the Basel Congress, he did not speak to me for three years. For the same reason it was not easy to be his political friend and colleague unless you blindly accepted everything he thought right. It took a certain amount of adroitness and humanity—you had to be a bit of a Weizmann yourself to stay close to him and yet maintain your own opinion.

Like many artists, Weizmann had a strongly feminine side, one positive aspect of which was the quite uncanny instinct for adapting himself to a situation or an opponent. He talked to lords like a lord, to labor leaders like a labor leader, and to Frenchmen like a Frenchman. In any situation he had an infallible sense of what was possible, an ability to assess what he could demand and conceivably attain. The disadvantage of his feminine traits was that he did not like to be contradicted. Actually he was brilliant and impressive only when surrounded by an atmosphere of admiration and approval. He needed warmth; he did not thrive in the glacial air that surrounds the outsider, the man who relies on himself alone. With an artist's creativity he set up the sort of world he needed, where he could best develop his qualities and talents. This explains the characteristics of his that have often been criticized. He was not what one could call reliable and often did not abide by political agreements, not because he wanted to deceive the other side but because he felt no obligation to honor something that belonged to the past and had no bearing on the present. In daily political work he had no sense of continuity; for him the world began anew every day and yesterday's agreements meant little in the new world of today. In politics he acted spontaneously and impulsively. Painting Weizmann's portrait as a statesman, you would not use sweeping brush strokes but rather the pointillist manner of applying one dab of color after another.

The fact that a consistent picture did after all emerge from his many different actions, contradictory as they were, can be attributed to the harmonious unity of his personality. His subjectivity in politics, which was in such contrast to his approach to scholarly work, affected his memory and his recall of past events. When he once asked me what I thought of his autobiography, I replied: "This autobiography will not be a document in the history of Zionism, but it will be a wonderful source for the history of Dr. Weizmann." Yet it would be unfair to say, as some do, that Weizmann falsified facts. He recorded the past as he saw it. Anything that was disturbing to him simply put his memory out of action. To some extent this is true of everybody, but it was especially pronounced in Weizmann, as it is in many artists.

His aristocratic spirit was also an artistic trait. He never sought easy victories and he hated the little tricks of internal politics. He preferred to provoke the opposition by stating his position too forcefully rather than seek the applause of the crowd through compromises and concessions. For this reason he performed very poorly in internal politics. Nearly all the crises in his political career that he took so much to heart might have been avoided if he had had a little more finesse and flexibility. But in spite of this heterogeneous nature—which was perhaps his true greatness—Weizmann was an overwhelming figure. Anyone who encountered him fell under his spell. He was self-confident, without being uncouth, charming but not obsequious, adaptable without ever losing sight of his own direction. He combined greatness and warmth to a rare degree. He became the natural center of any milieu he found himself in, and this explains the extraordinary fact that for thirty years he remained the undisputed—one might almost say God-given—leader of the Zionist movement.

Weizmann's inner circle included many people. One, Mrs.

Blanche Dugdale, a gentile, was the niece of Lord Balfour and a convinced Zionist. Through her family she possessed invaluable political connections, especially with the Conservative Party. She had a political talent unusual in a woman and admired Weizmann, who had converted her to Zionism. Naturally she regarded the Balfour Declaration as a sort of family institution and kept a strict eye on the Colonial Office to see that it did not distort what she held to be her uncle's intentions.

But the most fascinating figure in this circle was Lewis Namier. Namier came from a wealthy Jewish family in Galicia and was taken to England as a boy. With the fervor and devotion typical of some assimilated Jews, he had made English culture his own, including even its aristocratic, imperialistic aspects, which he considered its most productive ones. Nevertheless, he retained strong Jewish ties, probably not for religious reasons—he was said to have been baptized as a child—nor out of any knowledge of Jewish values, but out of a strong and not easily explicable national pride. He saw the solution to the Palestine question in terms of a permanent alliance between the Jewish state and the British Empire, a kind of synthesis of Jewish Zionism and British imperialism.

If ever there was a self-contradictory man, it was Namier. He was something of an anti-Semite, could not stand most Jews, and felt nothing but contempt and scorn for most of the Zionist Executive (probably in part out of slighted ambition, because he had tried unsuccessfully to become a member of it). He was a hero-worshiper by nature and had a boundless admiration for Weizmann. His remarkable talent as a historian is well known; not only was he one of the greatest English historians of his generation but the founder of a whole school that had an important methodological impact. It is difficult to reduce Namier's numerous contradictions to a common denominator. He was a snob and a humanitarian, a cynic and an idealist, proud and helpful, brilliant at formulation, devastating in his ridicule, extreme in his tactics, and at heart no politician.

But his excellent connections were entirely at the disposal of the Zionist movement. He used to come to the Zionist office several times a week, but he was interested only in foreign policy problems and had nothing but contempt for everything pertaining to internal politics, which, it must be said, he did not understand very well. Except for Weizmann, I was probably the only one of the Zionist activists who managed to establish friendly relations with him. We would often dine together at one of his clubs and he would unburden his mind to me. Since he knew that I did not take his attacks on my colleagues in the Executive seriously, I did not have to dissemble and could listen with amusement. I learned much from him about contemporary world problems and British politics. Later, especially after he married a Russian Orthodox Christian, which led to a break with Weizmann, he became estranged from Zionism. I have always been tolerant in these matters and saw no reason to break off relations with him. When the decisive phase of the dispute with Bevin and the Labour Party came, Namier was no longer active, but he welcomed the founding of the Jewish state from the bottom of his heart and visited Israel several times. I saw him there shortly before his death.

My involvement in concrete matters of Zionist foreign politics began in the later 1920's at the congresses in Prague and Karlsbad, to which I was a delegate, and more especially in the meetings of the Zionist General Council that I attended first as a deputy and later as a regular member. As a regular member of the Political Committee of the General Council, I came into closer touch with Weizmann and his circle, especially Selig Brodetzky. Brodetzky, for many years a prominent member of the Zionist Executive, was a versatile man, professor of mathematics at the University of Leeds and an active Zionist who divided his life between London and Leeds. Having come to England in early childhood, he fully understood the English way of thinking, and his method of working was cautious and deliberate rather than authoritative and assertive. At that time the Executive's political director was Leonard Stein, an English Jew and a lawyer by profession. He was very British in his attitude and was always prepared to understand and even accept the government's standpoint, which often brought him into conflict with the majority of the General Council. Weizmann found Stein's talent for formulation indispensable and would often defend him against his Zionist critics, to his own disadvantage. Stein and I often had drastic differences of opinion because he was an out-and-out minimalist in current political matters, but I always got along well with him personally.

However, my real debut in Zionist foreign politics occurred during the crisis over the Passfield White Paper of October, 1930, which severely curbed immigration into Palestine and was in fact an attempt to limit Britain's obligations under the Balfour Declaration to a bare minimum. Under pressure of Zionist protests, the British Prime Minister, Ramsay MacDonald, decided to appoint a cabinet commission headed by his foreign minister, Arthur Henderson, to negotiate with the Zionists in an attempt to interpret and improve the policy. The Zionist General Council elected a committee to negotiate with the cabinet commission, and I was one of its members.

Although I was busy in Berlin with the preliminary work for the *Encyclopaedia Judaica*, I spent several months in London in the winter and spring of 1930–1931 and really got to know Weizmann personally. I learned from him a sober, realistic approach to politics, although, of course, my party affiliation was with the opposition Radical Party. The outcome of our negotiations with the British government was Ramsay MacDonald's letter to Weizmann eliminating the worst hardships of the White Paper and establishing a basis for substantial immigration into Palestine in the coming years.

In spite of my budding friendship with Weizmann, I had become convinced that in the interests of the movement he ought to resign temporarily as president. In both English and Jewish eyes he stood for co-operation with the British government, and for the sake of Zionist unity it seemed to me desirable that he relinquish the formal leadership to somebody else, at least between the Zionist congresses of 1931 and 1933. The natural candidate for his position was Nahum Sokolow, who had been chairman of the Zionist Executive for many years, and I had come to a kind of gentlemen's agreement with Weizmann that he would voluntarily resign during the next congress. Of course he would remain the unchallenged political leader of the movement and would resume the presidency whenever it seemed appropriate.

However, when the Seventeenth Zionist Congress met in Basel in July, 1931, Weizmann did not seem inclined to observe our agreement. While he did not formally announce his candidacy, his strongest supporters, the Zionist Labor Party, refused to consider any other candidate and insisted that he remain president. Without the Labor Party a new president could not be elected. I repeatedly urged Weizmann to tell his friends that he would not in any circumstances be a candidate for the presidency, but he refused on the grounds that he could not issue instructions to the Labor Party. As a result, our relations at the congress were decidedly strained, although in the general debate I defended the policy that had led to MacDonald's letter—something that was not easy for me to do as a member of the opposition. In fact, Weizmann in his closing speech paid tribute to my defense as a courageous gesture.

The British government's attempt to reduce Zionism to a minor immigration movement led to the so-called debate on ultimate objectives. The Revisionist Party under Jabotinsky pressed strongly for the adoption of a new maximalist slogan: a Jewish state on both sides of the Jordan. In contrast Weizmann took an exaggeratedly minimalist position. He thought it dangerous to publicize the majority demand for Jewish preponderance in Palestine because it might be taken as a threat to displace the Arabs. With his tendency to phrase things too drastically, he went so far as to say, in a press interview: "I have no sympathy with the demand for a Jewish majority in Palestine. The world will only interpret this demand to mean that we want to drive the Arabs out of the country." This interview aroused a storm of protest at the congress. Even Weizmann's own Labor Party had to dissociate itself from it, and the party spokesman, Dr. Chaim Arlosorov, addressed a parliamentary question to Weizmann about it. In response, Weizmann tried to soften the harmful impact of his statement. The Labor Party then proposed that we proceed with the agenda.

At this I took the floor to second the Revisionist Party's proposal that the Political Committee be instructed "to prepare without delay a resolution on Zionist objectives and submit it to a plenary session of the Congress as soon as possible." This motion was passed. I was elected chairman of the subcommittee appointed to formulate our ultimate aims, and during the ensuing days and nights I learned how prone Jewish politicians are to attach excessive importance to formulations of this sort. I remember times when my briefcase contained ten or fifteen versions of the Zionist aims. We finally agreed on one version and asked Weizmann to accept it and at the same time to retract his interview. We had dropped the word "majority" and substituted the following wording: "The homeless, landless Jewish people, eager to emigrate, desires to end its economic, spiritual and political plight by rerooting itself in its historic homeland through continuous immigration and resettlement and to revive in Eretz Israel a national life endowed with all the characteristic features of the normal life of a nation." Weizmann refused to accept this wording or to retract his interview. A majority of the Political Committee then decided to submit the following motion to the plenum: "The Congress regrets Dr. Weizmann's statements to the Jewish news agency and considers his answer to the interpellation unsatisfactory." It was clear that the motion, if carried, would amount to a vote of censure and would inevitably lead to Weizmann's resignation.

The crucial session took place on a Sunday evening, and of all the clashes I have witnessed at Zionist congresses (which can compete with any parliament in the world for fireworks), this was the most exciting. Up to the very last minute I tried to reach an agreement with Weizmann, whereby he would withdraw his candidacy in writing and I would withdraw the motion of censure. But Weizmann, who relied too heavily on his advisers in matters of party politics, was convinced that the vote of censure would never get a majority and declined my attempt to avoid an open crisis in the plenary session. When the meeting began, the tension in the hall was electric. Before the permanent president of Zionist congresses, Dr. Leo Motzkin, gave me the floor, I again approached Weizmann. On the platform, surrounded by his circle of intimates, he was looking rather pale and nervous.

I said, "Dr. Weizmann, if you will give me a letter now, addressed to the Labor Party delegation, saying that you are not a candidate for president, I will on my own responsibility ask

Dr. Motzkin to postpone the session for an hour and to convene the Political Committee to drop the motion of censure."

"Please don't go to the trouble. Try to get your resolution adopted by the assembly," Weizmann replied.

I proposed the committee's motion and an extremely violent debate ensued. My opponent was Chaim Arlosorov, a close friend as long as he lived and one of the most brilliant leaders of the Zionist Labor Party. A politician and writer, he was born in Russia and brought up in Germany and would no doubt have become one of the outstanding figures in Zionism if he had not been murdered in Tel Aviv at an early age and in circumstances that have never been explained. After a dramatic verbal duel between the two of us, the motion of censure was passed by 123 votes to 106. The outcome was uncertain to the last. After the vote there was dead silence. Weizmann and his friends immediately left the hall and the following day left Basel. Nahum Sokolow was elected president of the WZO for the next two years. My relations with Weizmann were abruptly broken off and were not resumed until he returned to the presidency, when we gradually developed a political and personal friendship.

The debate on ultimate objectives followed the Weizmann resolution. As spokesman for the Political Committee I had to execute a very difficult and risky parliamentary maneuver. To get the vote of censure passed, I needed the Revisionist vote, but in the vote on objectives that was to follow it, I was opposing the Revisionists' motion, which I thought politically harmful and dangerous. I was thus forced to work with two different coalitions in the course of a single session. Nevertheless, the Revisionist resolution was defeated by a strong majority and this produced an indescribable uproar. Jabotinsky tore up his delegate's card; it was now the Revisionist Party's turn to walk out of the congress.

It was 2 A.M. when this dramatic session ended, but to go to bed was out of the question. The delegates sat around for hours in the cafés, and in the early hours of the morning I went to the park to swim and play tennis. Many of my political opponents resented this more than they resented my motion of censure against Weizmann, and I must admit that it is not in accord with the normal style of Zionist politics to relax on the tennis court after such excitement.

10

Preliminary Work for the World Jewish Congress

My role at the 1931 Basel Congress led, among other things, to an invitation from the Zionist Organization of America to accompany Nahum Sokolow on a visit to the United States to raise money for the Keren Hayesod, the fund that financed Zionist work in Palestine. Nahum Sokolow had played a leading role in the Zionist movement for years. In many respects he was Weizmann's opposite number and complement. He began a brilliant career as a Hebrew journalist very early and was for many years chief editor of the Warsaw Hebrew daily newspaper *Hatzefirah*, for which he wrote at least one article a day for decades. Thanks to his wide-ranging memory, he had all Hebrew literature and most European languages at his fingertips. In politics, science, and literature there was hardly a subject on which he could not write wittily and absorbingly, if not always deeply. His productivity as a writer was almost inconceivable. He once told me his co-editors used to ration the amount of paper delivered to his house every morning for his daily article in order to keep it short, and as a result he acquired a minuscule handwriting that was almost as legible as print. I have received letters from him that looked like blank pages until, in an upper corner, you finally discovered a few lines scribbled in his miniature hand.

In conversation he had a sparkling wit and an amazing capacity for adjusting to his partner. Talking to a Hasidic rabbi he turned into a Hasid; dealing with a French statesman he became a charming *bel esprit*, and, as somebody once said half in jest and half in malice, conferring with the Pope he became a Catholic. Sokolow was extremely cautious and deliberate and thus counterbalanced Weizmann's impulsiveness. He had a masterly way of stripping away the difficulties of a situation and reducing an apparently insoluble problem to simple terms through unshakable calm and dialectical wisdom. A mediator to the manner born, he was created to resolve conflicts, and here his superior, slightly ironic attitude to affairs of life and politics was a help to him. As a speaker he was conversational rather than rhetorical, as a politician, a negotiator rather than a creative statesman. He had no real opponents, but not many enthusiastic supporters either. In the difficult situation precipitated by Weizmann's resignation he was an ideal president.

The U.S. delegation to the Basel Congress was split, like American Zionism as a whole. On the one hand stood the great figure of Supreme Court Justice Louis D. Brandeis, one of the leading jurists and moral spokesmen of his generation who had come to Zionism quite unexpectedly from a strongly assimilated background. To be sure, his views were closer to Herzl's than to those of Weizmann. He was a statesman from outside the movement who had theoretically worked out the possible ways of attaining Zionist ideals without any regard for the moods and emotions of the masses.

Brandeis and Weizmann had clashed sharply in 1919, at the first annual Zionist conference to be held after the First World War and the publication of the Balfour Declaration. The conflict was based both on political issues and on personalities. The issues concerned the method of building up the *yishuv* in Palestine. Brandeis and his followers were in favor of private investments and liberal economic methods. Weizmann and his group—especially the Labor Party—preferred collective means and centralized, controlled, economic enterprises. These conflicting concepts derived from their particular backgrounds. Brandeis typified the spirit of American free enterprise, whereas Weizmann was inclined toward the collectivist programs that were representative of much of Eastern European Jewry.

It was this rupture that had split the American Zionist movement. One section of it, led by Stephen Wise, Judge Julian
Mack, and Robert Szold, stood behind Brandeis, while another
faction, that might well be called the more Eastern European
Jewish one, was led by Louis Lipsky and Morris Rothenberg
and sided with Weizmann. This split was again in evidence at
the Basel Congress. The group led by Stephen Wise voted
against Weizmann, and a smaller group under Lipsky voted for
him.

When Sokolow became president of the WZO, the American
Zionists, under the presidency of Robert Szold, invited him and
me to come to the United States. This was my first major tour
on behalf of the movement. I spent several months, partly with
Sokolow, partly alone, visiting the larger cities, and I had a
much better opportunity than before to get to know the more
important American-Jewish organizations and leaders. In my
first few weeks I made my speeches in Yiddish, but the American Zionist leadership gave me a time limit of four weeks, after
which I was supposed to switch to English. In my first speech in
English, delivered at a Hadassah conference in Baltimore, I
gained the sympathy of my feminine audience when I said: "I
am going to show you how one is making an English speech
with very few words and a lot of *hutzpah.*"

A few days after arriving in New York, I was introduced to
a remarkable figure in American Zionism, the notorious Chone,
a big, hulking man with huge feet. Chone had no profession, but
he was an omnipresent figure at Zionist meetings, living and
traveling at his friends' expense. He had a sound native intelligence and common sense and was on familiar terms with everybody, being completely ignorant of the proprieties of language
and the conventions of courtesy and good manners. Before I
made my first address, he told me that this speech would determine my political fate. If it was good, I was a made man, if not,
I might as well go back to Europe the next day. He had already
looked up suitable sailings for me. He was the only man whose
honesty I could rely on. He always stuck to the truth, while the
recognized leaders of the organization were far too polite to
tell me their true opinion. He said he would sit in the front row

and after ten minutes I was to glance at him. If he nodded, the speech was all right; if he shook his head, I should bring it to an end as fast as possible and leave the next day. After ten minutes I looked at Chone. He was nodding his head ecstatically.

In those days, when a prominent guest from abroad was to address a Jewish meeting, it was the tiresome custom to invite a number of local big shots to speak too. The proceedings would begin very late, and since there were usually five or six speakers before Sokolow and myself, it was often midnight before our turn came. I found this as exasperating then as I do today. On one occasion I arranged with the chairman that no one would speak before me because I had to leave the meeting at eleven o'clock. However, several other speakers were called upon first and by ten o'clock my turn had still not come. As I was preparing to leave, the chairman asked the current speaker to yield to me. Somewhat put out, I began with what I thought was an appropriate joke, the story of the uneducated Irishman who goes to the most elegant restaurant in Paris to regale himself on French cooking. Not understanding a word of French, he orders the first item on the menu, hoping it will be soup. He is brought soup and, hoping for fish, orders the second item. This proves to be another soup and so it goes until he has eaten five or six soups. This is too much for him, so he calls the *maître d'hôtel*, shows him his billfold and asks to have everything on the menu served up so he can select what he wants. The savory dishes are brought to his table, and when it is all spread before him he groans: "The chance of a lifetime and my stomach's full of soup!" Though somewhat embarrassing to the preliminary speakers, the joke made a bigger hit than the talk itself, and from then on I threatened to tell it whenever the number of introductory speakers was not kept to a minimum.

My greatest gain from this visit to America was the friendship of Stephen S. Wise, who was to be an important force in my life, personally as well as politically. I was his pupil and friend until his last hour and felt closer to him than to any other great personality of my generation. He was without doubt the most well known Jew in the United States, and there was hardly an elevator operator, taxi driver, or bellboy who did not know him at least by name. He was an intimate friend of President Woodrow Wilson and together with Brandeis did more than anyone else to gain for Zionism the sympathy of the Wilson administration, without which the Balfour Declaration would have been impossible. There was no sphere of Jewish life in which Wise was not active and influential. A rabbi by profession, he founded the American Jewish Congress and became the recognized leader of American Zionism, although he was just as active in defending the general rights of Jews. In fact, his interests were not by any means limited to Jewish problems; he was a powerful—and feared—figure in American politics as a whole. Any career in America would have been open to him. He had many offers of ambassadorships, but his boundless loyalty to the Jewish cause led him to refuse them all.

Thanks mainly to his unusual temperament, Wise was one of America's greatest speakers. He had a moving voice and an awe-inspiring presence that dominated a meeting from the moment he ascended the rostrum, but it was his personality much more than the content of his speeches that was so effective. He was far too impulsive to be a successful statesman. He despised political considerations and lacked the politician's indispensable ability to take the long view and to reconcile radically different positions. And so for decades he was one of the most admired and at the same time controversial figures in American-Jewish life, hated by many but loved and honored by millions. Ruthless in battle and in polemics, he could offend his opponents deeply by his outbursts of temperament, both in private discussions and on the speaker's platform, but his remarkable humanity and generosity always put everything right again. Political leaders are motivated by many things, some by will for power, others by a wish to utilize their talents, others by vanity and the desire for fame. Stephen Wise was motivated essentially by his human goodness. Not only did he love the Jewish people; he loved every individual Jew. He would turn his hand to finding help for a poor refugee, arranging for the adoption of an orphan, or providing for a destitute widow as willingly as to solving a great social problem. This also explains his unsurpassed popularity with the Jewish masses of America. Other Jewish leaders

may have been more revered, feared, or admired than he, but
none was so beloved.

I had made the acquaintance of Stephen Wise on my first visit
to America, but on this second visit I was much closer to him
politically because of our joint action at the Basel Congress.
During the winter of 1931–1932 he became my friend and my
protector at many difficult moments. He would accept criticism
from me, although I was his junior by many years. We were on
the same side in nearly all the major political issues of subsequent years, with the single exception of the first plan for the
partition of Palestine before the Second World War when,
against my advice, he let Brandeis win him over to the anti-
partition viewpoint. But he never held it against me and he
himself embraced partition wholeheartedly at the end of the
war.

The direct result of this friendship was that Wise drew me
into the work of paving the way for the World Jewish Congress. While I was no stranger to the problems of Jewish life in
the Diaspora, they had not previously been one of my consum-
ing interests. The *Encyclopaedia Judaica* made heavy demands
on me and I devoted such time and energy as I had left to
Zionist work. But even then Stephen Wise had both feet firmly
planted in practical Jewish politics. The purpose of the American Jewish Congress, which he had founded, was to protect
Jewish rights and enhance Jewish life in America, and this
brought it into conflict with some other Jewish social and charitable organizations. Wise was a radical democrat all his life. He
believed in "the people" and disliked nothing more than rich
Jews who condescended to help the Jewish masses but did not
identify with them. As a young man he could have become the
leader of this Jewish oligarchy, when at the age of twenty he
was offered the rabbinate of the richest and most prestigious
Jewish community in New York, Temple Emanuel. He declined because the president of the congregation, the great Jewish lawyer Louis Marshall, Wise's lifelong adversary, insisted on
the right to approve all his sermons. Since then he had been
fighting to democratize Jewish life, not only through his own
American Jewish Congress but also through the Paris-based

Comité des Délégations Juives, which, under the direction of Leo Motzkin, defended threatened Jewish rights all over the world.

During those years Stephen Wise had conceived the idea of a World Jewish Congress, and in 1932 he wanted to convene a world conference in Europe to prepare for it. Obviously he could not do this from New York, and he suggested that I take charge of the preliminary work. At first I resisted, partly because I lacked time, partly because of my wish to devote myself exclusively to Zionist work, but Wise's charm was hard to withstand and when he insisted that the conference could never take place without my help, I agreed, on condition that this was not to establish a precedent. Nothing led me to suspect this was the beginning of a long chapter of my life or that, moving upward through various steps and positions, I should become successor to Stephen Wise in the presidency of the World Jewish Congress.

The purpose of the WJC is so elementary and self-evident it is surprising that it should not have come into existence until the 1930's and that there are still Jewish groups opposed to the idea. The WJC has two simple functions: to symbolize and make a reality of the common resolution of the Jewish people to unite in defense of its rights; and to secure the co-operation of the various branches of this dispersed people in all matters of common interest. Nothing imperils the survival of the Jewish people more than its fragmentation. It has been able to survive the Diaspora and remain a people only because, during the centuries when it was fragmented geographically, linguistically, and in all kinds of other ways, it succeeded in retaining a sense of solidarity. In earlier centuries religion created this sense; its rigorous laws imposed a similar way of life on all branches of the people. Since emancipation, religion has lost its predominant influence, so that other methods of strengthening Jewish solidarity have become necessary. The most natural instrument for strengthening it is an organization comprising the innumerable Jewish associations all over the world and designed to provide the Jewish people with an address, enabling it to collaborate systematically on the solution of its problems. Needless to say, it could never be the function of the WJC to intervene in the internal problems of individual Jewish communities, but when it comes to defending against anti-Semitic attacks or to guaranteeing the civil rights of threatened communities, all branches of the Jewish people are equally obliged to take a stand. Nothing could be more senseless and harmful than a Jewish isolationism that would confine itself to defending the rights of one specific Jewish community without regard for those of the whole people. If it holds true for the world as a whole that every important political event affects all its parts and that isolationism is untenable even for a great nation like the United States, this holds doubly true for the Jewish people. Once this principle is accepted, there follows the inescapable necessity of co-ordinating the separate programs of all the various Jewish associations.

It should be added that the WJC is founded upon one additional principle: the democratic representation of the most diverse Jewish groups. The era when the privileged Jewish communities of Western Europe or their influential spokesmen could set themselves up as protectors of disfranchised Jews is over for good. The WJC is founded upon the principle of equality of all Jewish communities, regardless of their situation. It does not act in the name of any individual body, unless that body is represented in the WJC and is in full accord with its action. The only exception is the case of a Jewish community, suppressed and unable to speak for itself, like German Jewry in the Nazi period. In such a case the free parts of the Jewish people must defend the rights and speak for the community held in captivity. In this spirit a substantial part of the Jewish people was successfully organized within two decades. To be sure, there are still groups, particularly in America, that refuse, out of stubbornness or reasons of prestige, to accept the principle of common representation of the Jewish people. It has always seemed to me that the gentile world grasped the purpose of the WJC much faster than some of these organizations did, perhaps because it is not plagued by Jewish inferiority and anxiety complexes. Gentile politicians were always glad to have a body with which they could discuss Jewish questions, instead of having to deal with ten or more different organizations. Although the

WJC has not yet attained its goal of representing all the Jews of the world, it has become the most representative world Jewish organization, has played a decisive role in many critical situations, and can be said without exaggeration to have made a lasting contribution to the solution of many of the tragic problems of our generation.

What induced me to devote my energies to it increasingly after Stephen Wise first enlisted me was the historical situation. From the first I was one of those—unfortunately a minority—who took the phenomenon of Hitler very seriously. Most Jews in Germany and in other countries lacked the imagination to envisage in the twentieth century anti-Semitism as bestial as that of the National Socialists. They took Hitler for a passing figure and the German Jews in particular, mindful of their economic and cultural standing in the Weimar Republic, refused to recognize the danger he represented. In 1932 and 1933 Stephen Wise and myself were warning world Jewry and especially the German Jews. We were ridiculed as panicky, hysterical alarmists. If the Jews had taken Hitler more seriously from the first, hundreds of thousands, perhaps millions of them, might have been saved. I do not claim to have foreseen Dachau and Auschwitz; our imagination did not go that far. But I did realize that a full-scale attack on the whole Jewish people was in the making, and for this reason alone I thought the moment had come to create a world organization of Jews.

The task proved much more complex and difficult than Dr. Wise and I had thought in New York. Jews are individualistic, strong-willed people. In centuries of dispersal they have learned to co-ordinate their actions by uniting at the local, or at best the territorial, level but never in a world association. This has produced in them an unusual loyalty to the individual group at the expense of what might be called a sense of overall solidarity. This is still a severe handicap to the State of Israel, despite the existence of a state authority backed by sanctions and power, conditions totally lacking in the Diaspora, where everything is voluntary and where even the smallest group feels free to say no whenever it pleases.

There are many Jews afraid that excessively vigorous expressions of pan-Jewish solidarity might be taken for a lack of loyalty to their native or host countries. This problem of dual loyalty, with which Zionism has always had to contend, was a factor in the controversy over the establishment of the WJC. It was relatively easy to win over the Eastern European Jews, except for those of the Soviet Union who even then were cut off from any connection with world Jewry. We had more difficulty with the Jews of Western Europe, where there were old-established organizations unwilling to see their sovereignty infringed for the sake of co-operating with other Jewish groups.

After my return from America, I visited nearly all the European Jewish centers to urge participation in the first world Jewish conference. In Poland, the Baltic countries, Austria, the Balkan countries, and in Switzerland and Italy, I was successful from the first. My major difficulties were in England and France. In France there existed the Alliance Israélite Universelle, which did not, however, truly represent the French Jews. In England the main thing was to get the support of the Board of Deputies, the long recognized organization of English Jewry. I went several times to London to negotiate with its leaders, notably Sir Henry d'Avigdor Goldsmith and Neville Laski. The Zionist groups in all countries immediately supported the world congress, since its basic principle, the unity of the Jewish people, coincided with that of Zionism. But in England this support was insufficient, and when the Board of Deputies voted, a small majority rejected participation. I then proceeded to create an English branch of the WJC out of the elements favorable to us. This laborious, time-consuming work had to be carried out from Berlin, in close collaboration with a number of leading Jewish figures, as a part-time occupation along with my full-time direction of the *Encyclopaedia Judaica*.

In Paris there still existed the Comité des Délégations Juives, an organization that had evolved from the collaboration of all kinds of Jewish groups after the First World War for the purpose of guaranteeing the minority rights of Eastern European Jewish communities. After securing those rights in the peace treaties with the Eastern European countries, the Comité had lost much of its authority over the years; it was now directed by

Leo Motzkin, the semipermanent president of the Zionist General Council and of the Zionist congresses who was distinguishing himself more and more in Diaspora politics. Motzkin was a remarkably talented mathematician but had broken off his studies to devote himself entirely to Jewish activities. His lofty imperturbability, his humor and fatherly manner, made him an ideal president of international meetings. There was something professional about him, something of the lecture room, and he was one of those who in political debate are more concerned with presenting all points of view than with getting their own adopted. Motzkin was esteemed by everybody for his selflessness; with extraordinary devotion he kept the Comité des Délégations alive. The WJC was to have incorporated the Comité and put its ideas into effect on a much broader basis. Unfortunately Motzkin died very soon after our preliminary work began, and he was able to play a role in the WJC only at its early stages.

I had the full support of the Eastern European Jewish leaders, especially the Zionist groups. My most invaluable collaborators included Yitzhak Gruenbaum, Yehoshua Thon, Yitzhak Schipper, Henryk Rosmarin in Poland, and Mordecai Nurock in Latvia. In Czechoslovakia I was assisted by Emil Margulies, a courageous man; he and Angelo Goldstein were among the recognized champions of Czech Jewry. Robert Stricker and Isidor Plaschkes of Vienna brought the Austrian Jewish groups into the WJC.

In Germany we managed to win over only a Zionist splinter group; the main body, led by Kurt Blumenfeld, remained aloof because it wished to confine itself to Zionist work. In their refusal to participate, which indicated how much they underestimated the importance of political activity in the Diaspora, the German Zionists showed themselves to be true disciples of Weizmann who, with the one-sidedness that often characterizes great leaders, devoted himself exclusively to Zionism all his life. Although in theory he recognized the importance of the Diaspora's work to ensure Jewish survival, he refused to take part in it personally. (The only exception he made was rescue work for the German Jews during the Nazi era.)

Many leading Palestinian Jews supported the WJC from the outset, including figures such as Menahem Ussishkin, Ben-Zion Mossenson, and Joseph Sprinzak, the late president of the Israeli Parliament. But Ben-Gurion and Arlosorov deliberately held aloof.

Despite all these difficulties, which stemmed partly from vigorous dissent, partly from indifference, I succeeded in assembling a representative body of participants for the first world Jewish conference, which met in Geneva in August, 1932. This conference set up the International Committee for the World Jewish Congress, whose tasks was to bring in nonparticipating groups and to make the final preparations. Almost four years were to elapse and three more world conferences were to follow this one before the first session of the World Jewish Congress was convened in Geneva in 1936. The 1932 meeting was overshadowed to a great extent by the rise of National Socialism. It was still not certain that the storm would break, but many of us were at least reckoning with the possibility and were deeply concerned about the fate of the European Jews. But nobody, including myself when I returned to Berlin from this first world conference, had any inkling of the catastrophe that was at hand when Hitler was appointed German chancellor in 1933.

11

I Leave Germany

The last two or three years in Berlin before Hitler came to power were not pleasant ones. The constant brawls, the fighting and killings that occurred every day, the general tenseness, made life, previously comfortable and meaningful, difficult and unrewarding. I had toyed with the idea of leaving Berlin, but various factors persuaded me to stay. I could not simply abandon the *Encyclopaedia Judaica*, for which I was responsible and which provided the livelihood of about fifty families. The *Encyclopaedia* was tied to Berlin and could not be moved elsewhere, if only because of its financial dependence on Jakob Goldschmidt and other Jewish patrons. Besides, Berlin was still one of the greatest Jewish centers of Central and Western Europe—probably the most important of them in fact—and many Hebrew and Jewish writers lived there. When Hitler came to power in 1933 I was just as uneasy as all other Jews, but no one could foresee how rapidly Nazism would develop into a movement of mass murder. The world accepted Hitler calmly and even the majority of Jews did not feel themselves fatally threatened.

Even before Hitler became chancellor I was repeatedly advised to emigrate because of the frequent clashes I had had in the past with the Nazis and other extreme nationalist groups. But the fact that I did not fall victim to Nazism, as so many of my friends did, is not due to any foresight on my own part. After my mother died in Frankfurt in 1930, I had helped my father to realize his old dream of settling in Palestine. I took an apartment for him in Tel Aviv, where a distant relative kept house for him, and it was a joy to me to make these last years of his life free of financial worries. He could now devote himself to literary work, although even then he was not in the best of health. In late March, 1933, I received a telegram informing me of his serious illness and asking me to come at once if I wanted to see him alive. I had already received several telegrams urging me to leave Germany from Chaim Weizmann and Stephen Wise, both of whom had sized up the course of events more accurately from a distance than we did in Germany. My fiancée, Alice Gottschalk, whom I married a year later, was constantly begging me to leave. When I received the news of my father's illness, I packed a few things and, with my fiancée, went to Palestine by way of Italy. I found my father critically ill, and he died a few months later. Since I had expected to return soon to Berlin, I had left everything behind in my little apartment, notably my valuable library of two thousand volumes. I was already beyond the German frontier when I learned of the anti-Jewish boycott of April 1. A few days later the Gestapo appeared at my Eschkol office, which was in the same building as my apartment. If they had found me I would probably have wound up in a concentration camp, but as it turned out I was immediately informed of this unwelcome visit and never returned to Germany during the Nazi era.

When I was informed that the Gestapo was "interested" in me, I had to look for a new field of action. To continue the *Encyclopaedia Judaica* was out of the question as things were. When I told Stephen Wise I was not going to return to Germany, he asked me to represent the World Jewish Congress and the Comité des Délégations Juives in Geneva. I left Palestine for Geneva and lived there until 1940, when I moved with my family to the U.S.A.

The Nazis let me alone for two more years, although my travels and activities in Europe were under constant observation. But in 1935, Goebbels' Propaganda Ministry had me deprived of citizenship for subversive activities, and all my property was confiscated and sold at public auction, above all my books that were lying crated and ready to be shipped at the free port of Hamburg. During the lengthy process of having my citizenship revoked, which involved the interrogation of many acquaintances, I discovered how well informed the Nazi intelligence service was about my activities. To give just one example. I had postponed my marriage for a long time in order not to endanger my wife's relatives, who were still living in Berlin. When in 1934 we finally decided to marry, we went to Tel Aviv because Palestine under the British mandate was the only place where a rabbinical marriage was valid in civil law. I did not tell any of my friends of the marriage, which was performed by two rabbis in the presence of no one but the two relatives who served as our witnesses. The marriage was recorded in the Hebrew rabbinical register of Tel Aviv. Three days later, when the Gestapo paid one of its regular calls at the Zionist office in the Meineckestrasse, one of the directors was asked by a Gestapo official where Dr. Goldmann, the rabble-rouser, was. He replied truthfully that he didn't know and that the office was not in touch with me, whereupon the Gestapo man informed him of my marriage three days before to Fräulein Alice Gottschalk in Tel Aviv. This proves that the Gestapo had agents in Palestine who knew Hebrew and had access to the rabbinical register. Apart from the loss of my furniture and library, I suffered no personal harm at the hands of the Nazis. I no longer had relatives in Germany and was able to get my wife's parents and her only brother out before it was too late.

When my citizenship was revoked in 1935 and I had to acquire a new nationality, I was able, through the help of the French foreign minister, Louis Barthou, to become a citizen of Honduras. I was then appointed Honduran consul in Geneva and for the next ten years traveled on a consular passport, which I surrendered when I became an American citizen in 1945. Incidentally, it is worth mentioning, as a sidelight on the life of a twentieth-century Jew, that I have held seven different passports. I was born in Russia, and when Spain was looking after Russian affairs in Germany during the First World War, I received a Spanish passport. After the war it was assumed that the little town where I was born had become Lithuanian, so I was granted a Lithuanian passport. This I returned because it was made out to "Doctoras Nahumas Goldmanas." In the meantime it had been established that Visznevo belonged to Poland, so I was issued a Polish passport that, because of Poland's anti-Semitic policy, I soon relinquished in favor of German nationality. Deprived of citizenship by the Nazis, I became a Honduran. In 1945 I became an American and in 1964 an Israeli.

Although the Nazis kept an eye on my activities and, as a high Gestapo official had told my father-in-law in the course of the denaturalization proceedings, considered me the Jewish Public Enemy Number One, this did not prevent them from trying to get me to help them work out some kind of *modus vivendi* with world Jewry. This was during the years when the Nazis still felt relatively weak and feared world Jewish opposition. It was Mussolini who made the most ambitious of these attempts. One morning in the summer of 1934 Dr. Sacerdote, then chief rabbi of Rome and a member of the executive committee of the WJC, appeared at my home in Geneva, saying he had come at the request of the Duce. Mussolini had sent for him and explained that world Jewry's bitterly anti-German attitude was an obstacle to Italian policy, which was already leaning toward a rapprochement with Germany, and he wanted to try to soften the Nazis' anti-Jewish policy. To do this, however, he needed to know world Jewry's minimum conditions for ceasing to oppose the Nazi regime. Originally he had wanted to consult Weizmann, but Sacerdote had told him that Weizmann was concerned exclusively with Zionist problems and it would be more advisable to invite me, as one of the leaders of the WJC.

Dr. Sacerdote was thunderstruck when I refused to go to Rome with him. It was inconceivable to him as an Italian that one could decline a summons from the Duce. Besides, he feared unpleasant consequences for himself. I explained to him why Mussolini's project was impracticable in the proposed form. First, I thought it impossible that Hitler would make any concessions in his anti-Jewish program, and even in the highly unlikely event that he did, he would not under any circumstances restore the former rights of the German Jews. World Jewry could not conclude any agreement that was not based on complete and unrestricted civil rights because such an agreement would invite all anti-Semitic regimes to curtail Jewish rights in a similar way. Either equality of rights is total, I told Sacerdote, or it is not equality, and even if a compromise with Hitler were possible on the basis of curtailed Jewish rights, we could not possibly pay the price of jeopardizing the rights of all other Jews in the world. Therefore, Mussolini would do better to urge moderation on Hitler on his own account, without the participation of Jewish leaders. This was not likely to make world Jewry much more friendly toward Germany, but in the absence of tangible persecution its protest would become less violent. On all these grounds it was preferable that neither I nor any other Jewish representative should be officially involved. When the Duce was informed of this, he is said to have been much displeased, but when I called upon him on a later occasion with regard to the Saar, he acknowledged that my refusal had been justified.

A second Nazi overture was made by the German ambassador in London who, through mutual acquaintances, twice invited me to negotiate an arrangement with him about the treatment of the Jews. I gave him the answer I had already given Mussolini. In later years, when the Nazis began their great mass murder of the Jews, I asked myself if it would not have been more sensible to accept these invitations, despite my fundamental objections. But I am firmly convinced that nothing would have come of any such conversations because Hitler's hatred of the Jews was too great. He would never have been deterred from his fanatical excesses by agreements or formal pacts.

12

Jewish Minority Rights and the League of Nations

During my years in Geneva from 1933 to 1940, as representative of the Comité des Délégations Juives and of the planning committee for the World Jewish Congress, I was in a sense the official Jewish representative on all Diaspora questions. In 1934 I also became the representative of the Jewish Agency for Palestine, accredited to the Mandates Commission of the League of Nations, and this brought the whole complex of the Palestine question into my sphere of activity. Hand in hand with this went my work in the Jewish fight against Nazism and, from 1935 on, my growing involvement in the German-Jewish refugee problem. There was scarcely an important Jewish political problem with which I was not in some way concerned. In Geneva I directed two offices, the Jewish Agency's and the WJC's, dividing my time between them. In 1935 and 1937 my two sons were born. In 1935 I moved into a beautifully situated house in Geneva, but because of my wide activities, I had to travel a great deal and was away from home for months at a time. My travels took me to the major cities of Western and Eastern Europe, with the exception, of course, of Germany.

The Jewish community of Geneva, not very numerous but strongly Jewish, welcomed me with good will and I made many real friendships with Jewish families during my years there. As the seat of the League of Nations, the city was a center of international politics and for anyone who had chosen this as his field, as I had, there could hardly have been a better place of initiation. The League of Nations was almost an autonomous city within Geneva, but the intellectual atmosphere of Geneva itself, with its strong Calvinist traditions, was completely different from that of the international diplomatic colony. Since Geneva is not very big, the delegates and officials knew each other much more intimately than they can at the United Nations in New York. Moreover, in the 1930's the world was not yet divided into the two great blocs of East and West, and although the capitalist states naturally mistrusted the Soviet Union, the tension between them cannot be compared with that of today. Besides, common fear of the Nazi Moloch produced a kind of solidarity. Diplomatic manners were much better than they were to become after the Second World War. I think that by and large the world had at its disposal greater talent for statesmanship, greater finesse and political adroitness, than it has today. The most jarring note was introduced by Nazi Germany. After Hitler's Germany had dramatically walked out of the disarmament conference and the League of Nations in 1934, it was, of course, no longer directly represented in Geneva, but it continued to cast its increasingly menacing shadow over everything that went on there.

As Jewish representative I found myself in an anomalous situation. As representative of the Jewish Agency I had a status of some kind, since the British mandate for Palestine officially recognized the Jewish Agency and I was semi-officially accredited to the Mandates Commission of the League of Nations. But this position was by no means equivalent to that of a delegate of a member country. It was always a problem to decide what sort of ticket should be issued to me for League meetings, and at some sessions I had to use personal influence to be admitted at all. As representative of the Comité des Délégations and later of the WJC, I had, of course, no official function of any kind. I was an illustration of the anomalous and difficult situation of what might be called Jewish diplomacy, the diplomacy of a people that, until the State of Israel was established, enjoyed no official recognition whatsoever. Once, on my way from Geneva to Paris, a French frontier official, who had just passed an Italian traveling on a diplomatic passport without opening his baggage, asked me whether I too was a diplomat. My reply—*Un diplomate juif sans passeport*—made sense to him and he left my suitcase unopened. But privileges of this sort were not so easily obtained at the League of Nations.

Jewish diplomacy was still a very young art in those days. Weizmann had created it, so to speak, and Dr. Victor Jacobson, my predecessor as representative of the Jewish Agency at the League of Nations, had developed it with great tact. But our foreign policy was still in its infancy and lacked guidelines. The position a Jewish representative established for himself at the League depended chiefly upon his personal relations and manner. He had the prestige and power of no country behind him. A Jewish diplomat's greatest asset in those days was good will. None of the top League of Nations officials, no delegate of any country, was obliged by protocol to receive him at all, let alone negotiate or consider his wishes.

My work was made easier, however, by the increasing acuteness and international importance of the Jewish question. Now that Hitler was German chancellor, the difficulties of German Jews, and with them of all Jews, acquired international dimensions and no country could dissociate itself from them in the long run. Therefore, although my formal position was quite unsubstantial, I was supported morally by the urgency and tragedy of the fate of the Jews in the Hitler era. Before long I could get an appointment with any influential figure in Geneva without difficulty. From the outset I was firmly determined, as a Jewish representative, to keep out of all international disputes; to me the neutrality of the Jewish people was, and is, a firm principle. Because of Nazism I was anti-German, but I made it clear that otherwise Jewish questions alone interested me and determined my political position. The United States, which was not, of course, a member of the League of Nations, was outside my sphere of responsibility, and it fell to Stephen Wise to secure its support when this became necessary. With all other governments and their representatives I maintained political contact myself, either in Geneva or through their foreign ministries. In those days I was a constant visitor at the Foreign Office in London, the Quai d'Orsay in Paris, and the foreign ministries in Warsaw, Prague, Belgrade, Budapest, Copenhagen, and Bern, and there were few statesmen with whom I had not talked and negotiated. The Nazi example had encouraged anti-Semitic trends in other countries. In Poland and Rumania especially, where anti-Semitism had long histories, many parties felt inclined to follow Hitler's example. From the international and legal point of view, however, their situation was quite different from that of Germany, not only because the might of a great power did not stand behind their discriminatory practices, but also because in Poland and Rumania the rights of the Jews were guaranteed by international protective treaties.

Nothing illustrates the rapid change in the international scene and in political ideas more clearly than the fact that today, as I write these lines, few people in the Western world have any idea what minority rights mean. The appalling increase, in our own era, of restrictions on intellectual freedom and contempt for the rights of minorities is clearly demonstrated by the fact that in the political climate of today it would be almost unthinkable to demand minority rights for anybody, except in theory. Yet this concept and the system for safeguarding such rights by international treaty were among the most positive results of the First World War and the great achievements of international law. The principle of minority rights declared that in a state composed of various ethnic groups, not only must all citizens enjoy equal rights, but the individual way of life of the minority and the free development of its language and culture must be internationally guaranteed against infringement by the majority population.

The idea of minority rights had been developed long before the First World War, and naturally the Jewish minorities, particularly those of Eastern Europe, were deeply interested in the theory. After 1918 the demand for these rights became an integral part of official Jewish policy in the Eastern European countries, and even the non-Zionist groups concurred in it. In the peace treaties with Poland, Rumania, the Baltic states, and Czechoslovakia, minority rights were legally guaranteed to all groups, not only Jews, and came under the supervision of the League of Nations. As events proved, this arrangement did not offer an absolute guarantee, because no constitutional or international pledge can ultimately prevail in the face of reality. But for many years these protective treaties did represent an effective instrument in the countries concerned, and as will be seen from what I am about to relate, in many cases they had at least a deterrent effect.

I am convinced that the principle of minority rights, perhaps expressed in somewhat different form, must be a part of every truly libertarian legal order and that the world will have to return to this principle. In contemporary political life, which has created gigantic monolithic states where the overwhelming power of government threatens to stifle all genuine culture, in an epoch in which nonconformism and the struggle for freedom of thought grow harder in the democracies as well as the totalitarian countries, such rights are bound to seem anachronistic and quixotic. But I am convinced that the next few decades, certainly the next few centuries, will see the sovereign state superseded by larger political structures in which various ethnic groups will have to live together, and I am sure that the question of the rights and protection of minorities will again become a timely one. When the moment arrives, we shall be able to learn much from the experience of the interwar years. Paradoxical and even heretical as it may sound, I dare say that the question of minority rights has not lost its significance for Jewish minorities. True, the great compact Jewish minorities of Eastern and Central Europe no longer exist, but if the Jewish people want to survive as a people, if the Jewish minorities in the various countries of the world are to maintain their individual way of life, they will have to adopt a system in which these rights are recognized and, if necessary, internationally guaranteed.

When I assumed my duties as chairman of the Comité des Délégations Juives, whose primary responsibility was the supervision of minority treaties and the protection of Jewish minority rights, and when I became chairman of the WJC Executive in 1936, what one might call the golden age of minority rights of the 1920's was over, and the ideology and power of the League of Nations were on the decline. Hitler's arrogant attitude to the League was silently tolerated and his brutal per-

secution of all minorities, especially the Jews, encouraged all nationalistic and reactionary forces. These nationalists missed no
opportunity to weaken the guarantees and, wherever possible,
get rid of them completely. By 1933 the whole system was
extensively eroded and all we could attempt was a kind of rear-
guard action; and by September, 1934, the situation was so bad
that Foreign Minister Józef Beck of Poland could declare before
the League Assembly the *de facto* abolition of minority rights
in Poland. We did manage to prevent the implementation of this
Polish threat by convincing the Western powers to intervene,
but there could no longer be any question of real enforcement
of minority rights in Poland.

To give an account of all my undertakings during those years
would take me too far afield. I frequently went to Poland and
other Eastern European countries for discussions with their
governments and I kept trying, with less and less success, to
enlist Britain and France in the defense of Jewish minorities.
The growing might of the National Socialist regime was obviously undermining, more and more drastically, not only the
position of the German Jews (who were, in any case, not guaranteed by any protective treaty), but that of all Eastern European Jewish minorities. Here and there it was possible to slow
down the process, but ultimately it was ineluctable, and indeed
it was in keeping with Hitler's general barbarization and terror-
ization of the world.

Our only conspicuous success came in 1938, in the fight
against the anti-Semitic policy of the Goga government of
Rumania. Rumania had long been a country of notorious and
violent anti-Semitic tendencies, and during the 1930's anti-
Semitism began quite openly to influence even official government policy. In 1936 and 1937 the WJC was led to intervene
several times when the government tried to curtail civil rights
of Jews or to exclude them from economic life by law. In both
cases the WJC managed to have the measures rescinded. In late
1937 King Carol of Rumania appointed Octavian Goga as prime
minister. Goga was the representative of Rumania's radically
anti-Semitic National Christian Party, whose ideologist was the
well-known anti-Semite Alexander Cuza. Goga came into office

with a program for a complete revision of the Rumanian constitution. He proposed to transform the country into a corporate state, principally by excluding Rumanian Jews from economic life and from all the liberal professions, by depriving them of civil rights, and by adopting many other provisions of the Nazi anti-Jewish Nuremberg Laws. A royal decree of January 22, 1938, ordered a general revision of the civil status of all Rumanian Jews.

The WJC immediately took a number of vigorous steps and declared open war on the Goga government. I took the matter up with the British and French governments and with the secretary-general of the League and also tried, through Stephen Wise, to get the American government to intervene. On January 13, 1938, I submitted to the League Council a memorandum based on the Rumanian treaty of December 9, 1919, for the protection of minorities. The Rumanian government declared that the Rumanian Jews were not protected by this treaty, a declaration that gained us the intervention of the Western European powers, as they were the guarantors of the minority rights treaties. On January 25, 1938, in a letter to Dr. Wise, President Franklin D. Roosevelt vigorously condemned the racial persecution.

Nevertheless, it was extremely difficult to get the League Council to act. We asked that the petition be given emergency consideration. Lord Cranborne (now Lord Salisbury) was of decisive help to us; I spoke to him in Geneva on January 26, 1938, and he and Anthony Eden arranged an interview with the Rumanian foreign minister. The Rumanian government remained intransigent and threatened to revoke the minorities treaty altogether. After persistent efforts the League Council was persuaded to recognize the petition, though not on an emergency basis, and it appointed a committee of three, composed of the French and British foreign ministers and the delegate from Iran, to investigate the petition before the next session. We also arranged for a question to be asked in the House of Commons and succeeded in getting the French, British, and American ambassadors to call on King Carol. This pressure, reinforced by a press campaign, had its effect on Rumania. The king received the British and French ambassadors on February

9, and the next day requested Goga to resign. Leaving the palace after his resignation, Goga, who besides being an anti-Semite was also a poet of a kind, made a dramatic gesture to the waiting journalists and said: "Israel, you have triumphed."

Our drive to topple the Goga regime was a success, but even this could not halt the anti-Semitic policy of the Rumanian government. Changes in the civil status of the Jews were still being made. Despite continuous intervention by the WJC, some forty percent of Rumanian Jews had been deprived of their citizenship by November, 1938.

In other countries even the measure of success we attained in Rumania was not achieved. It became increasingly evident that a world in which National Socialism was practically acceptable had no room for the humane and liberal system of minority rights. The outbreak of the Second World War was the death blow to minority treaties, and in the radically different postwar climate, after Hitler's annihilation of European Jews, there was no possibility for demanding that the system be reinstated. Moreover, after the war all our efforts were concentrated on establishing a Jewish state in Israel.

In our endeavors of those years two countries offered particular problems: Italy because of its Fascist regime and especially after its rapprochement with Nazi Germany, and Soviet Russia because of its deliberate diplomatic isolation and intensely anti-Zionist position. In the end, however, I managed to establish tolerable relations with both of them—with Italy after my conversation with Mussolini and with Soviet Russia when Foreign Minister Maxim Litvinov finally received me on November 22, 1934, after several unsuccessful approaches on my part. This led to further meetings and then to a fairly good acquaintanceship that was later extended to other Russian diplomats, such as the Russian ambassador in Paris, Vladimir Petrovic Potemkin, and Marcel Rosenberg, deputy secretary-general of the League of Nations.

Among the international statesmen who frequented Geneva, I had many dealings with Eduard Beneš, Nicholas Titulescu, and Józef Beck, the foreign ministers of Czechoslovakia, Rumania, and Poland, with Louis Barthou, Paul Goncourt, and Pierre Laval, and with Arthur Henderson, Anthony Eden, and Lord

Cranborne. I also attached great importance to maintaining good relations with high officials in the League Secretariat, with the secretaries-general James Drummond and Joseph Avenol, with Deputy Secretary-General Sean Lester, and especially with the officials who were concerned with questions of mandates, minorities, and refugees.

The high points of my work were always the sessions of the League Council, the Assembly, and the Mandates Commission. In between, my duties usually took me to other cities and for this reason we kept an apartment in Paris, where we spent most winters, in addition to our house in Geneva. Looking back, I see these years as busy ones with heavy responsibilities. I had some successes and many failures. But my colleagues and I were never for a moment unmindful that we were confronted by historic tasks and that in all our undertakings much was at stake. I was fortunate in having talented, devoted colleagues, especially Dr. Menahem Kahany, whom I had taken on from Dr. Jacobson, in the Jewish Agency office, Dr. Gerhart Riegner and Dr. Max Baer in the WJC, and the internationally recognized authority on international law and legal counsel to the WJC, Professor Paul Guggenheim.

From the end of 1937 it was obvious that the League of Nations was about to disintegrate. Responsibility for this can be ascribed to the aggressive policy of Germany, but also to the weakness, defeatism, and shortsightedness of Western diplomacy in failing to resist Nazism. When, in the spring of 1939, the Zionist Executive began to prepare for the Zionist congress to be held that summer, I proposed that instead of waiting for August we should hold it earlier because of the possibility of war, but my advice was not taken, and war broke out during the session.

The League automatically fell apart once hostilities began, and my days in Geneva were numbered, especially since there was the real danger that Germany might occupy Switzerland. It was clear that with the collapse of Europe the political center of gravity had shifted to the United States, and when the Zionist Executive asked me to transfer my activities to America in June of 1940 I left Geneva for New York.

13

Fighting the Nazis

The chapter I am about to begin fills me with deep sadness and despondency. It deals with the most tragic period in Jewish history and with the total failure of what might be called the leadership of the Jewish people. After a long debate with myself about whether this is the time to say all I want to say, I have come to the conclusion that the bitter and painful facts must be set forth for the sake of honesty and truthfulness and in order to serve as a warning and lesson.

It is not merely that our generation and its leadership did not succeed in preventing the mass murder of six million Jews. No people can be held responsible for defeats and failures that happen because of unavoidable external circumstances. Yet for a people and its leaders shortsightedly to refuse to believe in an imminent catastrophe or to have denied its truth because they feared it is indubitably a sign of inadequacy and an inability to face facts. Surveying the Jews' efforts to defend themselves during the Nazi era, we are forced to acknowledge both shortsightedness and fear, painful as this may be. The majority of the Jewish people and its leaders were not willing to recognize or properly interpret the symptoms. Even the Jews directly threatened by the Nazis clung to the naïve illusion that the regime was transitory, that it would never dare to carry out its threats. The result was that hundreds of thousands who might have escaped stayed in the trap too long and that no large-scale attempt was made to combat the bestial anti-Jewish policy of the Nazis while they were still weak and unsure of themselves.

I lived through this era in all its day-to-day events. I do not pretend that either my close friends, like Stephen Wise, or I foresaw the full extent of the slaughter. It would take someone with the character of a Nazi, perhaps even of a Hitler, to foresee such a catastrophe, to visualize the extermination of the European Jews in our century as the Nazis were to effect it. Nevertheless, some of us clearly recognized, even before Hitler became chancellor and particularly thereafter, that Nazism represented a total threat to the entire Jewish people, a threat we should have resisted by all the means at our disposal. I issued this warning in every speech I made at world Jewish conferences in 1932, 1933, and 1934. Dr. Wise did the same, with greater authority than mine. The results were discouraging. Wise told me that in 1932 he sent a confidential representative to Germany to discuss the potential dangers of a Nazi victory with the leaders of German Jewry. With one honorable exception every one assured him that there was no grave danger and that he should not aggravate their difficult position by intervention and protests.

In the whole of our history the unfortunate Jewish tendency to take an excessively optimistic view, to mistake temporary improvements for permanent ones, has never had such devastating consequences. Even after the most extreme measures had been taken against the German Jews and their persecution was in full force, other Jewish minorities not directly affected refused to believe that the same thing could happen to them. I well remember a closed meeting in Paris in 1935, attended by some distinguished French Jews. I spoke of the fate threatening the German Jews and predicted the same destiny for French Jews if war broke out. Most of them looked at me sympathetically and behaved as though they were dealing with a hysterical, panic-stricken German Jew. Almost no one took my warning seriously. In 1940 and 1941 I sent emergency visas, and steamship tickets to the United States, to several of the participants in that meeting to enable them to escape. Even in June, 1940, shortly after I arrived in America, when I made the gloomy forecast that a prolongation of the war might mean the annihilation of half European Jewry, I was violently attacked by most of the press as a prophet of disaster and indignantly asked how anyone could bring himself to speak of such things.

Furthermore, most contemporary Jewish leaders were not prepared to defend Jewish rights by political means under any circumstances, but confined themselves to philanthropy and relief measures. I considered these methods not only ineffective in the long run but actually harmful, because ultimately they amounted to offering a financial compensation for the persecution of Jews. When the Nazis announced that they were going to deprive German Jews of their human rights, ruin them economically, and finally expel them, the reaction of the influential American-Jewish leaders was equivalent to replying to Hitler: We will send millions of dollars to Germany to aid the Jews and thus strengthen the German economy. Colonel Beck, the Polish foreign minister—no Nazi, to be sure, though an anti-Semite— confirmed this in a conversation I had with him. Hitler, he said, had received several million dollars in Jewish relief funds from America, in response to threats to Germany's six hundred thousand Jews. Why should Poland not do the same with its three million Jews and receive five times the reward?

We, the leaders of the WJC, tried desperately to mobilize the Jews and persuade them to fight Nazism by political means. If we had succeeded, in the first few years, in organizing an effective anti-Nazi boycott and mobilizing the influence of Jews, especially in America and England, against the Nazi regime when it was still weak and if, as I feel sure, though, of course, I cannot prove it, millions of gentiles would have joined us, we might have produced, if not the suspension of the Nuremberg Laws, at least a mitigation of the persecution and possibly an arrangement whereby German Jews could emigrate and take a considerable percentage of their assets with them. But all these proposals met with very little response in the world and, as Dr. Wise bitterly admitted, they were actually opposed by influential Jews in the United States. In fact, since even the leaders of German Jewry did not endorse them, they remained completely futile.

We complain today that the non-Jewish world did not take an effective moral and political stand against the Nazi regime but embarked instead upon years of appeasement and had to pay the price with the Second World War. Historically these charges are completely justified, but no less justified is the self-accusation of our people, which irresolutely and myopically watched the coming of the greatest catastrophe in its history and prepared no adequate defense. We cannot offer the excuse that we were attacked unexpectedly. Everything Hitler and his regime did to us had been announced with cynical candor beforehand. Our naïveté and complacent optimism led us to ignore these threats. In this mortifying chapter of Jewish history there is no excuse for our generation as a whole or for most of our leaders. We must stand as a generation not only condemned to witness the destruction of a third of our number but guilty of having accepted it without any resistance worthy of the name.

In those years of fruitless struggle against Nazism, with all their deep disappointments, I sometimes found more understanding among gentile leaders than among Jewish ones. An example of this is the conversation I had in Geneva with Eduard Beneš, the Czech foreign minister, who asked me to come and see him a few days after the promulgation of the Nuremberg Laws. I can still picture him, excited and almost shouting, pacing back and forth across his corner salon in the Hotel Beau Rivage, where for two hours he reproachfully demanded to know why the Jews did not react on a grand scale, why my friends and I did not immediately call an international Jewish congress and declare all-out war on the National Socialist regime. He assured me that he and many other non-Jewish statesmen would give us their full support. "Don't you understand," he shouted, "that by reacting with nothing but half-hearted gestures, by failing to arouse world public opinion and take vigorous action against the Germans, the Jews are endangering their future and their human rights all over the world? If you go on like this, Hitler's example will be contagious and encourage all the anti-Semites throughout the world."

I have been through many painful interviews in my life, but I have never felt so uncomfortable and ashamed as I did during those two hours. I knew Beneš was right. Nevertheless, I tried to defend the attitude of world Jewry by pointing out the difficulties of organizing politically a dispersed, homeless people and the reluctance of many Jewish spokesmen to take a hostile position toward Germany so long as their governments maintained friendly relations with it. None of my arguments had any effect and I left Beneš after promising to try, at least, to obtain some international action against the Nuremberg Laws, although, of course, I knew I would never succeed.

During those years we lost the respect of many well-meaning friends who expected a united, deeply perturbed world Jewry to proclaim a moral and political crusade against the Nazi regime. No one can tell what might have happened if we had done so. There were unquestionably cases, such as the Bernheim Petition or the dispute about Jewish rights in the Saar, in which political resistance proved effective in those early days of National Socialism. But in this context such success was irrelevant. What matters in a situation of this sort is a people's moral stance, its readiness to fight back instead of helplessly allowing itself to be massacred. We did not stand the test.

The small group that headed the WJC in those days carried on the fight against Nazism in three main areas. As much as possible, we tried to alert the League of Nations. We promoted international public debate about Germany and discussions within the organizations Germany still belonged to, trying to discredit the Nazi regime. As our third and most realistic measure we planned an economic boycott of Germany.

The two concrete cases I have mentioned came up in the League of Nations: the Bernheim Petition at the beginning of the Nazi era, and later the defense of the Jews of Danzig and the Saar, when those areas reverted to Germany. This is not the place for a detailed account of the Bernheim Petition, in which my role was secondary. The action was organized primarily by Leo Motzkin, chairman of the Comité des Délégations Juives, and Emil Margulies, the champion of Jewish rights in Czechoslovakia. It was based on a treaty between Germany and Poland concerning equality of rights for the minorities of Upper Silesia. Through the Bernheim Petition the Nuremberg Laws in their entirety were brought before the League Council, with the result that the rights of the Upper Silesian Jews were fully respected until 1937, when the agreement expired. Even in those days it was not easy to get the various powers on the Council to take an unequivocal stand against the German government, but this victory shows that it was still possible to enforce Jewish rights, at least in one part of Germany.

Later we tried the same thing with Danzig, and also, in 1934, with the Saar. After the plebiscite, when the return of the Saar to Germany after fifteen years of French occupation became inevitable, the Jews living there requested the Comité des Délégations Juives (of which I had by then become chairman) to protect their rights. Obviously it was hopeless to insist on their civil rights, now that the Saar would be reincorporated into Germany. The important thing was to obtain for them the right to leave the province, taking their possessions with them. This problem occupied me for many months and I managed to get the support of Italy, which held the chairmanship of the Saar committee of the League of Nations. In spite of vigorous resistance, Nazi Germany was finally compelled to grant the Saar Jews the right to emigrate, and not as destitute refugees dependent on Jewish relief but as welcome immigrants, with all their assets.

I realize that these two cases do not prove something of the sort could have been done for the whole of German Jewry, but they do show there was a chance of achieving by political means a good deal that would otherwise have been impossible. Specifically, had we relied on so-called philanthropic measures to help the Saar's Jews, their assets would have reverted to Germany, thousands of them would have gone into the world as penniless refugees, and Jewish charities would have had to spend millions to provide them with even the minimal means of subsistence.

All the same, the possibilities of anti-Nazi action within the League of Nations were very limited, since it would only intervene in a clearly defined case or a matter involving international law. How I regretted that nobody had thought to include in the Treaty of Versailles an international guarantee of the rights of German Jews as a minority like the guarantees covering the

Jews of Poland, Rumania, Czechoslovakia, and other Eastern European countries! I am sure this would have made anti-Semitic legislation much more difficult for the Nazis. But what German Jew would ever have dreamed of demanding minority rights after the First World War? Seldom has a Jewish population paid so dearly for its naïve feeling of security and its super-patriotism.

Of course, the more firmly committed Britain and France became to appeasement, the more difficult it became to get the League to take any stand against the Nazi regime. As the Geneva representative of the Jews, I found it increasingly intolerable to watch all the great powers, except the Soviet Union, submitting to every fresh provocation by Hitler and allowing him to increase his power and prestige. The atmosphere in Geneva grew more oppressive and hopeless with every concession the Western powers made to Germany. The climax was reached during the Munich conference. The League Assembly was meeting at the time. Russia had not even been informed of the meeting in Munich, despite its offer to make a common front with the West against Germany. In those days Soviet Russia was completely isolated, and when Litvinov made his prophetic speech to the League Assembly immediately after the Munich agreement, predicting that it would lead to new provocations and ultimately to world war, hardly anyone dared to give him the applause courtesy alone would have demanded. Litvinov concluded his speech in almost total silence; only a handful of members shook his hand. Although I was not even a delegate, I could not restrain myself from going up to him and expressing my admiration. Later he assured me that he had never forgotten this gesture, which took a certain amount of courage in the prevailing climate. This was not a declaration of support for the Soviet Union against the Western powers; it was simply a gesture of recognition for a man with the courage to denounce the moral cowardice and political shortsightedness of the Munich appeasement policy.

We at the WJC also tried to call Germany to account outside the League of Nations: before public opinion, in the press, and in international organizations. The main campaign was concentrated in two organizations, the European Minorities Congress and the League of Nations Union. The Minorities Congress had been established after the First World War, when the peace treaties recognized the principle of minority rights for numerous minorities in Eastern and Central Europe, including various Jewish ones. To enforce these rights against the opposition of governments that found them extremely inconvenient and tried to weaken or abolish them, it soon became desirable for all the minorities to work together. This was the origin of the Congress. Among the minorities it represented, two played a leading role from the beginning—the German minorities outside Germany and the Jews. During the Weimar Republic, Germans cooperated closely, both inside and outside the Congress. The Jewish spokesmen were Leo Motzkin, Emil Margulies, Mordecai Nurock representing the Jewish minority of Latvia, and Michael Ringel representing that of Galicia. Their legal adviser was Nathan Feinberg, a recognized authority on minority rights, now professor of international law at the University of Jerusalem. When I first went to Geneva in 1933 I worked with them, but their activities were not to continue much longer. When Hitler came to power the German minorities began to be subject to increasing Nazi influence. Although they included anti-Nazi elements, they were dependent upon the support of the German government and were obliged to accommodate themselves more or less to its policies. This naturally precluded continued co-operation with the Jewish minorities, and the Minorities Congress collapsed very soon after 1933.

Our fight against Nazism within the League of Nations Union was more dramatic. This organization, headed by men of the calibre of Lord Robert Cecil, was composed of groups in the various participating countries dedicated to propagating the idea of the League of Nations. In many countries, including England, these were very influential, and the Union itself was an international body of considerable importance. After the Nazis came to power we tried to get the Union to take a stand against their anti-Semitic policy and in fact succeeded in having a resolution censuring the Nuremberg Laws passed by the League of Nations Union in 1935. In early June, 1935, I attended a meeting of the executive committee at which my resolution against Germany was accepted after a dramatic battle. The German delegation immediately resigned from the League of Nations Union. On June 12 the resolution was passed. The result, as far as I personally was concerned, was the revocation of my German citizenship. While efforts of this kind achieved some measure of success in specific cases, in the general atmosphere of appeasement created by the great powers such success was, again, meaningless.

Simultaneously we were trying to damage Germany economically by organizing an international boycott. If we could only have enlisted all Jews throughout the world in this effort, we would have had a very powerful weapon in our hands. But many Jewish groups declined, in some cases because Jewish firms served as agents for German companies, but also because many Jewish organizations, especially in the United States, took the view that it was unpatriotic to organize an economic boycott of a country with which one's own country maintained normal commercial relations. Stephen Wise, Samuel Untermeyer, and other American leaders of the boycott movement fought a heroic battle, as did the leaders in other countries, but since their actual success was confined to a very small section of world Jewry, the effects were very limited. We did manage to get the boycott resolution passed by the WJC, although here too certain delegations created difficulties, notably the Italians because of the close relations between Fascist Italy and National Socialist Germany.

These widely ramified anti-Nazi efforts on behalf of Jewish rights, especially my work on the Saar problem, brought me into constant touch with leading statesmen. To conclude this chapter I want to describe in some detail three of the many conversations I had during that period. One was with the Italian dictator, Benito Mussolini, the second with the future Pope Pius XII, then Cardinal and Secretary of State Pacelli, and the third with Russian Foreign Minister Litvinov. All three talks were occasioned by the Saar.

The Italian delegate to the League of Nations was chairman of the three-power committee appointed to settle the Saar question, and when, as chairman of the Comité des Délégations Juives, I began to deal with the problem, it became important, in the course of negotiations, to see Mussolini.

But my wish to see the Duce was intensified by another factor. The Italian government, and particularly Mussolini himself, were by no means anti-Jewish at the time. Some six months before I saw Mussolini I was informed by a Viennese source that Chancellor Dollfuss of Austria, who was completely under the influence of Italy, intended to introduce a change in the constitution involving the clause that guaranteed the civil rights of the Jews. Through Baron Aloisi, the Italian delegate to the League, I requested the Duce to use his influence with Dollfuss to prevent this infringement of the rights of the Austrian Jews. The Duce informed me that through Baron Sovich, undersecretary of state in the Foreign Office, who was then on an official visit to Vienna, he had sent a handwritten letter to Dollfuss asking him not to interfere with Jewish civil rights. My Jewish friends in Vienna later confirmed this. However, in the winter of 1934, Mussolini's relations with the Italian Jews became strained because an anti-Fascist conspiracy had been discovered in Turin, and most of the conspirators had turned out to be Jewish students. He had refused to receive Chief Rabbi Sacerdote, with whom he was normally on very good terms, and Sacerdote, a member of the board of the Comité des Délégations Juives and a good friend of mine, asked me to use the opportunity of my interview with Mussolini to restore his friendly attitude toward Italian Jewry. He also asked me to allow him to accompany me to the audience if possible, so that he might get back onto his former footing with the Duce.

I asked Baron Aloisi for a personal interview with Mussolini and was very soon informed that the Duce would be pleased to see me on November 13, 1934, and that he had no objection to Sacerdote's accompanying me.

I arrived in Rome on the morning of November 13, conferred with the leaders of the Jewish community organizations and presented myself at the Palazzo Venezia with Rabbi Sacerdote, a tall man with a fine beard, older and more dignified looking than I. The reception of Mussolini's visitors was like some marvelous stage production by Max Reinhardt. We approached the Palazzo Venezia, the doors of which were locked. We rang the bell, whereupon a small window was opened and an officer asked what we wanted. Dr. Sacerdote presented our letter of invitation and replied, *Convocazione al presidente del Consiglio per il dottore Goldmann.*

The officer, who was, of course, expecting us, opened the door. We entered, past a line of uniformed soldiers and policemen. The officer accompanied us to the second floor, where the same ceremony was repeated: locked door, raised window, same question, same answer, this time shouted by the officer at the top of his voice. The door opened to reveal another line of marionettes in a different uniform, and another officer conducted us up to the next floor. Here we went through the same performance, except that on every floor *"Convocazione,* etc." was shouted still more loudly. Finally we reached the fourth floor, the floor of the Duce's famous room.

We were shown into an anteroom hung with magnificent Renaissance paintings. One of the Duce's secretaries waited with us. He told us something about Mussolini's way of life; he suffered from a stomach disorder and lived mainly on coffee and fruit. He also gave me a tip. "When you go in to the Duce," he said, "he will receive you standing up and he won't invite you to sit down right away. If he has no interest in you and considers this a purely official audience, he will not offer you a chair and you should take your leave in a few minutes. If he is interested, he will ask you to sit down and then you can have a leisurely talk with him."

We waited about twenty minutes and then the secretary took us into another anteroom where a lot of flunkeys, policemen, and secret service men were drifting around. One of them flung open the double doors and a footman announced us.

We entered the famous room. It was a huge hall, and at the far end the Duce was standing at his desk. It was almost six o'clock and getting dark; the only light in the room came from a desk lamp that illuminated Mussolini, leaving the rest of the room quite dark. As we entered, Mussolini raised his arm in the Fascist salute, which Dr. Sacerdote returned. I bowed courteously. We walked the forty or fifty paces separating us from Mussolini. Poor Sacerdote was quite agitated. I found the whole thing very funny and murmured, *C'est très drôle ici,* at which Sacerdote practically fell to the floor in his fear that the Duce might have overheard me. At last we reached Mussolini's desk. He was dressed with studied casualness in gray trousers and a gray belted tunic. On his desk was a big bowl of fruit.

"What language do you prefer to speak?" he asked.

"French," I replied.

"You requested an audience," he said, "and I am glad to talk to you. Thank you for coming. You have done this for the sake of your people, and one should be ready to do anything for his people."

"That is why I am here, Your Excellency."

"What do you want to discuss with me?" He was still standing, and we remained standing too.

"First I should like to give Your Excellency an analysis of the present situation of the Jews."

"I am quite familiar with it because I am extremely interested in the Jewish question."

"Then I can make my analysis brief. A word or two will suffice. Before the war millions of Jews in Eastern Europe were deprived of their rights. While we now possess full civil rights on paper, even minority rights, the economic situation of millions of Jews in Poland, Rumania, etc. is worse today than it was in the worst days of Russian Czarism."

"I knew that the Jews were in a sorry state, but I didn't know it was as bad as that. Aren't you exaggerating a little?"

Here Mussolini looked at Sacerdote, who said: "That is the exact truth, Your Excellency."

"Really?" said Mussolini, looking quite impressed.

Then I asked if I might give him some reports on the situation of the Jews in Eastern and Central Europe. Mussolini took them, leafed through the memoranda and said, "I promise to read all this carefully, and I keep my promises. I see there is a chapter on the Jews in the Soviet Union. Where did you obtain your information? Did the Russians allow you to send a representative to study the situation of the Jews in Russia?"

"No, they didn't, but we get information indirectly from time to time."

"Written in invisible ink?"

"What makes you think that, Your Excellency?" I asked.

"I'm an old revolutionary and I know all the tricks of the trade. Those were the good old days, when I used to write reports in invisible ink."

Here Mussolini looked at me and said: "Won't you sit down?" He was, however, looking only at me and not at Chief Rabbi Sacerdote.

"After you," I said.

"I prefer to stand," he announced in oratorical tones.

"Do you know Nietzsche?" I asked.

"Do I know Nietzsche? He's my favorite philosopher."

"Then you probably remember, Your Excellency, that Nietzsche says there are two kinds of thinkers, sitting thinkers and walking thinkers. You, Your Excellency, are a standing thinker."

The Duce was about to smile but the imperial role he was playing prevented him, and he suppressed the beginning of a smile.

"I'm not a thinker," he exclaimed. "I'm a man of action."

"But I hope you think carefully before you act."

He smiled for a moment, and offered me a chair again. I asked him if the Chief Rabbi might also sit down, and he said yes, if I wanted him to. So we both sat down.

"What do you want to discuss with me?" Mussolini asked.

"The fate of the German Jews," I replied. "The Saar question, the question of the Austrian Jews, and also the minority treaties and what Poland is doing to them."

Mussolini wrote down these questions on a scratch pad. "Very good," he said. "Let's begin. First, the Saar."

To start with, I gave him a report of the conversation I had had that morning with Biancheri, the official in charge of the Saar problem at the Italian foreign ministry. Then I outlined the problem of the Jews in the Saar and told him that if the province reverted to Germany a temporary defense of their civil rights would not be enough and that some permanent protection was required. I admitted this presented legal difficulties but

mentioned that Bourquin and Hudson, two internationally re-
nowned jurists, one a Belgian, the other an American, had prepared a good case to meet them. The whole question of the
Jews in the Saar was one of principle. If the League of Nations
approved the return of the province to Germany without guaranteeing Jewish rights, it would appear to sanction Germany's
anti-Jewish legislation. Whatever happened, we must get a
clause included in the Saar agreement obliging Germany to
allow any Jews from the Saar who wished to emigrate to do so,
taking with them all their assets in French currency.

Mussolini broke in. "You want the League of Nations to do
this? You want the League of Nations to act? Are you naïve
enough to believe that the League of Nations can take any
decisive action?" And he launched into a tirade against the
League that lasted two or three minutes and was one of the best
bits of acting I have ever seen.

"What are you saying, Sir?" he shouted. "That the League of
Nations ought to act? The League never acts! It's a debating
society, a senate of old windbags who talk and talk and talk.
Jews are intelligent people. You are certainly an intelligent man.
And you expect this academy of windbags to do something?
The League of Nations can only talk. It can't act."

"But you're a member of the League, Your Excellency. You
could act."

"How do you expect me to do anything in Geneva, where
fifty-two nations are playing politics? I act when I'm alone. I
proved it in the Austrian affair."

I reminded him of Italy's particular responsibility, since
Baron Aloisi was chairman of the three-power commission on
the Saar, and to this he replied: "I'll force Germany to let the
Saar Jews leave and take their money with them." He picked up
the large scratch pad and a pencil, tore off a sheet and scribbled,
"Saar. Jews. Emigration."

"That takes care of that," he said. "You can rely on me." And
he kept his word.

The conversation turned to the Austrian question. I told Mussolini I had seen Chancellor Schuschnigg in Geneva (which he
already knew). "What was your impression of him?" he asked.
"Is he an intelligent man?"

"Yes, I think he's very intelligent."

"Do you think he is a sincere Catholic?"

"I've never been present when he was saying his prayers, Your Excellency, so I can't say."

"I'm told that he is a very sincere Catholic, and I personally have great respect for people who are sincerely religious."

Then I explained to Mussolini what we wanted done about the situation in Austria, telling him about the government's harassment of doctors, public servants, and so on, and mentioning that Jewish public opinion was very uneasy and American Jewish groups were already proposing to make public protests that I had discouraged for the time being.

"That was very wise of you," said Mussolini. "Those American Jews and gentiles are always ready to make protests and outcries and meddle in European affairs, which they don't understand at all. This was true of President Wilson and it's no different today. It's a terrible habit."

I said that while I agreed this was not the moment for public protest against the Austrian government, we must nevertheless demand a change in its attitude to the Jews and here we were counting strongly on him. I reminded him of the handwritten letter he had sent to Dollfuss insisting on civil rights for the Jews. This had caused Dollfuss to drop his anti-Jewish plans, but I was informed by Viennese sources that the danger still existed. "Your Excellency," I said, "Could you not persuade Schuschnigg that it would be a great mistake for Austria to create its own Jewish problem and thus incur the enmity of the Jews all over the world?"

"I will certainly do that. It is madness for the Austrian government, which is in an extremely weak position, to quarrel with the Jews. Don't worry. I'm a friend of the Jews. We cannot permit the Austrian Jews to be attacked. Herr Schuschnigg will be here next week, sitting in the chair you're sitting in now, and I'll tell him I don't want to see a Jewish problem created in Austria. Don't worry about that any more. I'll speak to him very seriously. You can rely on me."

Again he took a sheet of paper and wrote: "Austria. Schuschnigg. Jewish problem."

"Third, Germany," he continued.

I spoke of the problem of the German Jews and told Mussolini why I had not been able to comply with his earlier request
to work out a formula of compromise with Hitler. "I represent
the interests of world Jewry," I said at length, "and I cannot
allow the principle of full civil rights for Jews all over the
world to be infringed upon for the sake of a possible improvement in the position of the German Jews. This principle of
equality of rights is a permanent one, as important for future
generations of Jews as for the present generation. We are an
ancient, historic people, and our policy cannot surrender our
people's future in exchange for slight benefits to one section of
the present generation."

Mussolini listened with great interest. "When Dr. Sacerdote
explained this to me in your name," he said, "I was angry, but
now I realize that you are right. You are a wise man and you
represent a great, indestructible people. Have no fear of Herr
Hitler . . ." (Although he was speaking French, Mussolini referred to Hitler as *Herr* Hitler, and as an Italian he had trouble
pronouncing the "H.")

"I know Herr Hitler," he continued. (A few weeks earlier
they had met for the first time in Venice.) "He is an idiot, a
vaurien, a fanatical idiot, a talker. It's embarrassing to listen to
him. You are much stronger than Herr Hitler. When there's no
trace left of Hitler, the Jews will still be a great people. You and
we . . ."—and as he shouted these words I was not sure if *we*
meant Italy or Fascism—"are great historical powers. Herr Hitler is a joke that will be over in a few years. Have no fear of
him and tell your Jews to have no fear of him either."

"Nonetheless, Hitler has a fleet, an army, and an organized
nation of seventy million people. We are dispersed and we have
no fleet, no army, and no power."

"That's true. But I said that you are more powerful than Herr
Hitler. The main thing is that the Jews must not be afraid of
him. We shall all live to see his end. But you must create a
Jewish state. I am a Zionist and I told Dr. Weizmann so. You
must have a real country, not the ridiculous National Home
that the British have offered you. I will help you create a
Jewish state, but the main thing is that the Jews must have

confidence in their future and not be afraid of that idiot in
Berlin."

We turned to the minorities question. "Please allow me to
speak freely and openly," I said. "Poland's attitude disturbs us
greatly. We are quite aware that the minority rights granted to
the Jews there have no great practical significance; they have
remained purely theoretical. Nevertheless, they do provide a
certain legal guarantee for the rights of the Jews." I quoted the
remark of Sir Robert Vansittart, under-secretary of state in
the British Foreign Office, to Neville Laski, that the difference
between the position of the Eastern Jews with minority rights
and without them was the difference between hell and bloody-
hell. "Poland," I continued, "intends to suspend minority rights.
The statement of the Polish foreign minister in Geneva represented the ceremonial initiation of this policy; its outcome will
depend upon the reaction of the signatories of the Treaty of
Versailles. I am sure of Britain's position and almost sure of
France's, but if I may say so, I am not sure of your position for
two reasons. You are no great friend of minority rights in general, and you are not opposed to revision of the treaty. Revision,
though, is a matter of high policy, with which we Jews do not
concern ourselves. But if the treaty is to be revised, a total and
radical revision will be necessary, and the Jewish question will
have to be dealt with so as to provide a firm basis for our
existence."

"Don't worry. I quite agree with you. Poland's move was a
paranoid gesture. Poland is trying to imitate me and play the
role of a great power. But Poland is not a great power. Thirty
million inhabitants: Ukrainians, Russians, Germans, Jews—
that's not a great power! I will never permit the revision of the
peace treaties to begin with a revision of minority rights. Baron
Aloisi issued a statement to that effect in Geneva. I stick to this
position. If we embark upon a revision of the peace treaties—
which is necessary—it must be a thorough revision that will
settle the question of frontiers, the Hungarian problem, and so
on. If the Poles come to me about the minorities question—
which they haven't yet done—I shall say no, no, no. You can
count on that."

"I thank you for this statement, which reassures us as to your attitude. May I thank you again, Your Excellency, after all that you have just said, for your good will and your understanding of Jewish matters. It has been very gratifying for me as president of the Comité des Délégations Juives to have received the close co-operation of Italian Jewry ever since the beginning of the movement to create a World Jewish Congress. I thank you for all the sympathy you have shown for our movement, and I hope that Italian Jewry will be represented at the world Jewish Congress that we hope to convene next year on the basis of democratic elections."

"Dr. Sacerdote is a living witness of my profound and enduring sympathy for the World Jewish Congress."

This brought the conversation to an end, and I was about to get up and leave, but Mussolini asked me to wait, saying: "Can you answer a question that puzzles me? The Jews are an intelligent people, a realistic people, a very practical people. Why have Jews everywhere always been such dogged supporters of formal democracy?"

This was a very delicate point. I did not want to antagonize the Duce, yet on the other hand I could hardly declare my allegiance to the Fascist creed. "First," I said, "there's a historical reason. Persecuted peoples always tend to be revolutionary, libertarian, and democratic. Democracy brought the Jews emancipation and civil rights, and they are naturally thankful to it."

"I can understand that," Mussolini agreed.

Seeing he was in a good mood, I decided to take the opportunity of re-establishing friendly relations between him and Sacerdote. "I took the liberty of bringing the Chief Rabbi with me," I said. "He would like to talk to you about a few questions concerning Italian Jewry, if you would give him the opportunity."

"Since you ask me, I'll be glad to do so. But not today."

He turned to Sacerdote and said in Italian that this audience had been intended for me and Sacerdote should request an audience for himself at a later date. Four weeks later he received him, and they were back on former terms.

Before we took our leave I added: "I would like to ask one small favor. It is important to me that Stefani, the official Italian news agency, should report that you have received me."

"What for? For the sake of your prestige?"

"My prestige, Your Excellency, rests on the Jewish people's opinion of me. I ask this of you because it is good for both Jews and anti-Semites to know that you have spoken officially to a representative of the Jews and seriously discussed Jewish questions with him."

"I understand perfectly. It will be done."

Again he tore a page from the scratch pad and wrote: "Dr. Goldmann. Stefani Agency." Next morning Stefani carried an official report of our conversation.

"This conversation," said Mussolini, "has clarified many points for me. Come again if you need me."

I could not refrain from saying: "Perhaps next time I'll see you in Geneva."

"In Geneva! Me?" he exclaimed. "I'm not going to appear in that academy of speechifiers. That's just a waste of time. I'm accustomed to taking action, not to wasting days in discussions."

"Very well," I replied. "If you promise to take action on behalf of the Jews every time I talk to you, I'll be glad to come again."

Mussolini smiled, pressed a bell and gave the Fascist salute. I bowed and a secretary showed us out.

At the same time as this meeting I was trying to establish a connection with the Vatican on the question of the Saar. It seemed reasonable to ask League of Nations protection for all religious minorities in the province and I hoped to interest the Catholic Church in this. Zionist and Jewish politicians had often tried to establish contact with the Vatican, but it was not always easy. Nahum Sokolow was actually the only Jewish leader to have had conversations with the Vatican before the Balfour Declaration and its ratification at the San Remo conference. The notion of the Wandering Jew, condemned to homelessness as a punishment for scorning Jesus, was an obstacle to political negotiations with the Catholic Church about Zionist matters. I

was put in touch with the Vatican by a member of the Hapsburg family who one day in Paris tried to enlist my support for
a Hapsburg restoration. With all his Viennese charm he suggested that this would be the best solution to the problem of the
German Jews. As soon as the Hapsburgs, traditional protectors
of the Jews, returned to power, they would offer the German
Jews a refuge in Austria. I was very cautious, since obviously I
could not pledge the support of world Jewry to the restoration
of the Hapsburgs. Nevertheless, these conversations led to a
meeting with Cardinal Innitzer of Vienna, a meeting I want to
record only one detail of. When I asked him whether the Catholic Church was really backing a Hapsburg restoration, the
Cardinal smiled and said: "In principle, yes—but only as a
long-range possibility. Naturally those young archdukes are
impatient. They want to get back their fortune and their position. But we and you—the Catholic Church and the Synagogue—
we are eternal powers. We have to look at things *sub specie
aeternitatis*. We both have to take the long view in politics."

"Your Eminence," I replied, "whatever you think of the
Jews, you must admit that in our history we have given proof
of both farsightedness and staying power."

"Indeed you have, but you must admit that the Church has
too."

I readily agreed but remarked that the Church had taken over
certain things from the Synagogue. At this the Cardinal bowed
and said: "Herr Doktor, I'm sure I may take your remark as a
compliment."

I was recommended to the Vatican by Cardinal Innitzer and
in June, 1934, had quite a long conversation with Cardinal and
Secretary of State Pacelli, in the course of which I several times
called upon the Vatican to protect the status of the Jews. (We
were discussing Catholic anti-Semitic movements in Argentina
and Austria.) Finally we came to the problem of the Saar. I
proposed a joint Catholic-Jewish front for the defense of religious freedom in the Saar in case the province reverted to Germany. The Cardinal listened attentively and said: "What would
be the point of League of Nations resolutions, given the character of the Nazi regime, which never honors its undertakings?"

In my reply I mentioned the Bernheim Petition, which had secured protection for the Jews of Upper Silesia. Cardinal Pacelli, who was not familiar with this case, asked me to tell him about it. Then he thought for a while and finally said: "May I speak very frankly, Herr Doktor? If you and your world Jewish organizations look to the League to uphold Jewish rights, I can well imagine that the Council may intervene, as it did with the Bernheim Petition. But when it comes to Catholic rights, I'm not so sure that such intervention would take place."

This answer irritated me and I replied: "I don't want to argue with you, but I'll make you an offer. As I sit here facing you, I'm ready to exchange places with you in terms of worldly power, but not religious beliefs."

He smiled and said: "That's a good answer, but I must ask you to take what I just said more seriously."

"Look, Your Eminence," I replied, "I asked you for an interview several weeks ago. I have made a twenty-four-hour journey from Paris to see you in Rome in order to ask you to protect the Jews in Argentina and Austria against Catholic attacks. I have yet to see one of your cardinals make the twenty-four-hour journey to Paris to ask me to protect the Catholics."

"Your reply is excellent but, believe me, many of my cardinals would have good reason to do so sometimes, if it were not for difficulties of dogma and protocol."

I mention this mainly to show how even such an intelligent, statesmanlike figure as Pacelli exaggerated the so-called power of world Jewry at that time, but also because it has some bearing on my first conversation with Litvinov.

Maxim Litvinov, as is well known, was of Jewish descent. For years Zionist policy had sought agreement with the Soviet Union but without success. Russian policy had been firmly against Zionism on the grounds that it was a counterrevolutionary movement. Having spoken to nearly all members of the League Council except Litvinov about Jewish demands in the Saar, I wrote to request an interview with him and was invited to come to his hotel in Geneva that same evening, November 22, 1934. When I entered the room his attitude was more than cool; it was icy. He began by saying: "If I am not mistaken, you are a Zionist." I replied that I was not only a Zionist but a member of the Zionist world executive. However, I had not come to see him about Zionist questions but Jewish affairs in general. At his request I outlined the problem and told him what I wanted the League to do. He listened attentively but was still very reserved. Then he said that he would probably support such a resolution but that he did not think it advisable to propose it himself. I replied that I was not asking him to, and that all I wanted was his support. "I think it would be best," he said, "to get Mr. Eden [then Foreign Secretary and British delegate to the League of Nations] to introduce it." I said that I had already spoken to Anthony Eden and received a favorable reply, though not a binding one.

"You must speak more strongly to Mr. Eden," said Litvinov.

"Yes," I replied. "But, you know, Mr. Eden represents the British Empire and I only represent the powerless Jewish people."

"Nonsense!" retorted Litvinov. "If your world Jewish organizations really want them to, the democracies will do what you ask."

Somewhat indignant at this answer, I said: "Mr. Litvinov, a few months ago I saw Cardinal and Secretary of State Pacelli at the Vatican and he said something similar about the great power of world Jewry. I was more amused than annoyed by it at the time. After all, why should a Catholic cardinal know much about these things? But when you, with your Jewish intelligence, make a remark like that, I really am annoyed."

Litvinov was very much taken aback and was silent for a moment. Then he stood up, walked around his desk, and said: "I apologize for my last remark. It was very stupid." This broke the ice; the tone of the rest of the conversation was very friendly, and from then on I remained in constant touch with him, saw him frequently in Geneva, and discussed many questions with him. Although he never did anything concrete for us in Jewish affairs—he was probably never in a position to—my acquaintance with him was more than merely formal and led to many interesting conversations.

Looking back at the years of struggle against Naziism, it must be admitted that the most we could do was administer a few pinpricks. There could be no question of a full-scale defense, which in the years between 1933 and 1936 would have had to consist of attack rather than defense, because influential sections of the Jewish people outside the WJC rejected such a policy. With the best will in the world we could not ask even our most devoted gentile friends to take a more pro-Jewish stand than the majority of Jews had taken. Those of us who never stopped agitating for an offensive of this kind, above all that great and fearless leader of our people, Stephen Wise, remained isolated. Year by year, with growing bitterness and horror, we were forced to watch Hitler extend his attacks on the Jews and prepare the greatest act of extermination in our history.

14

Refugee Problems

Parallel with the struggle against the National Socialist regime ran our efforts on behalf of the Jewish victims of Naziism, especially our efforts to find countries to which the growing numbers forced to leave Germany could immigrate. At the meeting of the League of Nations in September, 1933, this problem was already on the agenda. An attempt to create a special League of Nations commission for refugee problems was defeated by Germany, which still belonged to the League, so it was agreed to establish a High Commission for Refugees. A resolution concerning the treatment of Jewish minorities that we hoped to get passed simultaneously was also blocked by Germany, which left the League of Nations a few weeks later, on October 13. Jewish groups then began a feverish search for a suitable candidate for high commissioner and made plans to coordinate the work of the Jewish organizations with that of the commission. Several of us favored Lord Robert Cecil, one of the founders and early champions of the League of Nations, but unfortunately he declined. The Americans then proposed James McDonald. In this position McDonald was dealing with Jewish problems for the first time, but as a result of it, he developed a friendly attitude toward Zionism and later became the first American ambassador to Israel.

To prepare for collaboration with the High Commissioner, a conference of the major Jewish organizations met in London on October 29, 1933. Professor Brodetzky and Lewis Strauss, later head of the Atomic Energy Commission, and I made up a sub-committee for refugee questions. In addition, I was chairman of a subcommittee for political questions, and with Chaim Weiz-mann and Norman Bentwich I was elected, before the confer-ence closed, to the delegation that was to negotiate with the newly appointed high commissioner, Mr. McDonald. I flew to Geneva with Bentwich for discussions with top League of Na-tions officials. When McDonald appointed Professor Bentwich his assistant, negotiations with the High Commissioner were left to Weizmann and myself.

For all his good will, James McDonald had no idea what a difficult job he was undertaking. With the optimistic enthusiasm typical of so many American politicians, he was sure he could easily solve the problem of the six hundred thousand German Jews, most of whom would have to emigrate. As he indicated to Weizmann and me at our first meeting, he hoped first to obtain from Hitler a relaxation of the anti-Jewish measures and then to arrange for half the German Jews to be admitted to the United States and the other half to Palestine. Weizmann and I, more familiar with the difficulties, tried to dampen his excessive opti-mism a little without discouraging him. In a pun on the Euro-pean title of a then very popular movie, I nicknamed the big, blond, temperamental, but always good-tempered McDonald "Sunny Goy." As we were leaving after our first conversation, Weizmann said to me on the steps of the Hotel Bellevue, where McDonald lived, "You'll see, Nahum. The High Commissioner is not going to be able to do anything for the German Jews ex-cept get more immigration certificates out of the Jewish Agency." Several years later, after the complete failure of the High Com-mission, I was reminded of this during the final session of the advisory committee, when the last point on the agenda pro-duced a bitter discussion about the inadequate number of cer-tificates granted by the Jewish Agency.

This already suggests what was to come of that first interna-tional attempt to solve the German Jewish refugee problem. But it took several years of continuous disappointments and failures to convince McDonald, the governments represented on the High Commission executive council, and the Jewish organizations represented on the Advisory Committee that little could be achieved. In the first few weeks after the establishment of the commission we were all more or less confident that it was a major attempt to provide opportunities of emigration and resettlement for the German Jews and we went about our work with great enthusiasm.

The organization of the High Commission called for an Executive Council of government representatives and an "Advisory Committee of private organizations" composed of Jewish and certain non-Jewish organizations. The commission met for the first time in Lausanne, Switzerland, in December, 1933. The Jewish representatives were Chaim Weizmann, Louis Oungre of the American Jewish Colonization Association, Bernard Kahn, and other members of the American Jewish Joint Distribution Committee (JDC). In establishing the advisory committee a difficulty arose for me personally. Among the "respectable" Jewish organizations, such as the JDC, the American Jewish Council, and so on, I had the reputation of being a troublemaker and an extreme Zionist, and they were a little afraid of me. The representatives of the JDC in particular refused to work with me on the Advisory Committee. On the other hand, various members of the Executive Council supported me, among them the French Senator Béranger and the Italian and Polish delegates. McDonald himself wanted the organizations I represented to have a spokesman on the Advisory Committee. He told me later he had had to have a word on the telephone with Felix Warburg, president of the JDC, in New York to get the veto on my membership lifted. As our work proceeded, it became clear that the organizations I represented offered McDonald much stronger support than the philanthropic Jewish groups whose policies on many matters were far more timid than that of the High Commissioner.

In subsequent years I had constant dealings with the High Commissioner and attended almost all meetings of the Advisory Committee. This work grew more heartbreaking every month. It very soon became obvious that the various governments were not willing to open their doors generously to Jewish refugees. To put it cynically, all I got out of those meetings was a more

extensive knowledge of geography. Every session was a rehash
of the preceding ones. The High Commission officials had discovered a new country that might in theory accept German-
Jewish refugees. A report was written on the basis of a
thorough study of its absorptive potential and a representative
of the country in question was invited to state its position—
which in nearly every case was negative. There were a thousand
and one reasons for not admitting German-Jewish refugees. In
one country it was the infertile soil, in another local economic
conditions, in a third certain prejudices within its own population, in a fourth the climate. The reasons were varied enough,
but the result was always the same: There was no room for
sizable groups of German-Jewish immigrants.

Before a year had passed it was clear that the commission was
not going to achieve much. McDonald drew the courageous and
inevitable conclusion. On December 27, 1935, he sent to the
League of Nations a letter of resignation and protest that was a
truly historic document, placing on record diplomatically but
unequivocally the lack of good will, the heartlessness and hy-
pocrisy, of the great powers.

The next two High Commissioners were both Englishmen, and
since they were less hopeful at the start, they were not so disil-
lusioned. They approached the problem with their English *sang-
froid*, so that, even though they could not achieve much more,
they did not feel obliged to resign in protest. One of them, Sir
Neil Malcolm, reported, for instance, that in two and a half
years of office he had succeeded in placing five thousand
refugees. During that same period Palestine admitted many
times the total accepted by all other countries together. The
League of Nations Commission, however, had nothing to do
with immigration to Palestine; this was in the hands of the
Jewish Agency, which had to fight bitterly for every concession it managed to wrest from the British.

In 1938, with the persecution of the German Jews becoming
steadily more drastic, the consciences of the great powers began
to trouble them a little and President Roosevelt, in a new attempt, convened the Intergovernmental Conference on Refugees at Evian in France on July 6. The governments of twenty-

two potential countries of immigration were invited and a few others sent observers. Most of the Jewish organizations sent representatives, and although these were not actually delegates to the conference, they were given opportunities to state their views to a special subcommittee. As so often happened, it was not possible to get the twenty-one Jewish organizations represented at Evian to adopt a common position. On the contrary, each of them took an individual stand, which did nothing to enhance their efforts or the impression they made on non-Jewish governments. I attended of course and I could, if I wished, give a tragic-comic description of that conference. It was clear from the start that none of the participating countries contemplated any serious assistance. Since they did not want to offend Nazi Germany, the whole thing turned into a humanitarian rally. Resolutions were adopted and committees established, directors and officials were appointed—and they achieved little more than the High Commission had. After my experiences of the years 1933–1938 I went to Evian without any high expectations, but just the same it was shocking to see how ready all the powerful governments were to abandon the European Jews to their fate and to appease their sense of guilt by creating commissions and holding meetings. They were content with going through the motions of helping these refugees. I did not succeed in obtaining a visa for a single German applicant. All the government representatives I spoke to referred me to their country's normal immigration channels.

The fate of the high commission and the Evian conference, it seems to me, is an irrefutable indictment of the civilized world in its attitude to the Nazi persecution of the Jews. Historians of that era will have to confirm what had become increasingly clear to anybody living through the day-to-day phases of that persecution—that during this whole period the so-called democratic world made no large-scale effort to stop the murderous assault on the Jews or even to offer generous help to the victims of Naziism. There are individual exceptions to this indictment, but by and large all countries are equally guilty. Even an attempt to get visas to the Soviet Union for Jewish Communists forced to flee Germany was rejected on the grounds that the

German Jewish Communists were intellectuals suspected of Trotskyism.

This harsh charge against the civilized world is mitigated by two things, first, that its policy toward National Socialism as a whole was just as stupid and shortsighted as its attitude to its anti-Semitic aspects, and second, that the Jewish people itself lacked the vision, courage, and solidarity to set an example for the non-Jewish world that might have prevented this incomparable crime ending in the extermination of six million Jews.

15

Missed Opportunities of Founding a Jewish State

In addition to all these activities I continued my work in Zionist politics. Soon after the sudden death of Victor Jacobson, the first representative of the Jewish Agency at the League of Nations, I was asked by Chaim Weizmann, David Ben-Gurion, chairman of the Executive of the Jewish Agency, and Moshe Schertok, head of its political division in Jerusalem (who later Hebraized his name to Sharett), to represent the Zionist Executive in Geneva. My wife and I had intended to settle in Palestine in 1934 and were about to build a house in Jerusalem. When I received the invitation to Geneva I was hesitant, but Ben-Gurion and Schertok convinced me that there were more than enough Zionist leaders in Palestine but very few candidates for the position of League of Nations representative who had the necessary language qualifications, familiarity with international politics, diplomatic perseverance, and an intimate knowledge of Zionist problems. I finally accepted, and in 1935 my position was confirmed by the Zionist congress at Lucerne. I was given a seat on the Zionist Executive and the right to vote in all questions connected with my activities. A year later I became a full member of the Executive and belonged to it continuously until the Zionist congress in 1968, when I decided not to stand for reelection as president of the World Zionist Organization.

My Zionist work during this period was concerned with both internal politics and foreign policy. As to the former, I belonged to the small but not uninfluential Radical Party that I had helped found, took part in the unsuccessful attempts to unite the splintered General Zionists, as the central party of the world movement was called, and then joined the so-called Group A, the progressive prolabor wing as opposed to the more rightist, middle class Group B.

But my attention was focused more and more on foreign affairs. Our work centered on applying the rights granted us in Palestine under the Balfour Declaration and the mandate to immigration and colonization. Arab opposition grew from year to year in proportion to our success. There were constant outbreaks in Palestine. All attempts to reach an understanding with the Arab population miscarried, primarily because of the intransigence of the Arab leaders, who could not accept the idea of large-scale Jewish immigration, but also perhaps, as hindsight suggests, because the Zionist movement did not take this problem seriously enough.

We believed that the British government was the determining factor, and we concentrated our main strength on this front. The British, however, were trying to weaken the terms of the mandate from year to year, so as not to jeopardize their position in the Arab world. They evolved a theory whereby the rights of Jews and Arabs in mandated Palestine were equally valid, and this led to a policy of balancing one side against the other. If the Arabs caused a disturbance, concessions were made to them; if we protested, either in England or in Geneva, British policy yielded in our favor. With the appearance of Hitler on the world scene, the growth of National Socialist power, and the approaching danger of a world war, British policy almost inevitably became less and less pro-Zionist and more and more pro-Arab. The British government knew very well that if it came to war it could count on the support of world Jewry whatever happened, while the Arabs were free to choose sides. Because we were compelled to be pro-British in world affairs, our strategic and tactical position vis-à-vis the Arabs was seriously weakened. The continuous fight against the almost hostile policy of the British, however, increased the tension between us.

We became more and more of a nuisance to the British, especially in the eyes of their colonial officers in Palestine. Quite apart from the Arab-Jewish conflict, the average Colonial Office representative in Palestine resented us. Civil servants the world all over are alike in one respect; they prefer to keep things quiet. All bureaucracies resent dynamic local groups that jolt them out of their comfortable routine. In Palestine we were the dynamic element. We wanted to create something new, to develop the country at a constantly increasing tempo. This alone made us a nuisance to Colonial Office types accustomed to an easy-going life in the British colonies, to treating the local population as natives and keeping them in order by means of the stick and the carrot, that is, through oppression and bribery. With us, however, neither method worked. They could neither placate us with favors nor intimidate us with edicts.

A conversation I had with a high British official in Palestine about the constant deterioration in British-Jewish relations will illustrate this. He told me that years ago he had asked to be posted to Palestine because of his sympathy for the Zionist experiment, but that in time he had become anti-Zionist. His explanation for this was very simple. A particularly persistent Arab who had had his request rejected once might come back a second time, but a firm final *no* would end the matter once and for all. A Jew—he said—would come back countless times. If the official became nasty and threw him out, he could be sure that six months later London would raise an inquiry about the matter, either because a Member of Parliament had complained to the Colonial Office or because the Jewish Agency in Geneva had put the Mandates Commission on to it. "Why should I have any sympathy for them?" he asked at the end of his understandable though unsatisfactory explanation.

A member of the British cabinet once told me something similar. According to statistics, many times more questions were asked in Parliament about Palestine with its half-million Jews than about India with its four hundred million inhabitants.

The British government's anti-Zionist policy was most apparent in matters of immigration and land acquisition. It maintained a quite unreal conception of the country's "limited" capacity to absorb immigrants that was practically an article of faith and was always invoked when the number of immigration certificates, for which we had to apply twice a year, was curtailed. Britain sent commissions to Palestine that were supposed to prove, more or less scientifically, that there was no room for new Jewish immigrants in "overpopulated" Palestine. All in all they followed a *status quo* policy in contrast to our expansionist one that was based on the premise strikingly formulated by Weizmann: We would create the absorptive capacity of the country rather than accept it as fixed.

My part in this tug-of-war was to obstruct British policy from Geneva. The League of Nations Mandates Commission, a body that was highly respected legally and morally, supervised all mandates. It met twice a year, examined the reports of the mandated countries, and commented on them. Since the mandate concept was something new, created in the peace treaties after the First World War, the Mandates Commission had to acquire its authority gradually. The mandatory powers were naturally somewhat antagonistic to it, regarding it as a superfluous supervisory body whose idealistic, abstract, legalistic ideas impeded practical politics. The best known of the mandated countries and the one most subject to public discussion was without doubt Palestine. World opinion cared very little what went on in New Guinea or Tanganyika. But Palestine, in which millions of Jews and all the non-Jewish friends of Zionism took such an ardent interest, was constantly under discussion, and we made sure that the Palestine question was never allowed to die down. It fell to me, as the official representative of the Jewish Agency to the Mandates Commission, to substantiate our countless complaints against British policy. I was not allowed, however, to attend the meetings of the commission, at which the Colonial Office was always represented, often by the minister himself, nor to participate directly in the debates. I had to state our position in writing or, more often, in personal discussions with members. My predecessor, Victor Jacobson, had built up his position on a basis of personal respect and sympathy, but I had to establish my own contacts gradually.

In those days the League of Nations had more moral authority than the United Nations commands today. The world had not yet been demoralized by the barbarism of the totalitarian regimes and the Second World War. Moral principles played a more important role than they do in world politics today. Moreover, the Mandates Commission had become one of the most morally irreproachable and efficient organs of the League of Nations, thanks primarily to William Rappard, the original director of the Mandates Section of the League of Nations, who had prepared a solid basis for it. The commission consisted of representatives of the colonial powers and various neutral states and internationally recognized experts and authorities. Besides Rappard, the world-renowned Swiss jurist and sociologist, it included M. P. Orts, its chairman and a Belgian colonial officer of great experience and unquestionable fairness, and a number of others who, far from being willing to play along with the colonial powers, often had the courage to censure colonial policy and demand changes in it. While the commission could not force a government to change policy, its opinion carried considerable weight.

Every session of the commission witnessed a duel between the British Colonial Office and the Jewish Agency. Most members, especially those who represented the smaller countries, were experts in their field, morally independent men who frequently endorsed our criticism. They rendered us invaluable services, particularly in the difficult years when we had to struggle for every step forward in Palestine. As trustees of the mandate and of the Balfour Declaration, they were a judicial authority without which our position in Palestine, already bad, would have become much worse. In my opinion the Mandates Commission remained a more positive symbol of the great ideas the first League of Nations stood for than any of its other institutions. What we achieved in Palestine would have been impossible without it.

I realized that as long as the danger of Nazi Germany remained acute, time was not on our side. Our relations with the mandatory power were bound to become increasingly strained, since cold political facts forced it to try at any price to win the sympathies of the Arab world in the coming showdown with Germany. Obviously the British never used this argument, so we were both constantly evading the real issue. While we were always harping on our rights under the Balfour Declaration and the mandate, the British were forced to use specious arguments against us. Only once did Lord Halifax, then foreign minister, go so far as to admit that there were moments when "political expediency" took precedence over moral principles. (In an earlier debate over the Passfield White Paper, a colleague and I had once stated our view heatedly but, we thought, with such weighty and irrefutable logic that the other side would never be able to challenge it. After a moment's silence the British representative said: "Gentlemen, you have the logic but we have the Empire, and with your logic you would never have got our empire." Indignant as I was, I knew he was not entirely wrong.)

Another series of events from this period strongly influenced my political thinking. In fact, had it not been an isolated episode it might have prevented the extermination of six million European Jews. In 1936 the British government appointed a Royal Commission to examine the increasingly confusing Palestine situation and propose a solution. The history of this commission, which included some very eminent members, and of the Jewish case, especially as presented by Weizmann and Ben-Gurion, has been told many times. It all took place in Palestine, and I had nothing to do with it. On his return from Palestine, however, Weizmann asked me to come to his hotel in Paris and in the strictest confidence told me a great secret. Professor Reginald Coupland, probably the most intellectually distinguished member of the commission, had asked him unofficially what he would think of solving the Palestine problem by partitioning the country into separate Jewish and Arab states, since Arab and Jewish demands were incompatible. Weizmann had withheld his answer and was now on his way to London, where he wanted to discuss the question with some of his friends. He also wanted my opinion.

I said immediately that I was in favor of the idea, provided the area allotted to us would permit large-scale immigration. I have held to this opinion ever since, and when the war ended, I was the first to revive the partition plan and get it accepted by the Zionist movement and the American government. If there has been a tragedy in the history of Zionism, it is the fact that largely through our fault, partition was not put into effect the first time it was suggested, in 1937. When the Royal Commission proposed it officially, a passionate debate began, like the one that followed its second proposal, after the war. Many of the most respected Zionist leaders were ardently against it, including men like Menahem Ussishkin who, as I shall never forget, spent half a night in Jerusalem trying to change my attitude and that of the Radical Party. When I told him I was going to support the plan, he accused me of an unforgivable crime against the future of Palestine and the Jewish people. It was opposed by men like Berl Katzenelson, the most respected moral and intellectual leader of the Palestinian labor movement, and, for different reasons, by Louis Brandeis; Stephen Wise and all his friends were also against it.

The motives behind this violent opposition were the same ones I had to fight in 1945 and 1946: inability to compromise, determination to hold on to every inch of Palestine as something historically sacred, the obstinacy and fanaticism of a persecuted people that for two thousand years had set beliefs and ideals above reality and practical necessity, an unwillingness to recognize that a people not content with waiting, hoping, and having faith must reckon with realities, even if this means sacrificing some cherished historic ideas as a means toward shaping its own destiny. The debate almost ran wild. Weizmann and a majority of the Zionist Executive, led by Ben-Gurion, were for partition. So was the British government at first, especially the Colonial Minister, Sir John Ormsby Gore, an old friend of Zionism. I also managed to convince the Mandates Commission that the partition plan did not contravene the spirit of the mandate and a resolution to this effect was quickly passed. If the Zionist movement had accepted the proposal then, spontaneously and without delay, it is quite conceivable that it might have been implemented. We would then have had two years' time before war broke out and a country to which hundreds of thousands, possibly millions, of European Jews might have escaped. At the 1937 Zionist congress, at which I presided, after lengthy debates and several votes, a motion hedged with restrictive clauses was finally passed by a small majority expressing willingness to consider the partition plan. But it was already too late. The acceptance was too vague and the British government itself had begun to waver in the face of categorical Arab rejection. The plan died.

The Zionist movement's attitude toward this first partition plan was a major sin of our generation, second only to world Jewry's inadequate reaction to the Nazi peril and its irresponsible belief that Hitler would never carry out his threats. One of the motives that later led me to revive the idea of partition was the awareness that we ourselves bear some of the guilt for the annihilation of a third of our people. This may have been a decisive argument for many people, such as my friend Stephen Wise, who rejected the plan originally but later supported it vigorously.

In addition to fighting the British position in Palestine, we had our own problems in Zionist foreign policy during that period. I was actively involved in mobilizing sympathy and political support in the countries of Western Europe. As the unofficial representative of the Jewish Agency to the French government, I made a special effort in France to win friends within the various parties, and this was made easier for me by the preliminary work done by Dr. Jacobson and other Jewish and non-Jewish allies in Paris. I made the acquaintance of French politicians such as Paul Reynaud, Yvon Delbos, Senator Béranger, then chairman of the French Senate Foreign Affairs Committee, Emile Herriot, and that true friend of Zionism, Justin Goddard. I saw a lot of Léon Blum, not only a great Frenchman but a great Jew, a man always ready to help, whose intellectual vigor and nobility of character never failed to impress me deeply.

One question that gave us a lot of trouble, especially during my early years in Geneva, was how to facilitate the emigration of German Jews to Palestine. A related problem was *Ha-avarah*, the transfer of assets by which German Jews could emigrate to Palestine upon payment of a capital sum. While regulations stringently limited the number of Jewish immigrants to Palestine without means, there was no restriction, in principle, on capitalist immigration. Anyone who could transfer the equivalent of a thousand English pounds qualified as a capitalist. Since the German Jews could not transfer cash, an agreement was reached with the Nazi government, whereby emigrants could deposit money with the Jewish Agency in Germany. The Agency bought goods to be imported into Palestine, reimbursing the immigrants in pounds after their arrival in Palestine. This arrangement permitted eighty thousand German Jews to emigrate to Palestine, immigrants who made an essential contribution to the country and became one of the most creative elements in its development.

When the agreement came up for ratification by the Zionist Congress, there were stormy debates. Many thought it a national dishonor that the Zionist organization should do business with Germany. I, the man who had proclaimed the Jewish boycott against Nazi Germany at the World Jewish Congress, vigorously defended the transfer agreement because saving eighty thousand Jews and transferring Jewish assets to Palestine seemed to me worth doing, even if the German economy did benefit by it. At the Lucerne congress of 1937 the agreement was finally ratified, after a turbulent session over which I presided. When the majority had given its approval, the Revisionist delegates stood up and began to protest violently. To demonstrate their opposition they left their seats but remained in the doorway, shouting "Shame!" I was afraid it would break up the meeting, but I managed to outshout their leader, Robert Stricker. "Herr Stricker," I yelled, "shout all you want to, outside or inside, but at least close the door. There's a draft!" The laughter that followed ended the demonstration. I mention this episode because it too found an echo later, during the fierce Jewish controversy over the agreement with Konrad Adenauer's German government that I initiated in 1952. Here again similar considerations determined the course of the debate.

Participating in congresses was always a tricky business for German Zionists during those years. The German delegates were, in a manner of speaking, hostages, because they had left their families in Germany. Gestapo officials were usually present, and there was always a danger of reprisals if Hitler and his regime were denounced too violently. I had to see that speeches concerning Germany at Zionist congresses were uncompromising in content but parliamentary in form. My first difficulty came in 1935 with Stephen Wise, and I was not such a

Avigdor Leibmann, my paternal grandfather.

My father, around 1900.

Bar mitzvah, 1908. (l to r) Uncle Szalkowitz, my mother Rebecca, my father Solomon Goldmann.

The author, around 1920.

The author, in the mid-1920's.

My wife Alice, around 1930.

At the founding meeting of the World Jewish Congress, Geneva, 1936. To my left are Rabbi Alcalay, chief rabbi of Yugoslavia, and, beside him, Stephen Wise.

Stephen Wise addressing the World Jewish Congress, Geneva, 1936. I am to his right.

The World Zionist Congress, 1939. (r to l) My-self, Ben-Gurion, Menachem Ussischkin, and, to the right of the rostrum, Weizmann.

With Weizmann on the presidium of the World Zionist Congress, Lucerne, 1935.

The World Jewish Conference, Switzerland, 1935. (l to r)
Zionist labor leader Zerubawel, myself, Stephen Wise.

With my wife and sons in Lisbon, 1940.

With Stephen Wise in Mexico, 1942.

At the Zionist Conference, London 1946. Third row (l to r): Abba Hillel
Silver, Moshe Sneh, Yitzak Grynbaum. Second row: Moshe Sharett and
myself. First row (l to r): Two survivors of the Warsaw ghetto, Doctors
Sommerstein and Hartglass, leaders of Polish Jewry.

With Stephen Wise at War Emergency Conference, Atlantic City, 1944.

With Dag Hammarskjöld on a visit to Jerusalem.

Leaving Karlsbad after
the World Zionist
Conference, 1947.

In Rio, with leaders of Brazilian Jewry, after the war.

Casablanca, February 27, 1952.

(l to r) Noah Barou, an unidentified gentleman, Stephen Wise, and myself, in 1948.

Jewish leaders with President Truman, November 5, 1950. Beside me is Rabbi Irving Miller. To President Truman's right is Rose Halprin. Behind her is Henry Morgenthau, Jr., and to her left, Abraham Feinberg.

World Zionist Congress, Jerusalem, late 1950's. (l to r) Berl Locker, myself, Moshe Sharett.

At a dinner for the author, May 24, 1953. Rose Halprin, and a bust by Robert Berks.

Weizmann dinner, December 17, 1953. Front row (r to l): Meyer Weisgal, Louis Lipsky, myself, Abba Eban.

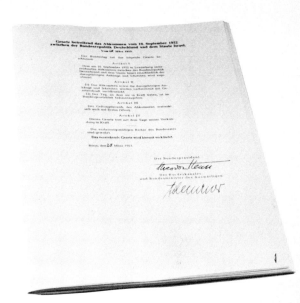

The ratification bill of the Luxembourg Agreement, signed by President Theodor Heuss and Federal Chancellor Konrad Adenauer, March, 1953.

At a dinner honoring Ben-Gurion, the Waldorf-Astoria, New York, 1957. (l to r) Rose Halprin, Ben-Gurion, Benjamin Brodie, myself.

With Ralph Bunche, around 1965.

At the World Jewish Congress, Geneva, 1953.

close friend of his then as I was later. I found out he was going to make a very strongly anti-German speech in the open debate. As president of the congress I told him that in accordance with a decision of the steering committee, he would have to submit this speech to me in advance and that I had the right to censor the passages concerning Germany. Wise, with his volcanic temperament, was furious. He declared that this was an insult and an outrage. Having refused the most prestigious rabbinical position in America because the president of the congregation wanted to see his sermons in advance, he would not put up with it. I remained quite calm and told him he would not get the floor unless he let me see his speech. When I pointed out how an indiscreet speech might jeopardize the German Jews and assured him that I only wanted to protect him from his own temperament, he gave in and allowed me to check the relevant passages.

In this connection I would also like to mention a less serious incident at the Lucerne congress. When the general debate was drawing to an end, after the numerous discomfiting speeches on Germany, and I was about to relinquish the chair to a colleague with great relief, an American delegate I did not know suddenly came up and asked for the floor. I asked him what subject he wished to speak on and he said: "Hitler." I told him the list of speakers in the open debate was closed. He replied with some heat that he had promised his constituency to speak on the subject of Hitler and could not possibly go home without having done so. However, since the list was full, he would be content with two minutes. When I asked him what he wanted to say in two minutes he replied: "I only want to say that Hitler is a wild beast and God should exterminate him as soon as possible." I told him he could not say this from the platform, at which he became hysterical. In the end, to prevent a scene, I had to ask the leader of the American delegation, Judge Morris Rothenberg, to escort his delegate from the hall. Many years later, when I was speaking in an American city, this man came up to me and told me how angry he had been with me all those years. Now, however, he could see how right I had been not to let him speak.

During those years I also tried to influence the Russian attitude toward Zionism. The most radical anti-Zionists were the Jewish Communists themselves. Within the Eastern European Jewish intelligentsia, especially in Russia, a controversy had been raging for years between the Zionist elements and the radical socialist (later Communist) group that looked to world revolution for salvation. When Communism came to power the Zionist party, like all others, was declared illegal and counter-revolutionary, and over the years thousands of Zionists were arrested, sentenced and deported to forced labor camps in Siberia. Although the prospects were not very hopeful, I tried to change this policy. There was no point in making any serious attempt with Litvinov. I do not believe he was basically anti-Zionist, but as a Jew in the exposed position of Russian commissar for foreign affairs, he could not permit himself the slightest deviation from the official line. Yet to my astonishment I encountered considerable flexibility in two other Communist representatives. One was Marcel Rosenberg, the Russian deputy secretary-general at the League of Nations. Rosenberg, a Jew, told me several times that he was sympathetic to Zionist efforts and sharply criticized the Jewish Communists in Russia who, in order to demonstrate their loyalty, were more radically anti-Zionist than their non-Jewish comrades.

The other was Vladimir Petrovic Potemkin, a gentile, then Soviet ambassador in Paris and later vice-commissar for foreign affairs and minister of education. He was a remarkable man, a descendent of the Potemkin princes, an idealist and a man of great education and charm, a *grand seigneur* but a convinced Communist and an extraordinarily candid diplomat. He had a really touching love of everything Jewish. As a young man he had wanted to be a theologian and had studied Hebrew. He could recite whole chapters of the Mishnaic tractate *Pirkei Avot* (*Sayings of the Fathers*), which he said was unequaled in world literature as a collection of wisdom. He once told me he had quarreled with Maxim Gorky, a friend of his youth, because Gorky dropped their joint plan to publish a Russian translation of the most important works in modern Hebrew and Jewish literature. His ideal was to become a professor of Hebrew literature in Moscow when he retired from politics.

Potemkin was pro-Zionist and claimed that it ought to be

possible to get Stalin to support the movement. He had anticipated all the arguments for partition and a Jewish state in Palestine that Gromyko later brought up at the United Nations
meeting of 1948. He maintained that Stalin had only become
anti-Zionist under the influence of the Jewish Communists and
suggested I go to see him, possibly with Dr. Wise. I readily
accepted the suggestion, and he promised to discuss it with
Stalin during his next home leave. But he arrived in Moscow at
the height of the great anti-Trotsky trials and told me when he
returned that in that atmosphere of panic and suspicion it would
have been impossible even to bring up the idea. He encouraged
me to hope for better luck next time, but the following year he
was recalled from Paris, and nothing came of my proposed visit
to Stalin.

In 1938 it began to seem unlikely that world tensions could be
resolved peacefully; war seemed inevitable. Western policy became increasingly that of appeasement, and the warnings
Litvinov issued in the League of Nations Assembly during the
Munich conference seemed to me convincing and justified.
Litvinov had often told me that if someday I read in the papers
he had resigned as Foreign Commissar, it would mean that an
understanding had been reached between Nazi Germany and Soviet Russia and war would soon follow. (In 1939, when
Litvinov resigned shortly before the Ribbentrop-Molotov
treaty, I telegraphed my fears of imminent world war to Dr.
Wise, who showed my cable to U.S. Under-Secretary of State
Sumner Welles. When I saw Welles for the first time in 1940,
he expressed surprise at my foresight. I told him what it was
based on and said the credit should go to Litvinov.)

In August, 1939, the Zionist congress met. Fearing war, I had
advised against convening it, and on the fifth or sixth day war
broke out. Weizmann immediately left Geneva for London
and the Congress was adjourned. However, many delegates
from Eastern Europe could not return home, and it fell to
me to arrange their return from Geneva. I succeeded in reaching an agreement with the Italian government whereby they
were taken in sealed railway coaches through Italy to Austria
and Poland. I knew that little more could be accomplished in
Geneva and shortly thereafter left for Paris.

16

Europe Goes Under

For the duration of the war our two major problems were obviously going to be the fate of the Jews in the countries over-run by the Nazis and the welfare of the Palestinian Jews, whose future the war had also plunged into uncertainty. For the time being I decided not to accept an invitation from the Zionist Organization of America (ZOA) to come to New York, feeling that it was my duty to remain close to both problem areas. Before long, in the fall of 1939, I was urgently called to Paris in connection with the French government's stupid and unfair decision to intern all former German citizens, which meant principally the German Jewish refugees. Thus, the most embittered enemies of the German regime were suddenly declared enemy aliens and imprisoned. My attempt to initiate action to have this policy rescinded by enlisting the support of the official leaders of French Jewry was fruitless; the French Jewish Consistoire, the supreme French religious body, declined, on patriotic grounds, to make strong representations to the French government. I decided to do this myself, in the name of the WJC, and found the military authorities more receptive to our demands than the spokesmen of French Jewry. While I did not succeed in getting all the internees liberated, I did manage to secure the release of a number of prominent Jewish figures on the basis of guarantees and character references from the WJC and other Jewish organizations. But of course, when the Germans invaded France in May, 1940, they were taken into custody again and in the

panic and chaos that overwhelmed France any further intervention was impossible.

During those months in Paris I also advocated the idea of a
Jewish legion as a separate unit within the Allied armies. The
purpose of this proposal was to give the Jewish people a military share in the war against the Nazis and to mobilize refugees
and the Jews of Palestine. As a mandated territory, Palestine
was neutral, and Palestinian Jews had no legal military obligations, but thousands of young Jews were eager to join in the struggle against Nazi Germany on the battlefield. Moreover, a commitment of this sort—that is, the visible presence of a Jewish
unit in the fight against Hitler—would be vitally important in
the postwar period, especially for Palestine. At the beginning of
the war I was thinking of a Jewish legion within the French
Army, because I realized that the British, who had to consider
the Arabs, were not likely to support the plan. France seemed
the most appropriate of all the great powers, if only because it
had the highest number of Central European refugees.

I discussed the idea with members of the French government.
In my search for influential people who could help me to realize
it, I met one of the strongest and most outstanding personalities
in French politics, Georges Mandel, the French colonial minister, who was Jewish. I had heard that he wanted nothing to do
with Jewish affairs. A pupil of Clemenceau and an extreme
French nationalist, he was authoritarian in his methods, stubborn in his ideas, and by no means easy to deal with. I was
introduced to him by a mutual acquaintance, one of my colleagues on the board of the WJC, a publisher of French financial papers and a man with wide connections, Robert Bollag.
The first time I saw Mandel he refused categorically to help,
but he impressed me at once as a man of stature, strong will, and
great ambition. He was the only French politician of my
acquaintance who appraised the situation realistically and foresaw France's downfall. In those months, when the French were
sustained by their blind faith in the Maginot Line, he admitted
that the French Army was demoralized and unfit to fight, that
the Germans would overrun France in a few weeks and most of
his associates were ready to make peace with them. He saw

France's only hope in forming a resistance government in Africa to carry on the struggle, together with England and possibly later with the United States.

At first the idea of a Jewish legion seemed utterly nonsensical to Mandel. As an assimilated Jew, he found the notion of a Jewish people absurd and argued that you might just as well create Catholic and Protestant legions. I talked at length with him about the nature of the Jewish people, about Zionism and Palestine—subjects he had been indifferent or even hostile to all his life. Our first talk was quite heated. He was unaccustomed to contradiction, and after a while he reprimanded me impatiently and irritably. I replied: "M. Mandel, I am very glad to have met you and I hope to see a lot of you. But further talks will be useless unless you understand that I am neither a member of your staff nor a citizen of France. I represent the Jewish people, and I can continue my conversations with you only as a partner on an equal footing. Whether we come to an understanding or not, both of us must have an absolute right to his own opinion. Otherwise I might as well say adieu to you right away." He looked at me in some amazement, then extended his hand and said: *Vous êtes un homme et je vous respecte.* From then on his tone changed and he was more responsive to my arguments.

Mandel finally assented to the idea of a Jewish legion for two main reasons, first, because thousands of young Jews, fanatical and eager fighters, would strengthen resistance to the Nazis, and second, because he recognized the far-reaching effect this was bound to have on American Jewry, since in his opinion the attitude of the United States would determine the outcome of the war. He opened the door for me to influential military figures, such as War Minister Edouard Daladier, and that spring I received a letter from the French government accepting in principle the idea of a Jewish legion. But before arrangements could be discussed the Germans invaded, France collapsed, and the project was buried for good as far as France was concerned. Later, of course, the Jewish Brigade was formed within the British Army, but it was restricted to Palestinian Jews.

When the German armies invaded Holland and Belgium I was

in Paris with my wife, but our children were in Geneva. We returned to Geneva immediately and I realized that there was little sense in my remaining in Europe. France was no longer a possible base of operations, and Geneva had become insignificant politically. We no longer felt safe in Switzerland, since we expected the German armies to occupy it, or at least to march through. I decided to take my family to safety in America. With the help of Stephen Wise, I obtained American visas for my family and myself (no easy matter in those days), and we decided to go to the United States via Paris and Lisbon.

Our reservations for Paris were already made. On the afternoon of our departure—it was in May—I went to the office to say good-by to my staff, turned on the radio and heard that panic had broken out in Paris. I suddenly had a vision of myself with two little children, aged two and four, caught up in that Paris maelstrom and probably unable to reach Spain and Portugal. Under the influence of this presentiment I telephoned my wife, asked her to unpack again, canceled the train reservations, and tried instead to get a flight to Spain. The only existing service, Locarno to Barcelona, was totally sold out, and only with the help of the Swiss authorities was I able to get seats on one of the last planes. Arriving in Lisbon with the naïve hope of flying on to New York via Pan-American Airways, we were told there were thousands of people on the waiting list and it would probably take months to get reservations. We spent several weeks in Estoril, near Lisbon, a delightful place, although at that time it was crowded with refugees. At last, again through the help of Stephen Wise and a State Department order, we were given a stateroom on the *U.S.S. Washington*—a favor to us as non-Americans, since this ship was supposed to be repatriating stranded American citizens.

Our eventful voyage began early in June. The first morning out we were awakened at five A.M. and told to man the lifeboats because a German U-boat was about to torpedo the ship and had given us twenty minutes to evacuate. Since the *Washington* was on a northerly course, on her way to an Irish port to embark Americans who had been stranded in England, the U-boat captain took her for a British ship flying false colors. We sat in the lifeboats for a while, until the captain finally convinced the U-boat commander that we really were the *U.S.S. Washington*, and after half an hour we were sent back to our cabins.

In the Irish port of Galway we had to wait three days, without going ashore, for the arrival of the special train bringing American passengers from London. The night before we sailed, the Galway police chief appeared with an order from the Irish Home Office to take me ashore as a suspected German spy. This misunderstanding had arisen out of a carelessly written letter a friend had sent me through one of the English passengers, a letter that had been intercepted by the Irish police. At first the chief of police would not see reason; he changed his attitude only when he found out that I was a friend of Sean Lester, the Irish deputy secretary-general of the League of Nations, and a school friend of his. After this was cleared up, our two-hour interview ended with a drink or two. On June 21 we landed in New York, to the joy of my friends, who had been worried by a report that I had been removed from the *U.S.S. Washington* by a German U-boat.

While still at sea, we heard on the radio of the armistice Pétain had concluded with the Germans. Many of the hundreds of Franco-Americans on board broke into sobs at this announcement and a discussion arose in which Professor Hans Kelsen, the great international jurist, later at the University of California at Berkeley, was a participant. Like most of the others, he was sure that after the collapse of France, England would also be overrun and the Nazis would control all of Europe for the indefinite future. I firmly contradicted this. For no logical reason, I simply refused to believe in such a course of events. I could not believe that England would behave like France or that the United States under Roosevelt could passively accept the Nazification of Europe. Even during those terrible months I never doubted the Nazis would lose the war.

However, I was much less optimistic about the fate of Europe's Jews. The real annihilation had not yet begun, but I already feared—and I said this openly soon after arriving in America and was strongly criticized for it—that millions of

European Jews would have to pay with their lives for the temporary victories of the Nazi armies. The only thing left to do, difficult and even hopeless as it might seem, was to save as many as possible from the holocaust. Exactly how this was to be done was by no means clear to me, but in situations like this one has to undertake the impossible; there is no alternative.

In this melancholy mood, aware of the momentary supremacy of the Nazis and the doom of millions of Jews, I arrived in New York. A return to Europe was out of the question for the present; no one could say how long the war would last; the fate of the Palestinian Jews was completely uncertain. I found only a little comfort in my resolve to do my part to rouse American Jewry and the Roosevelt administration for a rescue and relief operation.

17

American Jewry

For the next twenty-four years the United States was my home base, and a few remarks about my experiences with American Jewry will make many of the events I was involved in more intelligible. It is important for all who are concerned with problems of Jewish life to understand the American Jew. Historically, the same thing has happened to American Jews as to Americans in general: they have been placed, without any preparation, in positions of leadership they would probably have taken several more generations to attain had it not been for the catastrophes of two world wars.

Many of the difficulties in contemporary world politics are partly attributable to the fact that the United States, far from the center of world politics in 1914, was suddenly forced into a key position and became, after the Second World War, one of the world's two greatest powers. And in this respect an injustice was inflicted upon the American people; it was not given the time to grow into its position of leadership, to learn the business of international politics gradually, as the British had. Behind its basic isolationism lay a predominant desire to develop and to weld its demographic mixture into an organic whole. Suddenly, however, it had to assume responsibility for world events. It was America's destiny to be transformed overnight from a nation powerful but intellectually provincial in outlook into a world power. We must bear this in mind in criticizing the methods and mentality of contemporary American politics and in comparing the political maturity of Americans with that of other nations that through the centuries have learned to think on a global scale.

Hitler's extermination of European Jewry made American Jewry the most important Jewish community. Until then it had been, so to speak, a reserve army in the struggle for Jewish rights, while the shooting war was taking place in Europe. The European Jews were in the front lines; they determined strategy, set the objectives, and fought the decisive battles. In the rear were the millions of American Jews, reinforcements that could be called up in times of crisis. In the Second World War the front-line army was wiped out, and the reserves were forced to move up into its positions, whether they wanted to or not. Unprepared as they were, unaccustomed to leadership, American Jewry is still reluctant to assume responsibility for the fate of the Jewish people. Basically, it is trying to keep its reserve and reinforcement status, both with regard to Israeli affairs and in matters that concern the whole Jewish people. But American Jews can no more resist the call to the leadership vacated by European Jews than America can decline its responsibility as the leading power of the free world. Both are uncomfortable situations, painful to the leaders and to those they lead, but there is no alternative.

When the historic call went out to American Jewry, it was psychologically unready for it. In nineteenth- and early twentieth-century America, a community had emerged unlike any in previous Jewish history. Millions strong, more prosperous economically and more powerful politically than any other Jewish community of recent times, it was a diversified conglomeration of nationalities. Eastern and Western European Jews, Oriental Jews from various countries, all with their patrimony of Jewish tradition and ideologies, had arrived in a free country and encountered its unlimited possibilities. With no transition but a sea voyage, most nineteenth-century Jewish immigrants had come straight from ghetto life, persecution, and oppression to a country of apparently unrestricted freedom and opportunity. They did not need to struggle for their rights one step at a time for decades or even centuries, as the European Jews did; civil rights were suddenly bestowed upon them like an unearned inheritance. The moment they set foot on American soil they were free and enjoyed civil equality. An almost boundless horizon of success and careers seemed to lie open before them. This sudden gift of freedom made an overwhelming, inextinguishable impression upon most Jewish immigrants and inspired them with exuberant gratitude and love for what seemed a paradise when compared to the conditions from which they came. The tendency of many Americans to glorify their country, the consciousness that they are privileged to live in "God's own country," is found, perhaps to an even more marked degree, in many Jews.

Naturally most new arrivals were occupied at first with shaping their own lives and exploiting the great economic opportunities this free, aspiring country offered them. It was bound to take time before such diffuse elements could think of creating a synthesis, the basis for creative communal enterprises. Even under the most favorable conditions, such a process would have taken generations—and American Jewry was not given so much time. Still far from having coalesced into an organic whole, not yet able to make any distinctive contribution to Jewish culture, American Jews found themselves in a crucial position of leadership.

This all goes to show how difficult it is to portray American Jewry accurately. Apart from a few bold outlines, there is as yet really no such thing as American Jews. To understand them you have to go back to separate origins. In most cases it is easy to tell whether they came from Galicia or Hungary, Germany or France, Russia or Rumania. Consciously or unconsciously, many of them still carry with them the traditions and characteristics of their pre-American origins. Nearly all the ideas that nourish American Jewry had their birth in Europe, from strictest orthodoxy to radical reform, from Zionism to the cultural nationalism of the Bund and to assimilationism. Here and there we can discern attempts to create something approaching an independent American-Jewish ideology, but in addition to their weakness, these attempts are confined to the intellectual classes and have not become a motive force in American-Jewish life. Major Jewish problems in the United States are still basically those brought over from other centers of Jewish life. Their focus is directed abroad. Attitudes toward Israel, what to do for the Jewish state, how to help Jews in other countries—these are the questions the American-Jewish organizations argue and which, for the most part, determine Jewish schools of thought. The various factions within American Jewry have not reached the point of concentrating on their own specific Jewish questions. American Jewry is still a kind of reserve army directing its attention toward other Jewish communities.

Apart from this fundamental weakness in facing its responsibilities and tasks in the post-Hitler era, American Jewry has other shortcomings that often impede its behavior. It has acquired certain characteristics of American life in general, and, in contrast to European Jews, it reacts emotionally rather than ideologically. As a Jewish mass in a land of great masses, it is more susceptible to sentiment, slogans, and passions than to ideas. Among no other Jews in the world does the public speaker, especially the demagogue, play such a role; you have to speak to American Jews in superlatives before they will listen. Cool, balanced analysis makes no impression on them, and exaggeration is almost indispensable.

The Jews share another characteristic of the general American mentality: the excessive importance they attach to material assets, the dominance of the rich man. Public institutions, especially charitable ones, are, like those in other Anglo-Saxon cultures, far more dependent on private contributions than in Europe, where the state is the major source of support. In America and England, hospitals, universities, schools, and cultural projects are financed to a large extent by private funds. This state of affairs is even more obvious in American Jewry, which lacks any representative organization for dealing with government. Thus the "big giver" almost inevitably and automatically becomes a leader in Jewish life. Let us take one example. In the United States there are no real Jewish community organizations in which the whole Jewish population of a city comes together; there are synagogues supported by their congregations and a multiplicity of Jewish groups and institutions. These usually administer jointly a common welfare fund produced by the numerous fund drives for local and foreign Jewish causes. Since this fund is the backbone of every communal organization, the big giver obviously plays a decisive role. While we must respect and recognize the generosity of many wealthy Jews who year in and year out contribute not only large sums of money but also much time and energy to fund drives, from the sociological point of view their predominant position in the structure of American Jewry is a disadvantage. It makes organization on a really large scale impossible.

Any organization representing all of American Jewry must, by its very nature, be democratic. The handful of big givers will never assent to this—and it is quite understandable from the human point of view that they should want recognition. The more numerous the separate organizations, the more easily every philanthropist can acquire his own little world in which to be a leader. The result is a harmful splintering of American Jewry, dissipation of energy and money, duplication of effort in many areas, and ultimately a serious lowering of achievement. Instead of fighting over differences in their programs, which would be understandable and creative, the organizations compete for prestige, jockeying for position for themselves and their leaders. This is what makes exaggerated advertising necessary. Dependent on voluntary contributions and fund raising, they must try to attract attention because they have to keep people aware of their importance. This makes long-range political planning incomparably more difficult. You need publicity; whether or not *The New York Times* will publish a report becomes a fundamental problem.

I remember a dinner of the New York Foreign Policy Association in honor of the first visit of Chancellor Adenauer, at which I sat next to Arthur Hays Sulzberger, owner and publisher of *The New York Times*. Although very much a Jew, Mr. Sulzberger was very restrained in Jewish matters, chiefly in order to protect the *Times*, with its great influence, from any charge of favoring Jewish interests, and he took this opportunity to justify the paper's reserve on Jewish questions. I replied: "Mr. Sulzberger, there is one way in which you could do American Jewish life a great service, and it might even be profitable for your paper too. Except for a few special cases, stop publishing all those statements by Jewish organizations and so-called leaders of American Jewry. This would do a great deal to improve the internal organization of Jewish life in America and to limit the publicity-seeking which accounts for so many of its activities." Unfortunately Sulzberger did not follow my advice, probably because of the many Jews who read his paper.

Another consequence of the multiplicity of organizations is the great bureaucratic apparatus it requires. A whole class of well-paid "professional Jews" has emerged. Since they can devote full time to their work, these officials are steadily gaining the upper hand in the direction of their organizations, even though they are usually not much in evidence from the outside. American Jewry faces the danger of becoming professionalized and bureaucratized, with all the moral and intellectual disadvantages such a process inevitably involves.

One of the consequences of this situation is the quite inadequate, not to say negligible, role the intellectual plays in Jewish life in the United States. The reason for this is certainly not a lack of intelligence among American Jews, who have produced as many scientists, thinkers, and artists as their European counterparts. In fact, they have certainly produced more on a percentage basis, since the higher level of education in America and the prosperity of American Jews permit far more of them to attend universities. The intellectual's lack of influence in Jewish life parallels a similar situation in American life as a whole. But in Jewish life this has a much more detrimental effect, since the Jewish people in the Diaspora lives primarily by its spiritual values and capacities, not by its economic or political power.

Recently, of course, American intellectuals have been acquiring more and more influence. Professors and university students, writers and poets, eminent journalists, play a growing and often vociferous role in American politics—often a role of outspoken criticism and opposition. In this respect Jewish life still lags behind the general trend in America. Except for a few intellectual rabbinical leaders, there are almost no influential figures who do not owe their position to financial contributions and fund-raising activities. How often have I reproached

American-Jewish intellectuals for their inadequate participation in Jewish life, only to hear the answer: I'm not a big giver; what part could I play? But the whole thing goes much further. The aloofness of tens and hundreds of thousands of intellectuals impoverishes Jewish life, makes it boring, shallow, and devoid of spiritual impetus.

Differences exist, to be sure, between the three religious movements, Orthodox, Conservative, and Reform, but by common consent they are glossed over rather than accented. The fight over Zionism, which used to divide American Jewish groups, has become meaningless, as the vast majority not only accept the State of Israel but admire and actively support it. Theoretically there is a controversy between Jewish isolationism and the idea of world Jewry, but it is hardly evident to the public eye. As a result, American Jewry lacks the stirring calls to conscience and the great ideas that might recapture idealistic Jewish youth as well as intellectuals. Finding Jewish life shallow, boring, and devoid of worthwhile challenge, youth turns to general problems. In the struggle for civil rights for Negroes, for moral and pacifist principles, in the fight against poverty, in the Peace Corps, and in world politics, young intellectual Jews are playing a leading role. Their preoccupation with non-Jewish causes is steadily becoming the central problem of American Jewry, although the influential figures of the establishment still have their eyes closed to this reality.

For all that, American Jewry has some highly estimable qualities. Most American Jews have retained a link with their origins even in the second and third generations, and, of course, the Nazi era strengthened their Jewish consciousness enormously. Besides having felt compassion for the tragic fate of their fellow Jews in Europe, they felt guilty because fate had made them affluent Americans. This compelled them to help the victims of Naziism, to make it possible for Israel to take them in and establish a Jewish state that would make such catastrophes impossible. In the last two decades no single minority in America has raised such fantastic sums as the Jews, but the consequence of this achievement is, again, overemphasis on philanthropy. It is no exaggeration to say that American Jewry as a whole still does not pursue Jewish politics based on ideologies. In times of crisis there is plenty of political action, but it is confined to *ad hoc* protests and demonstrations and even these are restrained by the fear of appearing to constitute a separate group.

Summing up, I would say that American Jewry represents an inexhaustible reservoir of Jewish consciousness and readiness to help, but that these are still attributes of a reserve army. Before it can really take over the leadership of world Jewry, some essential prerequisites must be provided: democratic organization, genuine leadership possessing an authority that hardly exists today, and internal discipline, for which most of its members are still quite unready. American Jewry still lacks a full awareness of its significance and its responsibility. It does not take its equality of civil status for granted but seems to live in fear that the miracle might vanish. It still waits for calls to action from outside and lives, as it were, in the anxious state of youthful uncertainty. With all its generosity, it takes its situation too lightly, unwilling to recognize that it holds in its hand the fate of the whole people and of Israel. With great amounts of money and, I am sure, intellectual reserves as well, it must face its task of giving form, shape, and direction to its still basically chaotic and undefined status and answer the call of modern Jewish history.

18

War Years in the United States

My work in the United States during the war concentrated on two vital needs: saving European Jews from destruction and solving the problem of Palestine, which was obviously going to come to a head when the war ended. Upon arrival I was asked by the Zionist Executive in Jerusalem and by American Zionist leaders to direct the Zionist Emergency Committee, an organization founded soon after war broke out in Europe to act on behalf of all American Zionist groups. Since I was the only member of the Jewish Agency Executive in America, it was natural that I should act as its American representative and also take charge of the Emergency Committee.

For the first weeks and months our most pressing concern was to rescue at least some of the prominent Jewish personalities who were still in France and endangered by the Nazi occupation. With considerable difficulty we persuaded the State Department to issue emergency visas that cut through red tape. In this way the WJC and other Jewish organizations, such as the American Jewish Labor Committee and the Joint Distribution Committee, were able to bring to the United States a number of Jews who had been in hiding in France. During these negotiations, as in later ones over the rescue—never in fact effected—of larger groups of European Jews, I discovered that sympathy and assistance were more readily available from statesmen, especially President Roosevelt and Under-Secretary of State Sumner

Welles, than from administrative officials made inflexible by bureaucratic routine and their own infinite indifference.

One detail of those feverish negotiations in Washington is worth mentioning. A number of Jews in France who had somehow succeeded in getting Mexican visas sailed for Mexico on the *S.S. Quenza*. When they arrived—in Tampico, if I remember rightly—the Mexican government declared that its consul had not been authorized to issue them visas and refused to admit them, ordering the ship to return. Of course, if they had landed in France these people would immediately have been deported by the Nazi authorities. I received desperate telegrams from the Central Jewish Committee in Mexico and from the individuals in question, asking me to do everything possible to have them admitted to the United States when the ship stopped to refuel at Norfolk, Virginia. At the request of Stephen Wise, Mrs. Franklin Roosevelt, deeply sympathetic and eager to help, spoke to the President, who informed us he was prepared to instruct the immigration authorities in Norfolk to admit these refugees without visas, provided we could persuade Secretary of State Cordell Hull, who was very conservative in such matters, not to oppose the move.

Dr. Wise and I went to see Secretary Hull to ask him to agree to the admission of these unfortunate souls. At first he took a strictly negative attitude, explaining that under American law no one may immigrate without a visa. When I pressed him relentlessly, he exclaimed: "Do you see that American flag behind my desk? I have sworn by it to uphold the Constitution and the laws of the United States. You are asking me to break my oath." I told Mr. Hull that I read in the newspaper about some anti-Nazi German seamen who had jumped ship rather than return to Germany. The Coast Guard had had to send out a cutter to pick them up and take them to Ellis Island, where all immigrants whose papers were not in order were held.

"If you like," I said, "I'll send the *Quenza* refugees a telegram, and I guarantee they'll jump overboard at Norfolk. Then the Coast Guard will have to send boats to pick them up. Some of them may catch pneumonia. In the end you'll have to do the same with them as you've done with the German seamen. I personally have nothing against the idea of these unfortunate people sitting out the war in safety on Ellis Island. But why do you want me to go about it in this devious, complicated, expensive, and insalubrious way?"

Hull gave me an angry look and said: "You are very cynical, Mr. Goldmann.

"I wonder who is more cynical," I replied, "the Secretary who wants to condemn hundreds of Jewish refugees to certain death, or he who tries everything to save them."

My argument seemed to impress him, because finally he said, in a grumbling tone: "Tell the President that if he issues the orders on his own authority I won't make any difficulties." The order was issued; the refugees were allowed to land at Norfolk, sent briefly to Ellis Island, and later legally admitted as immigrants.

Despite our efforts, only an infinitesimal number of Jews could be saved. All this time, but especially in 1942 and 1943, when it became clear that the Nazis would systematically exterminate the Jews—the first reports to this effect came from reliable German sources through the WJC representative in Geneva, Gerhart Riegner—I kept urging the Jewish organizations to negotiate with the Nazis and offer them large sums to ransom some of the Jews. Of course, this could not have been done without the consent of the American government, especially after America had declared war and all traffic with the enemy was prohibited. I took the view that American Jewry had a right to ask the government to make an exception in this case. Even if the Nazis made several million dollars on the deal, this would not affect the astronomical cost of their war effort. On the other hand, hundreds of thousands of human lives might be saved.

However, I failed in these efforts. The difficulty of finding countries to which these people could immigrate, Britain's refusal to admit large numbers of Jews to Palestine, the difficulty of finding shipping for refugees in wartime, and above all, a psychological reluctance to ask the American government to sanction something that was against the law and might somehow help the Nazis—all these dilemmas were so insoluble that the project had to be abandoned. I still feel sure that President Roosevelt would have been generous and humane enough to agree to it if it had been submitted to him in an appropriate form.

In 1943 we received a report that for a large sum of money the Rumanian Gestapo was prepared to let a number of Jews, mostly children, emigrate. We went to Secretary of the Treasury Henry Morgenthau Jr. to apply for a permit to transfer this money. Since President Roosevelt had no objections, Morgenthau readily assented. Unfortunately the State Department's permission was also required and negotiations with Cordell Hull and his staff took so long that by the time we finally got their reluctant consent, it was too late. In connection with this tragic episode I can only repeat what I have already said about the attitude of the Jewish leaders and organizations. They lacked the courage, vision, and resolution to risk a radical and drastic move. In all my years in Jewish politics I have never felt so impotent, so grimly bitter, as I did over this. All of us who spoke for the Jewish people in those days—and I emphatically include myself—bear a share of the guilt, some of us a heavy share, some a lighter one.

The extent of our responsibility was brought home to me poignantly one day early in 1943 by a desperate call for help sent over a clandestine radio transmitter. It came from the resistance committee in the Warsaw ghetto; it was addressed to Dr. Stephen Wise and myself and it urged American-Jewish leaders to take dramatic rescue measures. Why, asked the telegram, did not a dozen or so Jewish leaders sit on the steps of the White House or the State Department until the American government declared itself ready to take action to save Polish Jewry? This may sound naïve today, but I still believe, as I did then, that a desperate, unconventional gesture might have achieved something. Besides, in certain situations leaders have a moral duty to make quixotic gestures.

To go into all the details of our activities during the war years would take much too long. I was in constant touch with the State Department, where Sumner Welles showed understanding; but he could not do much to offset the bureaucracy, the indifference to the fate of European Jews, and the British

Mandatory's cruel policy of keeping Palestine more or less closed. We tried to keep in touch with the leaders of the Eastern European Jewish underground, and of course we exchanged intelligence with the governments-in-exile. The Jews of Eastern Europe were given some assistance, but it was a drop in the ocean, and in the long run it was ineffectual. The regular apparatus of Jewish charity was totally inadequate in this situation.

Worthwhile help could not be given until the war was over and Nazi power had been smashed. The Allies, and above all the United States, did a great deal for the liberation and relief of the Jews, especially in the early postwar period. Legislation made it possible to help destitute Jews and those in concentration camps and American Jewry backed up the legislation with fund drives and extremely generous contributions. But by this time it was merely a matter of rescuing the few hundred thousand survivors; the millions who had been destroyed were gone forever.

Parallel with these never-ending wartime attempts to save something from the holocaust ran my Zionist work, which was essentially of a preparatory nature. If Palestine could be saved from a Nazi invasion, a new plan for its future would have to be worked out within the over-all design of postwar international politics. It was American Zionism's task to offer the Palestinian Jewish community, the *yishuv*, all possible help and support in the coming decisive struggle and to prepare influential American groups to take a pro-Zionist stand when the war was over. Since there was no telling how long the war would last, it was important to begin preliminary approaches to the government and the U.S. Congress as soon as possible. As head of the Zionist Emergency Committee, I was responsible for the preparation and day-to-day execution of this agenda. I used to spend half the week in Washington, and here Dr. Wise was indispensable; his authoritative status among Jews and gentiles paved the way for me and opened all doors. He himself maintained our contact with President Roosevelt, with whom he had been collaborating for many years.

It is my impression that the President, whose attitude to Zionism has been the subject of much recent debate, was not actually pro-Zionist. His approach to Jewish problems was primarily humanitarian. A real humanitarian and a man of genuine good will, with an instinctive sympathy for the persecuted, Roosevelt was deeply affected by the Jewish tragedy in Europe and ready to help save Jewish lives, particularly to prevent a repetition of such bestiality. He was chiefly interested in Palestine from this point of view, and we could therefore count on his help in getting British immigration policy liberalized. Here his deep convictions led him to repudiate Britain's restrictive policy. But with regard to purely political Zionist questions and the creation of a Jewish state, he was inclined to be reserved.

There can be no doubt that the inflexible resistance of the Arabs, as he encountered it in his well-known conversation with King Ibn Saud of Arabia during his return from Yalta, made a deep impression on him. Hence, it is difficult to say what his position would have been during the final phases of the struggle for the Jewish state. I am not sure whether he would have taken such an unequivocally political line as his successor, President Truman, did. After his talk with Ibn Saud, he was always very dubious of the ability of a Jewish state to survive in the face of Arab hostility. Perhaps we could have changed his mind, but this we shall never know. In the war years, when we were concerned with immigration and the creation of a Jewish brigade rather than a sovereign state, we could usually count on his sympathy and often on his willingness to give active support to our requests.

In the State Department, which bore the major responsibility for American policy in Palestine, the situation was much more difficult. The only high State Department official who had an understanding of the Zionist concept was Sumner Welles. As I have indicated before, of all those members of the department with whom I dealt for fourteen years, Welles impressed me most as a truly internationally minded man, an aristocrat and a gentleman with the courage to be decisive. In my opinion his early resignation from government service was a great loss to American diplomacy and over the years I have often had reason to regret it. The other officials with whom I conferred about Zionist problems and questions of general Jewish interest were much less open-minded.

What I have already said about America in general also applies to its diplomacy. The rapidity of the United States' advance to the position of a leading world power after the First World War had many injurious consequences. A provincial America was suddenly called upon to make decisions on universal political problems without having acquired, through experience, an instinctive sense of direction. But lack of familiarity with the world's problems is not America's only handicap; it also suffers from a fear of making decisions and a tendency to pass the buck and hide behind bureaucratic routine. The result is the accumulation of reports, data, memoranda, and blueprints and a terrible rigidity and duplication of procedure. What we wanted to do in Palestine was something revolutionary, quite outside normal diplomatic routine. It is easy to understand why the average State Department official did not support our efforts with alacrity.

I once complained to Sumner Welles about the attitude of some American officials in the Near East, saying that they nearly always followed the line of their British colleagues blindly. He replied: "Don't forget that our officers come from backgrounds where they probably never even heard of the existence of these countries before they began their State Department training. You take a typical Middle Westerner and make him American minister in an Arab capital where his British counterpart has been more or less at home for centuries. Is it surprising that he unconsciously acknowledges the Englishman's superiority and regards him as an authority?"

Again, State Department officials are naturally influenced by embassy reports, six or seven of which reflect the Arab standpoint, while one at most—and that only since Israel has existed—gives the Jewish point of view. This does not exactly promote a friendly attitude toward the Jews. The whole thing is further complicated by the fact that the Zionists carry a lot of weight in American domestic politics and, like all other groups, quite properly use their position in that great democracy to influence their government. Anti-Zionists may complain, but that is the way the game is played in the United States and it is not fair to single out Zionist pressure for censure. Democracy consists of a multiplicity of pressure-exerting forces, each of which is trying to make itself felt. Diplomatic officials abroad, however, do not like to have their plans disrupted by domestic considerations, by protests and delegations or by intervention on the part of political parties or even the White House. This makes them resentful and bitter, so that in exerting political pressure at home, one must always be cautious and tactful or risk incurring the hostility of influential diplomatic figures. I had many differences of opinion wih Zionist colleagues, particularly in the postwar years, when the great question of the partition of Palestine was being fought out in America, because I was against using excessively drastic tactics in American home politics and always stressed the importance of maintaining correct or, if possible, friendly personal relations with State Department officers. Anyone who has not had years of practical political experience usually fails to realize what a difference the personal attitude of an official in a foreign ministry can make.

When one thinks of the tremendous scope and ever growing ramifications of foreign policy, it is naïve to assume that every high official is fully informed on something that may be a mere detail in the total picture. One should not be too ready to run to the foreign minister or to the president himself with complaints. In practice the decision is often actually made by the man who writes the reports, assembles the data, and submits the proposals. For this reason I have never been in favor of attacking unfriendly officials personally, as Jews unfortunately are sometimes inclined to do. This is what I call the "Haman syndrome." They blame everything they don't like on a villain, whereas in reality even the worst villain is only a spokesman for factors, forces, and tendencies. From the propaganda standpoint it is always tempting to pick out a culprit and direct all your protests at him, but this is usually unfair to the man in question and in any case it has the negative effect of forcing him into an increasingly hostile position.

Of all the personalities of American Jewry with whom I was in constant touch then and later the first I want to write about is Louis Brandeis. An outstanding jurist and eminent member of the Supreme Court, a pioneer fighter against economic and political privilege in any form, a close friend of Woodrow Wilson and, later, of President Roosevelt, Brandeis was a great figure in American life long before he had anything to do with Jewish affairs. Converted to Zionism by Jakob de Haas, secretary-general of the then quite insignificant Zionist Organization of America, he remained faithful to the idea even after the clash with Weizmann following the First World War—a chapter of Zionist history with which I had absolutely nothing to do.

When I began my work in America, Brandeis was no longer very active in Zionism, partly because of his Supreme Court position, partly because of his advanced age. Nonetheless, he remained the most important figure in American Zionism of his time. If he had not been so prominent and famous, he might have been one of those thirty-six unknown just men on whom, according to the well-known Jewish legend, the world's moral welfare depends. Although he was wealthy, he lived simply and modestly and despised fuss and ostentation. The moment one came face to face with him, one felt the moral strength his personality radiated. He had a way of paring down every question to its essentials. When the first news of the extermination of the Jews in the concentration camps reached us, he said to me: "Now we don't need to make a case for Zionism any more. Hitler has proved that a Jewish homeland is necessary and the Jews in Palestine have proved that it is possible"—one of the briefest and most striking formulations of Zionism ever made. His closer friends, particularly Stephen Wise, who considered himself his pupil, never undertook anything without asking his advice.

Brandeis occupies a major place in the Pantheon of Zionist leaders. If it had not been for his influence on Wilson, who in turn influenced the British government, the Balfour Declaration would probably never have been issued. And it is he who deserves the major credit for the essentially pro-Zionist policy of the American administrations of Roosevelt and Truman.

Of similar background but very different in personality was Viennese-born Felix Frankfurter, who was appointed to the Supreme Court after a brilliant career as professor of law at Harvard. A convinced Zionist from his early days, Frankfurter had made his name chiefly through his efforts to promote Arab-Jewish understanding during the negotiations in 1919 between Weizmann and Emir Faisal. Unlike Brandeis, Frankfurter was not a puritan or a moralist, and the range of his education and interests was much wider. A brilliant stylist and a connoisseur of many literatures, open-minded to intellectual trends of all kinds, sparkling in conversation, and a man of unusual charm, he knew most of the eminent personalities of his time, was a close friend of many of them, and was active in many areas of American public life. Through his recommendation, many of his students had attained important positions in the Roosevelt administration, and since he was very close to Roosevelt, Frankfurter was for years one of the most influential men in Washington. He was a friend of Stephen Wise, and along with Justice Julian Mack, they belonged to the Brandeis inner circle.

Wise arranged for me to meet Frankfurter, and from then on I saw him regularly two or three times a month in Washington, where I kept a small apartment during the war. His advice and assistance were invaluable to me. Frankfurter was a great political tactician, and above all he understood the psychology of the capital's prominent personalities. He was a mediator by nature rather than a fighter. In my conflict with the more extreme wing of American Zionism, led by Rabbi Abba Hillel Silver, he was firmly on my side. When the controversy between Silver and me was fought out at the first Jerusalem congress after the creation of the State of Israel, he sent a telegram to Weizmann, saying that "if Zionism went off the Gold and on the Silver standard" he was through with it. A talk with Frankfurter was an intellectual and esthetic pleasure. He would make the same brilliant formulations he made in his writing, and since his interests were so diversified, his conversation ranged over a multitude of problems and subjects. Although he was not active in Zionism except during the First World War and the Versailles peace talks, on occasion he exerted an influence that should not be underestimated. His friendship was of inestimable value to me in my work in Washington—a world I entered as a complete stranger—and a source of perpetually self-renewing enrichment.

During the war, and more especially the postwar years, I also had many dealings with Henry Morgenthau Jr., Secretary of the Treasury under Roosevelt. I came to know this shy man only gradually. His father, American ambassador to Istanbul during the First World War, had been one of the leading Jewish personalities of America, but he himself had held aloof from Jewish affairs until the Second World War. It was the impact of Hitler's atrocities that brought him to Judaism. He helped wherever he could, and having personal access to Roosevelt, he was able to do a great deal. When the war ended and he resigned his cabinet post, Morgenthau became one of the leading supporters of the young State of Israel. He brought to his chairmanship of the United Jewish Appeal (UJA) all the authority of his family and his political position and carried out his duties with the utmost dedication.

When Morgenthau became involved in a conflict with Rabbi Silver, who was attacking the Roosevelt administration for a lack of active support for Zionism, I led the campaign to keep him on the UJA and became very close to him. My task during those months was not easy. Often his supporters were not willing to accept my tactics and urged more extreme ones, but he always instructed them to follow my proposals unquestioningly, and he was grateful when I secured his re-election. But for all his interest in Israel and his Jewish loyalty, Morgenthau remained an outsider in Jewish affairs, which were often too complicated for him. Once he asked me to explain a complex transaction of the Israeli government and when I had finished he said: "Tell Mr. Ben-Gurion that I could never be Finance Minister of Israel."

Louis Lipsky was a Zionist leader of quite different background and social position. For years he was the great opponent of the Brandeis-Wise group and an unconditional supporter of Weizmann. After the latter's victory over the Brandeis group he became president of the ZOA and one of the foremost leaders of American Zionism. By nature and disposition Lipsky was an artist and writer rather than a politician. He began his career as a dramatist and probably sacrificed a very successful career in the theater. He possessed a great talent for organization and apart from his activity in Zionist affairs was a leader of the

American Jewish Conference, an organization created during the war. This organizational talent was an unusual offshoot of his artistic gifts; he could not stand chaos; his esthetic sense demanded order, co-ordination, and teamwork. He liked to build up an organization as a great dramatist constructs a play. His supporters were wholeheartedly devoted to him and he himself showed a high degree of loyalty to the leaders he recognized, such as Weizmann, and to friends, associates and co-workers. He played a decisive part in shaping American Zionism and preventing it from becoming too antithetical to its European counterpart, as it might easily have done to the detriment of the movement as a whole.

Lipsky was active in many areas of American Jewish life, as president of the American Jewish Congress, as spokesman for the American Jewish Conference, and as a long-standing member of the world Zionist Executive. To me he was for many years friend, colleague, and indispensable co-worker. He retained his unusual intellectual liveliness until his old age, and I would like to repeat here a tribute I paid to him on his eightieth birthday: "To grow old is a blessing, but to grow old and remain mentally young like Lipsky is a virtue. It is the result of a wise way of life and the creative use of the gifts with which one is endowed."

Among my early helpers and personal friends in America was Meyer Weisgal, one of the most colorful and striking figures in Jewish life of recent decades. A journalist by profession and a passionate Zionist since his youth, he, along with Louis Lipsky, dedicated many years of his life to the ZOA. Soon, however, he too came under the influence of Chaim Weizmann. This affected his whole life and he became Weizmann's closest associate in personal, though not in political, matters. The project nearest to Weisgal's heart was the development of the Weizmann Institute in Rehovot, of which he is now president. Without his boundless dynamism and his extraordinary ability to charm or terrorize donors and to influence people, the Weizmann Institute, one of the jewels of modern Israel, could never have been established. More endearing than all the characteristics that equipped him for such a successful career in public life are his human qualities of unfailing helpfulness and loyalty to his friends. During my years in the United States he helped me on many occasions, especially in preparing the historic Biltmore Conference in 1942. His closeness to Weizmann and my agreement with the main lines of Weizmann's policy formed a sound basis for our co-operation.

I can make only brief mention of three other important leaders. Rabbi Solomon Goldman, for years one of the most forceful and original minds in American Jewry, was the man who, as president of the ZOA, insisted when war broke out that I come to America without delay. In Goldman qualities of intellectual and political leadership were combined in a way that is unfortunately very rare. The final phase of the struggle for the Jewish state was deprived of his support by his early death, but in the first few years of my work in America he was a valuable friend to me.

Later Herman Schulman became my tireless helper, especially in my political work for the Zionist Emergency Committee. Schulman had no liking for the limelight, but he was a most sympathetic, loyal co-worker behind the scenes and later in a top elective position as temporary president of the Zionist Council executive. In the controversy over our tactics in Washington, when I opposed Rabbi Silver's violent attacks on the Democratic administration, and in my conflict with Rabbi Silver (which to some extent grew out of this controversy), Schulman was entirely on my side. Despite failing health, he devoted all his time and energy to the Jewish cause and through his early death became, like so many others, a victim of unremitting work for Zionism.

Finally a word about Robert Szold, one of the oldest Zionists in America. As a former president of the ZOA, he was a member of the inner circle of the Brandeis group. Although he took an active part in matters of foreign policy, particularly during the war, and sometimes accompanied me to interviews at the State Department, his main interest was the economic development of Palestine, and he became one of the most important figures in the Palestine Economic Corporation. Like Schulman, Szold did not like public polemics and factional fighting, although he had very clear-cut, firm convictions in all Zionist controversies. A gentleman of incorruptible objectivity, with a strong sense of justice, he was not the type to be popular with the masses, but among the top Zionist leaders he was very highly regarded, even more highly in Palestine than in the United States. I collaborated with him for many years, as long as he remained in politics, and we never had any disagreements.

Two more Jewish personalities who have given me valuable support in my work in the United States also deserve mention. The first is Sam Bronfman, one of the most successful Jewish financiers and industrialists of my generation, whose wealth and eminent social position in Canada have never detracted from his interest in all Jewish questions. President of the Canadian Jewish Congress for many years, Bronfman is also one of the leading figures in the World Jewish Congress, of which he is vice-president. Our close relationship in practical affairs is reinforced by our personal friendship.

A man of a very different type is Philip Klutznick, an American Jewish leader of great political understanding and unusual tactical skill. A friend of Adlai Stevenson, Klutznick has been active in American political life and served as the United States ambassador to the United Nations. At the same time, he has maintained a great interest in the problems of Israel and world Jewry, a concern which his presidency of the B'nai B'rith bespeaks. Klutznick's help was invaluable to me in my attempts to unite American Jewry through the Conference of Presidents of Major American Jewish Organizations and the creation of the Conference of Jewish Organizations (COJO). He is remarkable for his broadminded approach to Jewish problems, an approach which is the antithesis of provincial and which never loses sight of the world context—something that unfortunately cannot be said of the attitude of all American Jewish leaders.

In conclusion I must say a few words about one of the leading non-Zionists, Edward M. M. Warburg, for many years president of the Joint Distribution Committee and the UJA. I worked closely with Warburg for many years, during which I learned to esteem him not only because of his eminent position in American Jewish life and as an important colleague but as a man with few equals. A member of the Warburg family that has been prominent in international banking for decades and has attained high status in Germany and America, a son of Felix Warburg, with whom Weizmann established the enlarged Jewish Agency, Edward Warburg has for years taken an active interest in Jewish philanthropy and in Palestine and Israel. For him a position of leadership in Jewish life was not, as it was for many American Jews, a substitute for complete acceptance by American society, nor was it a way of attaining publicity and prestige. Any career in America was open to Warburg. His loyalty to everything Jewish and his almost daily activity in the positions he held stemmed from his desire to help and his deeply felt obligation to continue his family's tradition. Unfortunately in this respect he is the last of his kind. Warburg is a true aristocrat and, as I have often told him, one of the few great gentlemen of the Jewish Establishment—modest, uninterested in publicity, a man who does more than he promises and hates fine talk for its own sake. While he is inwardly strongly critical of the weaknesses of American Jewry and of Israel, he does not let this affect his loyalty or his fulfillment of the tasks he has assumed. American Jewry would be much richer if it had more figures like Warburg at its head. To discuss current problems with him was always a satisfaction and a pleasure to me and I was frequently struck by his unusual sense of humor, which has nothing sharp or caustic about it but reveals a profound knowledge of mankind.

What we achieved we owe to the co-operation of these and many other figures in American Zionism, not all of whom can be mentioned here. It is not easy for a European Jew to acquire influence within American Jewry and only a few of those who came to America during the Hitler era managed it. If I achieved some success, this is partly attributable to the fact that through my adaptability I was able to gain the confidence of several American leaders, notably Stephen Wise and Felix Frankfurter. From them I learned to understand the American Jews, unique in the history of our people, and although I never really became one of them, I learned to assume a stance that helped involve American Jewry in the great problems of my generation.

19

Preparing for the
Postwar Era

The news streaming in about the Jewish catastrophe in Europe
made it increasingly clear what tasks Jewish leadership would
have to face when the war ended. The more obvious it became
that the bulk of European Jewry was irretrievably lost, the
more necessary it was to draw the conclusions from this tragedy
and create a basis for the continued existence of the Jewish
people after the Allied victory, that had been beyond question
since 1943 or 1944. This work had two goals. One was to rehabilitate the European survivors and obtain restitution from
Germany, the other to seek a definitive solution to the problem
of Palestine.

Discussion of the first problem was carried on mainly within
the World Jewish Congress. In addition to Dr. Wise and the
leaders of the American Jewish Congress, we managed to enlist
a number of European Jewish leaders to participate in the direction of the WJC, which had been transferred from Geneva to
New York at the beginning of the war. Through bold ideas that
were revolutionary in human as well as Jewish terms this group
rendered services of enduring value, and I want to mention a
few of its members by name. Jacob Robinson and his brother
Nehemiah Robinson combined great originality of mind with
singular legal knowledge. Leon Kubovitzky, secretary-general
of the WJC and formerly one of the leaders of Belgian Jewry,
was a most dynamic man with a thoroughgoing knowledge of
European Jewish affairs. He later became Israeli ambassador to

Prague and then Buenos Aires and, after he left the diplomatic service, director of Yad Vashem, the Jerusalem institution dedicated to the study of the Jewish tragedy during the Nazi era. With them were associated other Jewish politicians and scholars, including Arieh Tartakower and later Isidor Schwarzbart, who shared their conviction that the conventional prewar methods of Jewish politics had become inadequate for solving postwar problems.

Among their early co-workers I can mention only a few names: Rabbi Maurice Perlzweig, head of the WJC's division for international questions and for many years its most authoritative representative at the United Nations; Noah Barou, a Russian Jewish idealist whose role in paving the way for negotiations with the German Federal Republic I shall deal with later; Dr. F. R. Bienenfeld, an eminent Austrian lawyer whose special field was the League of Nations and the United Nations commissions concerned with human rights; and the Marchioness of Reading, Sir Alfred Mond's daughter and the daughter-in-law of Lord Reading, who showed great skill in political work and was for years a leading member of the board of the WJC. In England the Labour Member of Parliament, Sydney Silverman, rendered inestimable help, thanks to his temperament and incomparable courage and to his moral authority in Parliament and government circles, while the political flair of Alex Easterman, a gifted English journalist who for years has devoted himself wholeheartedly to the WJC, was, and still is, a valuable asset.

The WJC established the Institute of Jewish Affairs where the groundwork was laid for two main objectives: ensuring that the Nazi criminals did not escape punishment and obtaining maximum restitution from a defeated Germany. It was in this institute that the idea of punishing Nazi war criminals was first conceived, an idea later taken up by some great American jurists, notably Justice Robert H. Jackson of the Supreme Court, and implemented in the Nuremberg Trials. The idea of prosecuting and sentencing political and military leaders for crimes against humanity was completely new in international justice. Many jurists unable to see beyond the concepts of conventional jurisprudence were dubious or categorically opposed it; also, the principle that one cannot be punished for a crime not prohibited by law at the time it is committed and that subordinates cannot be penalized for carrying out the orders of their superiors seemed to argue against it. But these arguments were outweighed by the importance of exacting retribution for the Nazi regime's monstrous crimes against Jews and gentiles. The precedents had to be established that national sovereignty is no defense against infringements of the most basic principles of humanity, and obedience to a superior is not a valid excuse for individual and mass crimes. From this point of view the Nuremberg Trials were a momentous event in the history of international justice and morality. Not only did they prove their worth in bringing the top Nazi criminals to justice; they also served as an effective warning and deterrent for the future. Under the direction of Jacob and Nehemiah Robinson the WJC put great effort into the intellectual and moral groundwork for these trials, and it is one of the triumphs of the Roosevelt administration that it consistently accepted these principles despite all the misgivings of some influential Allied circles, particularly in England.

Important as it was from the moral and international standpoint to convict the guilty, obviously this alone was not going to save the survivors of European Jewry. No less important than the principle of punishment was the prompt proclamation and establishment of the principle of restitution, and not to the Jews alone. This too was something completely new and almost revolutionary. The idea that conquered states should pay tribute to their conquerors is as old as war itself, but that a so-called sovereign state should be forced to compensate an unorganized minority was a revolutionary idea. That the WJC was the first to come forward with this proposal is one of its enduring achievements.

Two principles of compensation were involved. One applied to every individual whose family had been destroyed or robbed of its property. The other was the principle of collective restitution to the Jewish community—something unprecedented in world history as well as in the history of the Jews. When my friends and I first came out with this compound proposal, the usual response to it was an ironic smile, but events proved that what had at first been called a utopian fantasy could be put into practice on both the individual and the collective levels. The measures taken by the Allies and later legislation by Germany, culminating in the Luxembourg Agreement between the German Federal Republic and Israel, as well as with the Conference on Jewish Material Claims against Germany, transformed it into reality.

This was one aspect of our Jewish demands; another was the necessity, in the light of the catastrophe we had suffered, of guaranteeing the rights of Jews in all European countries and preventing future attempts to rescind them. It quickly became clear that the conventional formulations, as they had evolved after the First World War, needed radical revision. After that war Jewish demands, apart from civil rights in general, were limited to the proclamation and guarantee of their minority rights in Eastern Europe. After the Second World War, it was more than doubtful that a demand for Jewish minority rights had any point, since a minimum numerical strength is an obvious prerequisite for specific minority status for any group. Whether it was even worth talking about such legislation for the minute numbers of the Jews that had survived was a question that would have to be examined in the light of postwar realities. Unfortunately the reality more than justified the doubts. The Jews who had survived in Poland, Czechoslovakia, Hungary, and Rumania were not large enough in number to substantiate a claim to minority status. Besides, the establishment of Communist regimes in those countries made the enforcement of minority rights and international guarantees impracticable. Unhappily this item in the program of Jewish demands had become obsolete.

On the other hand, clauses safeguarding the Jews' equality of rights were almost automatically embodied in all constitutions and peace treaties after the Second World War. But in this postwar world a system of international guarantees had little chance of success. Here, as in the protection of minorities, the situation had gravely deteriorated. Rights of surveillance, such as the League of Nations enjoyed to some degree, are not accorded to the United Nations. In view of this general trend, which even the most vigorous demands and protests were not able to halt, it became increasingly clear that Jewish politics must concentrate on alleviating the aftereffects of the Nazi holocaust and providing a means of existence for the tragic remnant of European Jewry. For this reason, practical considerations of compensation and restitution became more pressing than the theoretical program of equality of rights.

The first thing to do was to win over public opinion and the governments concerned. Jewish public opinion was roused chiefly at two conferences called by the WJC: the Pan-American Conference that took place in November, 1941, in Baltimore, and the War Emergency Conference held in November, 1944, in Atlantic City. Jewish delegates from every state took part in the Baltimore meeting and the later one was also attended by representatives of European Jewry. Within American Jewry our program was impressively sponsored by the American Jewish Assembly. It was first submitted in conversations and memoranda to the top men in American government, and I can say today with great satisfaction that the responsible authorities involved accepted these concepts, novel and daring as they were, with little hesitation.

The Palestine question weighed equally heavily on my friends and myself. As the only representative of the Jewish Agency Executive in America and as head of the Zionist Emergency Committee, I was constantly involved with this problem. During the war it was primarily a matter of doing everything possible to enable the Jewish population of Palestine to survive, but the *yishuv* also wanted a chance to contribute to the war effort. We in America could do little about the first problem. There were many moments, particularly during the battle of El Alamein, when we were all haunted by the fear that the Nazis might successfully invade Palestine, which would certainly have meant the destruction of its Jewish population. That Hitler held back, against the urgent recommendations of his generals, must be reckoned a stroke of luck for the Jewish people in those tragic times.

From the very beginning of the war, the leaders of the Jewish Agency in Palestine had been trying to make it possible for the Palestinian Jews to participate in the fight. This could only be done on a voluntary basis, since the provisions of the mandate prohibited military conscription. The British authorities might have been expected to support these efforts with enthusiasm, but in fact the opposite was the case. The reason for this reserved attitude on the part of the mandatory authorities was their fear of augmented Zionist demands after the war—a fear that increased when the Jewish leaders insisted that the Palestinian volunteers be assigned to separate units, that is, to a kind of Jewish legion. A long political battle was fought over the formation of this unit; finally, after Churchill's personal intervention, a positive decision was reached, and the Jewish Brigade was formed. In my search for support among American statesmen I had met widespread sympathy, but, of course, the decision always rested with the British government.

It goes without saying that our efforts to get European Jews out of countries conquered or threatened by the Nazis and into Palestine never ceased. In a few cases they bore fruit, but we could not achieve much. The most exciting episode was the 1944 mission of Joel Brand, a Hungarian Zionist the Nazi authorities had sent to Constantinople with a proposal whereby a large number of Hungarian Jews—100,000 or more—would be allowed to emigrate in return for the delivery of 10,000 trucks. One day I was urgently summoned by Secretary of State Stettinius who, under the seal of absolute secrecy, read me a telegram from the American embassy in Turkey, informing him of Joel Brand's mission. Stettinius did not want me to confer with my colleagues but merely asked for my opinion. Although I strongly doubted that the Allies would accept the terms—despite the fact that, in view of the imminent collapse of Germany in the occupied countries, the trucks would not have been of any significant help to the Nazis—I unhesitatingly approved the transaction, for it was in line with the Allies' moral duty to save the Jews. The British authorities took an absolutely negative attitude from the outset, not only because they refused to give the German war effort such a boost but also because they were afraid of the Arab reaction. Further negotiations were left in the hands of Chaim Weizmann, Moshe Schertok and other members of the Zionist Executive in Jerusalem and London. As we all know, nothing came of these, and even this faint hope—assuming that the Nazi proposal was meant seriously—flickered out.

In Zionist politics too the main task was to prepare for the postwar period. Up to now I had been among those who went along with Weizmann in opposing any official demand for a Jewish state. This, of course, was a matter of practical politics, not principle. As long as there was no realistic prospect of attaining a Jewish state in Palestine, if only for the simple reason that we were outnumbered by the Arabs, it would have been harmful to issue such a demand. In principle, of course, I had always been convinced that a sovereign state in Palestine was the only possible solution and that it was just a matter of waiting for the right moment to make the demand. When the British government had suggested partition in 1937, I had strongly favored it, and I still feel that the tardy decision by the Zurich congress was an irredeemable mistake. The massacre of the Jews made me more certain than ever that after the war we would have to come out with a demand for a Jewish state. Of course the great obstacle was that we were still a minority in Palestine. I never doubted for a moment that our demand would have to be based on the premise of a divided Palestine, though I shared the opinion of like-minded friends that it would be tactically inadvisable for us to propose partition. Therefore we began to prepare public opinion for the idea of a Jewish state or, in the more flexible phrase we used in America, a Jewish commonwealth.

The first move was to win over the Zionist movement, and after lengthy preliminaries this was done at the Biltmore Hotel Conference held in New York on May 9, 1942. Besides the American Zionist leaders, Chaim Weizmann and David Ben-Gurion were present. Here the Biltmore Program, with its demand for a Jewish state, was worked out. Constitutionally, the Biltmore Conference lacked the authority to make such a decision binding, but it was impossible to convene a regular Zionist congress in wartime, and since the platform was quickly ratified by all branches of the movement, it acquired the validity of a congressional resolution.

After this step forward it was necessary to get the support of non-Zionist Jews. Here our first move was to initiate talks, in the winter of 1941–1942, with the American Jewish Committee, the most representative organization of American non-Zionists. In the beginning we got a favorable reaction from a number of its leaders, especially the chairman, Maurice Wertheim, but at the last minute Judge Joseph M. Proskauer and others formed an opposition group within the Committee, with the result that Wertheim resigned and Proskauer assumed the chairmanship. The fact that Judge Proskauer later changed his attitude did not help us at the time.

After this failure, Dr. Weizmann, Stephen Wise, Louis Lipsky, and I conceived the idea of convening a democratically elected conference of all American Jews, where the chances that a large majority would vote for a Jewish state were much better. Such a broadly based assembly representing American Jewry would also serve a very useful purpose in formulating postwar demands concerning restitution, compensation, and Jewish rights all over the world. Given the proliferation of American Jewish organizations and the lack of any body that could claim to represent all of them, it was necessary to find a conspicuously non-Zionist personality to head it. The selection of the dynamic young president of the B'nai B'rith, Henry Monsky, proved a fortunate one.

Monsky, who combined a superb tactical instinct with fighting spirit, took to the idea with alacrity and invited representatives of all the most important Jewish organizations in America to a conference in Pittsburgh on January 23, 1943. I represented the Jewish Agency Executive, and at this preliminary conference we managed to get a motion passed that a representative conference of American Jews be convened, consisting of both appointed and democratically elected delegates of constituent organizations. Nearly all the Jewish organizations in America responded to this call. We had difficulties with the American Jewish Committee, which was—and still is—opposed in principle to any over-all Jewish representation and still refuses to recognize majority decisions of such conferences as binding. It took months of hard work to organize the elections for this American Jewish Conference, but in the end even the American Jewish Committee was persuaded to participate.

On August 29, 1943, the conference was opened in New York, and the first session turned out to be one of the most impressive demonstrations ever organized by American Jewry. As far as our demands in Europe were concerned, there was little difference of opinion, but the question of the Jewish state aroused violent controversy. I reported on the Palestine problem and voiced the demand for a Jewish commonwealth. Debate then centered on it. After an emotional debate, in which Abba Hillel Silver made one of his most effective speeches, the idea of the Jewish commonwealth was accepted by an overwhelming majority over the opposition of the American Jewish Committee and a few other delegates. American Jewry, the most influential Jewish community in the world, had gone on record in favor of a Jewish state.

The American Jewish Conference then proceeded to set up machinery for promulgating this demand, as well as Jewish postwar claims in general. Here it worked in constant collaboration with the WJC and the Jewish Agency and during the next few years was extremely successful in implementing both sections of the Jewish postwar program. The later withdrawal of the American Jewish Committee did little to diminish the impact of the Conference, whose voluntary dissolution after a few years was a mistake of historic dimensions. It meant the abandoning of the first attempt ever made to organize American Jewry as a whole.

All this time I was also participating in efforts to organize world Jewry more effectively, and especially to establish links with the Jews of Soviet Russia. Since Russia was an ally, there seemed to be some prospect that this could be done. In the absence of any other organization, the WJC got in touch with the Soviet Russian Committee of Jewish Artists and Writers, at first in connection with the search for relatives of Jews who had fled from Poland and other countries. In 1943 a Russian delegation finally visited America. I managed to convince the State

Department of the value of such an exchange and procured the necessary visas, and the delegation spent June and July in the United States. It was led by the famous Jewish actor Shlomo Michoels and the poet Itzik Pfeffer, and the visit led to resounding declarations of solidarity between American and Russian Jewry. An enthusiastic audience of over 100,000 attended its first reception at Yankee Stadium in New York, where I spoke. I had high hopes that this event would help to bring Russian Jewry back into contact with world Jewry and thus halt the process of assimilation that was threatening the existence of Russia's more than three million Jews. With this in mind, I kept in constant touch with the representatives of the Soviet Union in America, including Maxim Litvinov, the Russian ambassador in Washington, his successor Konstantin Oumansky, and later Andrei Gromyko. Of course, all these expectations were blighted when the postwar era, far from bringing co-operation between the Soviet Union and the Western powers, brought growing estrangement and the cold war.

Once Jewish public opinion had been persuaded to endorse the demand for a Jewish state, influence had to be brought to bear on the American government, although obviously at this point it could not commit itself to such a far-reaching measure, especially since the decision on this question rested with its British ally. Nevertheless, in talks with the State Department we tried to pave the way for its endorsement, and the fact that I was able, without too much difficulty, to induce the American government to accept a partition plan in 1946 is mainly attributable to the preliminary work of the years 1943–1945.

All this work was important in creating the apparatus for radically changing the situation of the Jews when the war ended. By 1943 even the worst skeptics and pessimists were beginning to realize that however long the war might last and however many victims it might still devour, an Allied victory was assured. We were kept going by the hope that it would all end soon, so that at least some of the European Jews might be saved and the Palestine *yishuv* might escape. On the *yishuv* depended all possibility of writing a new chapter in Jewish history.

20

The Partition Plan

With the end of the world war the problem of Palestine entered a very acute phase. Relations with the British had been strained even during the last years of the war, but so long as the war lasted the Jewish Agency avoided open conflict with Britain at any price. The "White Paper policy" formulated in 1939, which practically kept a stranglehold on immigration and colonization, was rigorously enforced by the British government, and this put the Jewish Agency in the difficult position of co-operating with Britain while at the same time rejecting the White Paper. As David Ben-Gurion neatly expressed it, Palestinian Jewry fought on Britain's side against the Nazis as if there had been no White Paper and against the White Paper as if there had been no war.

After the defeat of the Nazis, when the number of Jews surviving in the occupied countries could be estimated, it was immediately obvious that a maintenance of the *status quo* in Palestine was bound to lead to bitter conflict. There were more than a half-million Jewish survivors of Naziism in concentration camps in Germany, Austria, and Italy. The Allies, and the United States in particular, gave a great deal of direct aid to these survivors, notably through the establishment of the U.N. Relief and Rehabilitation Administration, but it was clear that the only possible solution to the refugee problem was large-scale emigration. In the light of past experience it was no less clear that most of the people in these camps would not be able to go anywhere but Palestine. There were simply no other countries ready to accept hundreds of thousands of Jewish refugees, and in any case the great majority of them ardently wished to go to

Palestine. The British government, which had allowed itself to be forced more and more into a policy of consideration for the Arabs, was unwilling to recognize this elementary fact. It continued to restrict immigration, so that the Jewish Agency found itself compelled to agree to a plan for taking these refugees to Palestine without the permission of Britain. This grew into the large-scale Aliyah Beth, or second immigration movement, that brought thousands of refugees into the country in defiance of the British authorities.

Of course there were physical clashes. Terrorist groups emerged advocating open war against the British because this seemed the only possibility of ending the mandatory regime. The Jewish Agency tried to some extent to stop the terrorism, but it could not passively accept the White Paper policy either. Extreme differences of opinion developed within the Zionist Executive over methods of resisting British policy, and these came to a dramatic climax in a conflict between its two leading personalities, Chaim Weizmann and David Ben-Gurion. The former firmly rejected all terrorist or activist resistance and continued to hope for an understanding with the British government. Ben-Gurion was equally against terrorism, but he tacitly supported a policy of active resistance, a distinction not always easy to maintain. My own position was somewhere between the two and my primary concern was to prevent an open rupture that would have seriously weakened our cause.

This friction had its inevitable effect on American Zionism. The events of the Nazi era had naturally aroused great sympathy for the Zionist movement. Gentile Americans of all groups, including the most important government leaders, were deeply moved by the tragedy of the six million murdered Jews and eager to see the problem of Jewish homelessness finally solved. Above all, everybody realized that something drastic had to be done to reintegrate the five or six hundred thousand survivors of the concentration camps into normal life. As things stood, this meant taking them to Palestine. The fight the Zionist Executive was forced to wage against British policy was therefore wholeheartedly supported by the vast majority of American Jews and by many non-Jews.

As inevitably happens in crises of this sort, the tension increased steadily. In Palestine something like a state of war existed between the Jewish population and the British authorities, while the Jewish Agency's relations with London grew ever more distant and strained. The British foreign minister, the temperamental, stubborn, and not always very diplomatic Ernest Bevin, refused even to receive representatives of the Jewish Agency. The whole process reached a climax in London's decision to arrest the leading members of the Jewish Agency in Jerusalem, intern them, and in effect impose a state of siege on Palestine. Ben-Gurion escaped arrest because he happened to be abroad at the time, but I myself and other friends of his had to use all our powers of persuasion to restrain him from the useless gesture of flying back to Palestine and sharing the fate of his colleagues. The American government, for all its good will, refused to take an anti-British position, so that our relations with the State Department were also subject to growing strain. I did my best to stay on friendly terms, but most American Zionists, who followed the lead of Abba Hillel Silver, an advocate of more drastic methods of propaganda and political pressure, were against me.

Here I would like to say a few words about Dr. Silver from my own point of view. Besides playing an important role in this phase of Zionist activity, he was for years the most influential figure in American Zionism. He had all the characteristics of a leader. He was an excellent speaker, to whom emotional appeal and applause were important. He had an acute mind; he was brilliant in debate; above all he had unyielding strength of will. He was a typical autocrat, possessing the authority and self-confidence to command but not the flexibility to understand his opponent. He was an Old Testament Jew who never forgave or forgot and who possessed no trace of the talent for keeping personal and political affairs separate. Once he had adopted a movement or an idea, he served it with the utmost devotion, and he was a loyal friend to all those who followed his orders absolutely. Anyone who fought him politically became his personal enemy. He could be extremely ruthless in a fight, and there was something of the terrorist in his manner and bearing. I myself never reacted to his overpowering aggressiveness and generally responded to it ironically or with a joke, which used to incense him. But not everyone felt like this; Stephen Wise, for instance, who was also a born leader, though of a quite different kind, and who was more sensitive than I to Silver's aura, once admitted to me that he began to tremble when the man entered a hall.

The cause of the one really bitter, ruthless fight I ever had to undertake in my whole career was the disparity in Silver's and my nature. Ideologies are usually only a superstructure erected on a given psychological outlook, and at first our differences expressed themselves in the matter of tactics toward the American government during the war. Silver favored very outspoken criticism and opposition whenever the policy of the Roosevelt administration was not a hundred percent pro-Zionist, which was most of the time. I, more flexible and diplomatic than he, tried to compromise and to influence Washington rather than fight it outright. Silver's resistance became even more rigid when he went over to the Republican Party and extended his attacks on Roosevelt and Truman to the domestic political front. He was sure that vociferous protests and the mobilization of American Jewry could force Roosevelt into a position quite foreign to him. Once in a conference with me he said in his blustering way: "We'll force the President to swallow our demands."

I replied: "Unfortunately, Dr. Silver, you're confusing the White House with the sisterhood of your congregation."

Our differences then spread to the problem of activism and terrorism in Palestine. I was in favor of illegal immigration, even if it led to skirmishes and armed clashes with the British police. However, I was basically opposed to terrorist methods, such as those of Revisionist armed groups like the Etzel and the Stern Gang. Though he was not a Revisionist, Silver was more sympathetic to their activities and often condoned them. This produced a certain antithesis between his political position in American life, where he was often on the progressive side, and the stand he took on Palestine, where he endorsed the most prominent right-wing leaders and anti-labor Revisionists.

Our ideological conflict emerged again when I actively began to support and promote the partition plan. Silver opposed it and insisted that we demand a Jewish state in an undivided Palestine. When I asked how such a state could be established democratically without a Jewish majority, he could give no reply. The more strongly I supported partition, the more irreconcilable our differences became. He refused to attend the crucial meeting of the Zionist Executive in Paris where, on my motion, the partition plan was discussed, and at the Basel Congress of 1946 he campaigned for its rejection, although he loyally accepted the decision in favor of partition and later helped to implement it. At Basel, Silver was elected chairman of the New York section of the Zionist Executive and became the most important advocate at the United Nations of our demand for a Jewish state. Diplomatic negotiations were left more or less to Schertok and myself, but Silver was not only our official spokesman on the United Nations committees, he was also an extremely effective one.

However, the long-standing conflict between Silver and myself reached its climax when he tried to oust Henry Morgenthau, Jr., the president of the UJA, and take over its direction. Along with the majority of my colleagues on the Executive, I took Morgenthau's side. We were afraid that if Silver became president, fund drives would suffer, since the top administrators of the welfare funds disapproved of his methods. Moreover, we were not willing to hand him a potential pressure instrument on the Executive by giving him control of the funds its existence depended on. The conflict assumed dramatic proportions. Despite Silver's great popularity with the Jewish population of America, I had the support of Hadassah, the women's Zionist organization, and of my associates on the Zionist Executive, including Ben-Gurion. By a complicated tactical maneuver I managed to oust Silver from his powerful position in the UJA, and in consequence he resigned as New York chairman of the Zionist Executive. At the first Jerusalem congress he tried, without success, to regain his former position of power, but even the ZOA, for years the basis of his authority, followed the lead of its president, Israel Brodie, and took my side.

This marked the end of Silver's official Zionist activity. He withdrew in bitterness, and despite my attempts to get him elected to the Zionist Executive, he refused to accept any position. This was in keeping with his character. He could only function when he had absolute authority. He lacked the gift of working under someone else and in collaboration with people who felt themselves to be on an equal footing with him. The two of us were formally reconciled at a subsequent annual conference of the ZOA in New York and met from time to time thereafter, but we were never again to work together.

Silver was a great figure in American Jewry and in Zionism, and there is no doubt that he performed historic services during and after the war in converting the Jewish masses to the idea of a Jewish state. Since I do not carry political antagonisms into the personal realm, I think back on him as a great leader of the Zionist movement and as one of the most fascinating Jewish personalities of my generation—in spite of the frequent vexation and more than one defeat he caused me.

After the war, one committee after another was appointed, American and Anglo-American, but none of them achieved any success in finding a way out of the Palestine dilemma. Even President Harry Truman's relatively modest demand that 100,000 refugees be admitted to Palestine immediately was refused by the British government. As things moved toward a crisis, it became increasingly clear to me that only a radical solution would work. I was afraid for the future of the movement and for our work in Palestine. In the long run, the British were bound to take drastic measures against terrorism and illegal immigration. One high commissioner, Sir Alan Cunningham, no enemy of Zionism, had already threatened that the British would destroy half Tel Aviv if they were forced to. I was also afraid that the incessant American-Jewish attacks on Great Britain and on the State Department would lead to conflict with the American government. For all his friendship and sympathy, President Truman had indicated several times that he saw no way out and would like to withdraw from the whole thing, which would have been a worse catastrophe than an open state of war with England.

In these circumstances it seemed to me that the only way for us to regain the initiative was to come out with a drastic plan. As I evaluated the situation, we would have to propose the partition of Palestine and the creation of a Jewish state. Since we were only a minority, democratic principles made it impossible for us to ask for all of Palestine for ourselves. On the other hand, our relations with Britain during the past few years had reached a point that rendered the continuation of the mandate impossible. With their vital interests in the Arab world, the British would never be prepared to risk conflict with the Arabs for the sake of Jewish immigration. Therefore, the only alternative was to terminate the mandate and hand over full autonomy and responsibility in the area of Palestine that would be allotted us.

Although the most influential Zionist leaders agreed with me, including Weizmann, Ben-Gurion, and Schertok, the political head of the Jewish Agency in Jerusalem, I knew that I would have to overcome strong resistance inside the movement. Palestine is a small country, and the Jewish people holds every part of it sacred for its historic associations and traditions. I realized that a movement like Zionism, not trained in realistic political thinking but quick to react emotionally, would not easily be persuaded to relinquish part of Palestine of its own free will. But it seemed to me that we were forced to choose between such a compromise and continually escalating the conflict with England, which might easily lead to the destruction of the *yishuv* and the decades of work in resettlement, as well as to a political weakening of the Zionist movement all over the world.

Confident of the support of the Zionist Executive, I tried, before any official decision was made, to sound out some key figures on the prospects of a partition plan. I could not do this in the name of the Jewish Agency but only on a personal basis. My inquiries showed that there was a substantial prospect of securing, in any case, the assent of the American government, since it would welcome a chance to get out of a blind alley and was anxious to avoid conflict with either Britain or the Jews. Therefore I began openly to advocate partition. Here I was vigorously opposed by Dr. Silver and his friends, who saw this as a surrender of our right to the whole of Palestine and a betrayal of what they called classic Zionism. The dispute reached its head in a verbal duel between Dr. Emanuel Neumann and myself at a Hadassah conference in Boston on November 13, 1946.

Ever since 1945 I had been urging the convening of a plenary session of the Zionist Executive to discuss partition. This was not easy. Moreover, for internal political reasons Ben-Gurion hesitated to commit the Executive to an official stand on partition, but it was becoming increasingly clear that there was no point in temporizing. The Anglo-American Committee of Inquiry, that met in Montreux and included some good friends of ours, such as James McDonald and Bartley Crum, was, after much soul-searching, inclined to the idea of partition. The Zionist Executive finally met in Paris at the end of July, 1946. I outlined at length the compelling reasons for considering an acceptable plan of partition and for informing the American government that we were doing so. During the passionate discussion I received a telephone call from David Niles, one of Truman's assistants in charge of Jewish questions and one of our best and most loyal friends in Washington, informing me that as a result of the British government's rejection of the Anglo-American Committee's proposals and the permanent attacks on him by American Zionists, the President was threatening to wash his hands of the whole matter unless the Jewish Agency Executive came up with a reasonable, realistic plan. After several days of debate the vote was finally taken. The resolution, which I proposed on August 5, 1946, read as follows:

> 1. The Executive of the Jewish Agency finds the British proposals originated by the Committee of Inquiry and announced by Mr. Morrison in the House of Commons unacceptable as a basis of discussion.
> 2. The Executive is prepared to discuss a proposal for the establishment of a viable Jewish state in an adequate area of Palestine.
> 3. For the immediate implementation of Paragraph 2, the Executive submits the following demands:
> a. The immediate issue of 100,000 immigration per-

mits and an immediate start on the transportation of the
100,000 Jews to Palestine.

b. The immediate granting of full administrative and
economic autonomy to the area of Palestine designated to
become a Jewish state.

c. The right of the Jewish administration of the area
of Palestine designated to become a Jewish state to supervise immigration.

The crucial second paragraph was accepted by ten members
of the Executive. One voted against it and another abstained.
Without doubt the resolution was of historic importance and
paved the way for the ultimate acceptance of partition by the
United Nations and for the proclamation of the Jewish state.

Following the vote I was sent on an urgent mission to Washington to secure the American government's support for partition. The meeting of the Executive was suspended for a few
days to await my return. Secretary of State James Byrnes, who
was in Paris at the time, arranged for me to fly back to the
United States without delay, and I arrived in New York on
August 6. First I had a talk with Dr. Silver and asked him, in
spite of his opposition, to go along with the majority resolution
and refrain from interfering with my negotiations in Washington. To this he agreed. Then I flew to the capital, where I got in
touch with David Niles and Bartley Crum. President Truman
had already appointed a Palestine committee consisting of
Under-Secretary of State Dean Acheson, Secretary of the
Treasury John W. Snyder, and Secretary of War Robert P.
Patterson. My principal task was to secure the support of these
three cabinet members for partition, so that the President could
make the final decision on their recommendation. I stayed in
Washington from August 6 to August 11 and managed in three
long, exhaustive conversations to convince Acheson that the
partition plan represented the only feasible way out of the
ominous situation.

Although Dean Acheson was never strongly pro-Zionist, he
was a statesman of stature and an unusually candid man. In
presenting my case I found him responsive to the argument
that if the present state of affairs continued, the terrorists would

gain the upper hand in Palestine and an actual war between the Jewish population and the British administration would become inevitable. A development of this sort would place not only American Jewry but also the American government in an extremely difficult situation, quite apart from the disastrous consequences for England if it had to appear in the eyes of the world as the enemy of the Jews so soon after the war and the Jewish tragedy. For Acheson the decisive issue was one of a modus vivendi between the Jewish state and its Arab neighbors. He assured me that a state of war might easily persist for years, with constant border incidents and a permanently unstable Near East. Unhappily events have shown how justified his objections were, but I replied that the Jewish state would be prepared to enter a Near Eastern confederation in which Jews and Arabs could work together in developing the region. When I made this suggestion, I had no way of knowing that the establishment of the Jewish state would immediately precipitate war with the Arab countries. On the contrary, I hoped that with the help of the United States and the United Nations the Palestine problem might be solved in a purely peaceful way. Acheson agreed to recommend my proposal to the President and, with the President's approval, to inform the British government officially of the American decision. At the end of our talk Loy Henderson, Assistant Secretary for the Near East, prepared a résumé of my proposals that I initialed. Acheson then requested that I submit my ideas to Secretary Snyder and Secretary Patterson, since their agreement was necessary before the Palestine committee could present a joint recommendation to the President.

On August 8 I talked to Snyder, who quickly gave his approval. I expected to have more difficulty with Patterson. Soon after arriving in Washington, I had learned that Judge Proskauer, president of the American Jewish Committee and an opponent of the idea of a Jewish state, had interrupted his vacation when he heard of my visit in order to exert his influence against our plan. Proskauer had excellent connections, especially to Patterson who, as a former New York judge, was a colleague of his. I decided to try to reverse Proskauer's stand and asked him for an interview. I met him on August 7 in his hotel and we talked for several hours. I made a particular appeal to his Jewish conscience, arguing that he could not take the moral responsibility of blocking the decision of the Jewish Agency and the will of Palestinian Jewry. Above all, I reminded him of the conflict of conscience that would afflict American Jewry if a prolongation of the Palestinian Jews' struggle against Britain would force it to choose between Jewish solidarity (and hence, having to attack America's first ally) and stabbing the Palestinian Jews and the concentration camp refugees in the back out of loyalty to American policy.

I managed to change Judge Proskauer's mind and he declared himself ready to shift his position, even at the risk of having to resign the presidency of the American Jewish Committee, which was committed to opposing a Jewish state. He even offered to go with me to see Patterson the following day. I was deeply impressed by his moral courage in relinquishing a life-long position and told him that to me this change of mind was a demonstration of true greatness. From that day on Proskauer supported the policy of a Jewish state and placed his great influence and his wealth of political experience at the disposal of the cause. That same night he informed the chairman of the American Jewish Committee board of his change of attitude. The Committee later followed his lead and gave the Jewish Agency valuable support. The next morning Judge Proskauer told Secretary Patterson in my presence that he endorsed my ideas and I proceeded to outline the plan. The conversation ended with Patterson saying that he would gladly accept a program sponsored by two people holding such generally opposing views.

And so the President's committee had accepted partition. All that remained was the approval of the President. I conferred with David Niles about the most effective way of submitting the plan to Truman, and we decided it would be best to leave this to Acheson and Niles himself. On the afternoon of August 9 Niles asked me to come to his hotel and told me with tears in his eyes that the President had accepted the plan without reservation and had instructed Dean Acheson to inform the British government.

In our first talk Acheson had broached the question of what was to be done about the British government if the United States accepted the plan, since relations between London and the Jewish Agency had practically been broken off. Members of the Jewish Agency Executive had been imprisoned. Had he returned to Palestine, Ben-Gurion too would have been arrested, and he could not, of course, go to London. Weizmann and Foreign Minister Bevin had not even seen each other for months. Acheson suggested that while my negotiations with the American government were still in progress, I should keep the British ambassador in Washington continuously informed. Luckily for us, the ambassador, Lord Inverchapel, was an old friend of Zionism. I went to see him on August 8 and told him of the Executive's decision and of my hope of getting the American government to support partition. He immediately gave his personal approval and asked me to keep him informed during my Washington visit. In our final talk he said that I ought now to go to see Bevin and submit the proposal to him, but to this I replied that without being authorized by the Executive, I could not enter into such communication with the British government and in any case, the more than strained relations between the Executive and Bevin made it doubtful that he would even receive me. Lord Inverchapel then offered to cable the gist of my proposals to Bevin and to recommend that he invite me for a series of talks.

Those few days in Washington, momentous ones for our foreign policy, were thus crowned with success. What was going on in internal Zionist politics, on the other hand, was less gratifying. Dr. Silver, chairman of the Zionist Emergency Committee, remained opposed to partition on principle, and as I have said, relations between the two of us were strained. No doubt Silver had expected me to include him in my conversations with members of the American cabinet. This I did not do because I could not be sure that he would sincerely uphold the partition plan he privately rejected. Besides, I knew that Acheson preferred to confer with me alone, having had an embarrassing clash with Dr. Silver a few months earlier. I was even doubtful whether Mr. Acheson would receive me with Silver, and if he did the atmosphere would certainly not be conducive to the candid talk that was necessary if he was to accept our proposal. The Zionist Executive had defeated a motion that Dr. Silver accompany me to the interviews in Washington and I was authorized to conduct the negotiations as I saw fit.

After securing the U.S. government's agreement to the partition proposal and satisfying myself that the British foreign minister had been informed, I flew back to Paris to report to the Executive, which was awaiting the result of my mission. It endorsed the Washington negotiations and authorized me to get in touch with Bevin forthwith. I telephoned him the next morning and was told that he had been expecting my call. I saw him on August 14 for the first of a series of talks that ended inconclusively. I was not able to persuade him to accept partition.

Ernest Bevin was one of the great British trade union leaders, not a trained diplomat. He was a heavy-set man, in personality as well as physique. In one of our conversations I remarked that it was a pity that in the matter of Palestine he reacted like a passionate, headstrong Jew rather than a cool, compromising Englishman. Having come to world politics as an outsider, he was more dependent than most cabinet ministers on the advice of his staff, which, like the whole Foreign Office, was violently anti-Zionist at the time. He was not well briefed on the extremely intricate details of the Palestine problem, and in addition, he was personally offended by the tone of the political struggle and particularly by the publicly leveled charge that he was anti-Semitic. He had a completely illusory conception of the power of New York Jews and believed that they had President Truman and the federal government in their pocket. In an intimate conversation with me he once burst into a towering rage over American Jews. I kept quite quiet and when he had finished merely remarked: "Well, that takes care of everything except the carpet, Mr. Bevin"—an allusion to Hitler's outbursts of rage that are said to have ended with his biting the carpet.

The redeeming features of Bevin's character were his absolute frankness and his great sense of humor. It was not easy to negotiate with him. He was quick-tempered and in his anger would launch into long monologues that usually had nothing to do with the subject at hand. I always suspected that his irascibility stemmed from his seeing no way out of a difficult situation. Sometimes I was able to avert outbursts by making a joke at the right moment. Once I had to transmit the Jewish Agency's written answer to a proposal dear to his heart, and although I had expressed it in very diplomatic language, the answer still amounted to a rejection. After reading it twice he said: "Your answer is couched in very beautiful verbiage, but if I strip it of this verbiage, it amounts to a simple refusal."

"Mr. Bevin," I replied, "respectable gentlemen don't strip either girls or proposals." Bevin burst out laughing.

With regard to the longer subject of our talks, Bevin told me that while he was not personally opposed to the partition plan, he could not accept it without the assent of the Arabs. It was axiomatic in Britain's Palestine policy that proposals were acceptable only if the Jews and Arabs had agreed on them in advance, which, of course, never happened. But the immediate subject of our negotiations was the British government's invitation to the Jewish Agency to take part in a conference with the Arabs in London. In view of our experience at the St. James's Palace conference in 1939 the upshot of which had been the White Paper, we declared we would negotiate only if the principle of partition was recognized as the basis of discussion. We also stipulated, as conditions for attending the conference, the release of the imprisoned members of the Executive and the right to choose our representatives without restriction. Conversations with Bevin dragged on for weeks, some of them between just the two of us, others with Dr. Wise and Berl Locker. Dr. Weizmann was in London, and I kept him constantly informed, but for the first few weeks he did not participate in the talks, and it was not until September that he intervened personally. On the British side, Secretary for War George Hall, Colonial Secretary Creech-Jones, and several high Foreign Office and Colonial Office officials participated, in addition to Bevin.

From the first I had managed to establish an atmosphere of personal trust with Bevin and could speak to him with complete frankness, something he appreciated very much. He fully realized the significance of the partition proposal and what the establishment of a Jewish state would mean, even if it were only in part of Palestine, and he was afraid that this state would be anti-British and would undermine Britain's position in the Near East. He had great respect for Jewish ability, and sometimes an unholy fear of it. Once when I was advocating the founding of a Jewish state as the only practical solution and explaining that the coast of Palestine must be Jewish because the Jewish population was concentrated in that area, he looked at me and said: "Do you know what you are asking of me? You want me to hand you the keys to what is strategically the most important region in the world."

"Mr. Bevin," I replied, "I have studied both the Old Testament and the New thoroughly, but I can't recall where it says that this key was forever entrusted to the hands of Great Britain." He laughed and said that even a clever answer was not going to persuade him to hand me the key.

These Paris talks with Bevin were continued in a series of conferences with British officials in London, but these too ended in failure because of our procedural stipulations.

The London talks were still in progress when the first Zionist congress since the Second World War met in Basel early in December. Increasingly heated debate of the partition plan had also been going on within the movement and the time had now come to let its highest authority, the Zionist congress, make the ultimate decision. I had been designated chief sponsor of the plan. My friends in the Executive held back somewhat and did me the honor of letting the opponents of partition concentrate their fire on me. I mention this in no spirit of complaint; on the contrary, I sometimes enjoy being the target of attack in fair debate, and in any case, leaders such as Ben-Gurion and Schertok and of course Dr. Weizmann supported the plan. As I have said, the spokesman for the opposition was Dr. Silver. The decisive vote was taken on a resolution reiterating the Biltmore Program and its demand for a Jewish state. The opponents of partition insisted on the insertion of the words "inside Palestine as a whole." This amendment was not carried, and in this indirect form a majority of the Zionist Congress accepted the plan of partition.

Although this victory was gratifying, in other respects the Basel congress was one of my most disagreeable political experiences. Three figures had united in a kind of coalition out of motives that were in some ways quite antithetical. One of these was Ben-Gurion, who was motivated by a desire for activist resistance to the current British policy in Palestine, a position opposed by Dr. Weizmann. The second, Rabbi Silver, went even further than Ben-Gurion in his sympathy for the terrorists but took the opposite view on partition. The third was Moshe Kleinbaum (who later changed his name to Moshe Sneh). Sneh eventually became a Communist but at that time was quite influential in the General Zionist Party. He supported Ben-Gurion in advocating radical resistance to Britain and opposing the policy of Weizmann and the majority of the Executive. At Basel I myself belonged to the Weizmann group. I rejected terrorism in Palestine because I felt it changed and to some extent destroyed the moral character of the Zionist movement. I had still not given up hope that with American help an agreement with Britain might be reached, and I thought this essential in the interests of a peaceful settlement with the Arabs.

The practical question the conflict centered on was our acceptance or refusal of the invitation to the London conference. Weizmann and I favored conditional acceptance; the Ben-Gurion-Silver-Sneh group was for outright refusal. David Remez, the Palestinian labor leader, was in the chair at the crucial session which, following the tradition at Zionist congresses, was held at night. In most of the parties represented at the congress opinions were divided and the majority of Ben-Gurion's own Mapai was pro-Weizmann. However, the vote resulted in a small majority for refusal of the British invitation. During the heated debate and the voting I sat on the platform, angry and upset because I felt that different tactics could have obtained a majority for Weizmann. But a clumsy voting procedure and the dogmatic, politically inept stand of Hashomer Hatzair, a socialist Zionist movement, resulted in defeat of the resolution. The result was that Weizmann resigned as president and I too thought seriously of withdrawing from the Zionist Executive, in disgust over the personal rancor displayed at the congress. What restrained me was the fear that my resignation might jeopardize the whole policy of partition. In any case, it was obvious that my influence in the Executive was going to be much diminished for the next few years, because Dr. Silver would return to America with the feeling that he had won a victory and, as the newly elected chairman of the New York section, would exert a decisive influence on Executive policy. I stayed on in order to continue my defense of the policy of partition but decided to transfer, for a certain while, my political work to London.

21

The Struggle for the Jewish State

Soon after the Basel congress, the attempt to reach an understanding with the British government that had now dragged on for months was recognized as hopeless. Looking back, perhaps we ought to thank fate or Bevin for being so intransigent, because if the British government had been more accommodating, I doubt whether 1948 would have seen the founding of the Jewish state. Bent on avoiding open conflict, the Jewish Agency was in fact ready to make extensive compromises, both in the matter of autonomy without sovereignty and on immigration and resettlement. All these concessions, however, were frustrated by the rigid British position on Arab acceptance.

When the British government declared that it could no longer carry the responsibility for the Palestine mandate and would have to turn the whole matter over to the United Nations for settlement, the political center shifted to New York and I became a member of the Jewish Agency Executive delegation charged with presenting our demands to the United Nations. Those of us who were residents of New York were joined by Moshe Schertok from Jerusalem; Dr. Silver and Schertok were our principal spokesmen at the United Nations. Ben-Gurion remained in Palestine. My job was mainly behind the scenes in Washington and in the U.N. Secretariat, where I worked closely with Schertok.

I was also supposed to win over the Western European and Latin American countries to our cause and sound out the Russian delegation. In the first debate on the Palestine question in the U.N. Assembly the Soviet Union unexpectedly came out in favor of a Jewish state. Gromyko's speech to this effect caused a great sensation, since Jewish and non-Jewish opinion alike had considered the Soviets implacable enemies of Zionism. Zionism had been treated as an illegal movement in Russia and hundreds, if not thousands, of Russian Zionists were languishing in Siberian concentration camps.

Personally I had never completely given up hope that Russia might be reconciled to the idea of a Jewish state. This hope was based on my conversations with Litvinov and Potemkin in my Geneva days and with Gromyko and Oumansky in Washington. When President Eduard Beneš of Czechoslovakia went to Moscow in March, 1945, he had promised Weizmann and me to raise the Palestine question with Stalin. Upon his return he told us that he had indeed spoken briefly about Palestine to Stalin, who had said that he knew serious wrong had been done to the Jewish people in recent years and he would do everything he could to make up for it. Beneš was to assure his Jewish friends that they need not worry about the position of the Soviet Union.

While this was not a definite promise, it offered reason not to be entirely pessimistic. Nonetheless, Gromyko's unequivocally pro-Zionist statement was a wonderful surprise, and I am still not sure that a two-thirds majority for the partition resolution could have been obtained without the assent of the Soviet Union and the other Communist members of the United Nations. The essential two-thirds majority was, of course, the goal of our feverish efforts. Every little country became important, and we turned our attention to the entire membership of the United Nations. Since I was responsible for paving the way for our policy in many countries, I inevitably did a lot of traveling. Twice I flew to Paris for two days. I made several visits to South America, and, of course, I assisted my colleagues in New York. A close relationship was soon established with Trygve Lie, secretary general of the United Nations. Although Lie, as the highest U.N. official, could not take any official stand, in his heart he was very sympathetic to our cause. Indirectly he gave us some vital help. Another asset was the friendly relationship I established with Oswaldo Aranha, the Brazilian foreign minister and president of the U.N. General Assembly, where the final verdict rested.

It would be impossible for me to give an account of the approaches we made to almost every one of the sixty member states. The history of our political struggle in the United Nations has not yet been written; some day it will fill an exciting book that will show, among other things, on what remote and often irrelevant factors historical decisions may sometimes depend. More than once chance played an important role. I remember how we waited in breathless suspense for the vote on an Arab motion to submit the whole question to the Hague Court of International Justice. This would have amounted to postponing the resolution until doomsday. As I recall, the motion was defeated by one vote.

Even in the final debate, which took place in November, 1947, we could not count on a two-thirds majority. Britain refrained from any statement during the whole discussion. Among the great powers, the United States and the Soviet Union supported us. France's position was unclear, probably because of her Arab interests, but France was extremely influential in determining the stand of the Benelux countries. The widespread sympathy for our cause among South Americans was offset by strong Catholic interests; there were also influential Arab colonies in many of these countries, for instance, in Argentina and Chile. Other small nations, such as Liberia, Haiti, the Philippines, and Thailand, had no immediate interest in the whole problem, and their position was determined by completely extraneous considerations.

This uncertainty made the Assembly debate intensely dramatic. The vote itself was a nerve-racking affair. It took place on November 29, a Saturday. Actually it was supposed to have occurred three days earlier, but when we arrived at the meeting on Wednesday afternoon, various items of information indicated there was no hope of a two-thirds majority. The faces of my associates revealed worry and uncertainty. Trygve Lie took me aside and asked me to say a word to Schertok about the expression on his face, which plainly indicated that the partition plan was done for. Fortunately it was possible by prolonging the debate and with the help of Mr. Aranha, the president of the Assembly, to postpone the vote for a few days. By a lucky chance the next day, Thursday, was Thanksgiving Day, so the Assembly could not meet, and the next session was set by President Aranha for Saturday. In the intervening days we campaigned frantically. President Truman himself lent a hand by conferring with various delegates. All the good will we could count on was mobilized to secure the votes of a few undecided delegations. Early on Saturday morning Schertok and I went to see the French delegate, Alexandre Parodi. While he did not give us a binding promise, I left him feeling confident that France would vote for us. Schertok was more skeptical, but I telephoned my wife and told her that the champagne we had ordered on Wednesday for a celebration but later canceled could now be delivered.

That afternoon the Assembly hall was packed. Hundreds of Jews filled the spectators' gallery and even the delegates' lounge was crowded. The suspense was unbearable, particularly when the roll-call began, and hundreds of delegates and guests sat there with crumpled lists of members, checking off the results. Since members vote in alphabetical order, France was called fairly early. Parodi's *Oui* produced an ovation lasting several minutes. When the result was announced the Arab delegates began to make angry protests, but the vote was final. The delight of our delegation can hardly be described. Scenes of jubilation and tears were still going on in the U.N. corridors several hours after the session had been adjourned. In New York the Jews celebrated the decision with spontaneous dancing in the streets. The Jewish Agency delegation, led by Dr. Weizmann, celebrated in my home, and although I had invited only my closest colleagues, hundreds of friends and journalists, including many non-Jews, joined us.

Of course it was naïve to think that the battle was over. The innumerable details of partition remained to be worked out. Even if things went well, execution of the plan, which provided for Jewish and Arab states linked in an economic union, was bound to be a lengthy and tedious process. The hope that the

Arab states would accept the U.N. decision soon proved illusory. The Arabs inside and outside Palestine declared their intention of obstructing its implementation by sabotage and force. Because of the hostility the British administration had encountered from Palestinian Jews during the years of terror and active resistance to its policy and in the hope of being able to prevent the establishment of the Jewish state, it was not prepared to co-operate fully in the changeover from the mandatory regime to the new one.

The second phase now began: the struggle to put the Assembly's decision into effect. The more obvious it became that co-operation with the Arabs was out of the question, the more difficult our situation became. Possibilities of securing Arab agreement by amending the U.N. resolution were explored. The most concrete plan of this sort was that of Count Folke Bernadotte, the Swedish U.N. mediator who proposed significant concessions at the expense of the Palestinian Jews. His murder by Jewish terrorists in Jerusalem only weakened our moral position in the United Nations, but the greatest danger was an obvious reversal of the American position, indicated by the United States' proposal to the Security Council that partition be postponed and a new trusteeship for Palestine be proclaimed instead. For a time we seemed to be confronted by a closed front, consisting of the United States, Britain, and the Arabs, with only the Soviet Union to support us.

The situation was becoming steadily more critical. In April, 1948, in Tel Aviv, important meetings of the Jewish Agency Executive and the Zionist General Council were held, coinciding with the first acts of aggression by the Arab states. Nevertheless, we felt unmistakably that the Jewish population of Palestine was determined to establish the Jewish state, come what might. When we returned to New York the American government made all kinds of proposals for compromise. Opinions were divided in the Executive, particularly in the New York section. In Palestine Ben-Gurion and the majority were determined to proclaim the state, and this view was shared by most of their New York colleagues, including Dr. Silver and Mrs. Rose Halprin. I myself had great misgivings. I was afraid that a *fait accompli* of this sort might cost us America's support, and above all I feared the effects of a real war—even if it ended in a Jewish victory—on our future relations with the Arab world. However, I did not succeed in carrying my point. All attempts to postpone the proclamation of the state and arrange talks with the Arabs (which I shall describe in detail in Chapter 23) failed because the majority of the Executive and, even more, the people of Israel would not wait.

The uncertainty was terminated by the proclamation of the State of Israel in Tel Aviv on May 14, 1948. No less momentous was President Truman's spontaneous decision, made entirely on his own initiative, to recognize Israel the very same day. The U.S. representatives on the Security Council, which happened to be in session at the time, were as astonished as we were. President Truman may have saved the Jewish state by his bold move, and for his action he, of all our friends, gave us the most decisive political support.

After the state had been proclaimed and the machinery of parliamentary government was being established, my political party asked me to represent it in the provisional government. After extensive consideration I requested them to appoint someone else. For both personal and practical reasons I was not prepared at that point to break off my work in America. Whether a decision of this kind is right or wrong can only be determined at the end of a lifetime, when it can be considered in perspective. I feel sure that I was able to do more for the young country in my American and international position than I would have been able to do in Israel. From the moment independence was proclaimed I was never in doubt that it was going to be as difficult to safeguard and develop this country, born into such a terribly unsettled global situation and surrounded by the hostility of the Arab world, as it had been to call it to life. The naïve belief of many Zionists inside and outside Israel that establishing the machinery of statehood guaranteed the survival of the state soon proved to be an illusion, and a quite dangerous one.

An event of interest in this respect took place during the celebration of the U.N. vote at my home in New York on

November 29, 1947. I was sitting with Dr. Weizmann and some other friends, and as we talked excited journalists kept coming up to tell us about the reaction of the Jews in New York. One of them told us that ten thousand Jews were singing and dancing in the streets of the Bronx. A second one reported demonstrations of hundreds of thousands of Jews in Brooklyn and on Broadway. Everybody was very happy about this, but I told Dr. Weizmann that such a reaction worried me. He looked at me in amazement and said: "Nahum, are you so hardhearted that you begrudge the Jews this happiness after the Hitler era?" I replied that I did not begrudge it at all but was afraid that in the years to come the Jewish people might be too busy dancing and singing over their new country to think about ensuring its survival.

My fears proved all too justified, and because I believed I could do more by remaining outside Israel and helping to mobilize the Jewish people on behalf of the infant state already beset by danger, I decided to decline the great honor of participating in the first provisional government of Israel and for the time being to continue my work in the Diaspora.

22

Negotiations with the Federal Republic of Germany

My negotiations with German Chancellor Konrad Adenauer and his associates, which culminated in the Luxembourg Agreement of 1952, make up one of the most exciting and successful chapters of my political career. From the beginning these negotiations were a subject of great ideological and emotional controversy among Jews. The premises they were based on represented something quite new and unique. There hardly was a precedent for persuading a state to assume moral responsibility and make large-scale compensation for crimes committed against an unorganized ethnic group lacking any sovereign status. There was no basis in international law for the collective Jewish claims; neither Israel nor the Jewish people could use power politics to force Germany to recognize them. This was a moral problem from the first, although post-Hitler Germany had an understandable political interest in allaying the enmity of world Jewry. That Germany could be persuaded to recognize and satisfy this predominantly moral claim is a triumph of momentous significance.

Obvious as it may seem today, many years after the signing of the Luxembourg Agreement, many Jews found it very difficult to recognize its positive side at first. Any question concerning relations between Germans and Jews was highly charged with passion, and I was always aware of the emotional nature of the problem. Even during those critical months, when I was reviled by a large section of Jewish opinion both in Israel and abroad as a betrayer of Jewish honor, when I had to travel accompanied by an Israeli bodyguard, I stated publicly and privately that I understood and respected the hostility my position aroused. But I have always maintained that nations must not let their relations be dictated by emotion. Their own interests require them to find a way to live together and not be dominated solely by feelings, however justified these may be. Every foreign policy determined by emotion sooner or later ends in catastrophe. One nation can conquer another and destroy that defeated enemy, morally reprehensible as such an act always is. But to hold a permanent grudge against yesterday's enemy is impossible in the face of historical change. Only groups that do not engage in foreign politics and are aware of their powerlessness can allow themselves the easy luxury of living for emotions. The Jews did this during their centuries of ghetto and Diaspora life, but a people that has succeeded in establishing its own state, that wants to acquire positions of power and have its claims satisfied can no longer permit itself such indulgence. Be that as it may, the emotional complexion of the problem was for many years an obstacle to any active discussion of restitution.

As I have mentioned earlier, the idea of demanding compensation from a conquered Germany had been brought up long before the war was over. In 1942 and 1943 the leaders of the WJC, who were formulating postwar Jewish demands, had worked out a program to this end. In my opening speech at the Pan-American conference of the WJC in Baltimore in 1941 I had said: "Who can doubt that we Jews have every right to international help for European Jewry after the war? If reparations are to be paid, we are the first who have a claim to them." Two years later, at the international Jewish conference convened by the WJC in Atlantic City and attended by a number of representatives of European Jewry, this demand was formulated in concrete terms, principally by the Congress's resourceful legal adviser, Dr. Jacob Robinson. Paragraphs 4 and 5 of the resolution passed at this conference contained demands for restitution and compensation for losses suffered by surviving Jewish communities and by individual Jewish victims of Nazi and Fascist murder and robbery; recognition of the principle that the Jewish people has a right to collective compensation for the material and moral losses sustained by the Jewish people and its institutions or by individual Jews who (or whose heirs) cannot make their own claims.

German authorities and individuals who had wrongfully acquired German property by expropriation or duress during the Nazi era would be forced to relinquish it. But we went even further on behalf of disadvantaged or persecuted individuals who had survived the Nazi era and their heirs. We demanded that Germany pay compensation wherever possible for any infringement of health, liberty or the opportunity to practice a profession suffered by individual victims of the Nazi regime, Jewish or gentile. Although these demands may well have been unprecedented in scope, their legal, moral, and intellectual basis was more or less in line with contemporary ideas. What was truly revolutionary was the fact that the new Germany was to make global restitution to the Jewish people as a whole to help it secure a new life and establish new institutions in the devastated communities of Europe. According to international law, the Jewish people was not at war with Germany, since only sovereign states can wage war. To ask reparations for this people was as audacious as it was ethically justified.

When the war ended, leading Jewish organizations tried to put part of this program into effect without delay. For the first few years their demands had to be addressed to the Allies. In New York an unofficial committee came into existence, consisting of the WJC, the Jewish Agency for Palestine, the Joint Distribution Committee, and the American Jewish Committee. This body worked successfully for several years and persuaded the Allies to enact legislation consistent with Jewish demands. But the American occupation authorities and the government in Washington needed little persuasion. The American military commanders in Germany, especially the first and most influential of them, General Dwight D. Eisenhower, but also his successor General Lucius Clay and later High Commissioner John J. McCloy, showed great understanding of this and other Jewish questions. As a result of our efforts, the American occupation authorities soon passed regulations compelling individual Germans who had acquired Jewish property during the Nazi era to restore it to its original owners or their heirs. In addition, an American decree established the Jewish Restitution Successor Organization (JRSO), which was declared the legal successor to all heirless Jewish property in the American-occupied zone of Germany and empowered to dispose of this property and use the proceeds for general Jewish purposes.

The British and—considerably later—the French occupation authorities passed similar though less far-reaching regulations. Even in those days, however, there was no hope of the Russians' following suit. In line with the Communist policy of nationalization, the Russians refused on principle to recognize individual claims for compensation; as far as global Jewish demands were concerned, the Soviet government, and later the German Democratic Republic, regarded themselves as the representatives of their own Jewish citizens. As time passed, laws awarding material compensation to the victims of National Socialist persecution were also enacted in the individual German *Länder,* or states, that were steadily acquiring autonomy. These laws varied from state to state and represented no more than a modest beginning in their scope and execution.

As postwar Germany recovered and gradually regained its autonomous rights, while the plenary powers of the Allied occupation authorities became in consequence more restricted, I realized more and more clearly that in the long run any large-scale satisfaction of Jewish claims could come about only by agreement with a German government. I did not believe that during the intensified cold war the Western Allies would compel a strong Germany, against its will, to commit itself to any large-scale fulfillment of the Jewish demands. On the other hand, I was under no illusions as to how difficult it would be to persuade the Jewish people to enter into direct relations with Germany. Understandably enough, any approach to the Germans by Jews was taboo during that period. In fact, hundreds of thousands of Jewish refugees in German camps refused to do any productive work because it might directly or indirectly help the German economy. To suggest, therefore, that the Jewish public deal directly with Germany would have aroused infinite indignation and absolute refusal, thereby prejudicing future policy. In any case, there was no hurry. The Allies themselves had deferred any such demands while they tried their best to revive the German economy. For the time being there was nothing to do but wait.

As far as Germany was concerned, our most pressing interest between 1945 and 1950 was to provide for the half-million Jewish victims of Naziism still in German camps, and above all, to liquidate these camps through immigration to Palestine. I cannot give a detailed account here of this heroic chapter of the postwar period, especially as I did not play a very large role in it myself. But the major credit for all that was done to take care of the camps belongs to the directors of the London branch of the WJC and to people like Noah Barou, the British member of Parliament Sydney Silverman, Lady Eva Reading, and Alex Easterman. The Joint Distribution Committee fulfilled its mission by philanthropic relief work in the refugee camps, but the most important contribution was that of the many representatives from Palestine and the leaders of the refugees themselves who defied all opposition, in particular that of the British authorities in Germany and Palestine, to effect the large-scale "illegal" immigration of thousands of these displaced persons. Today it can be openly stated that the American occupation authorities including General Eisenhower displayed tacit but unmistakable sympathy for this emigration—and sometimes made no secret of it. While this drama was going on, little thought was given to problems of indemnification and restitution. Yet with great tenacity a small group of leaders in the WJC, principally Barou, chairman of its European board, kept the idea alive and tirelessly sought ways of obtaining satisfaction for our claims.

Slowly the picture in Germany began to change. The camps were liquidated, except for a few. After the German currency reform, the German economy recovered almost miraculously. Above all, the State of Israel was established and some half-million refugees found a new existence. During this period, the question of restitution was raised by various parties, though often in a quite insufficient and inept way. For instance, soon after the end of the war, a group of German Jews persuaded Dr. Adenauer to state that the German government was prepared to make an appropriation of ten million dollars. This offer was of course declined as completely inadequate; in fact, it was not even seriously discussed. In addition, several private Jewish individuals and unauthorized groups approached members of the German government with proposals and suggestions of all kinds, and to the credit of the German chancellor, it must be said that he recognized the magnitude of the problem from the first. He knew it could be solved only by negotiation with representatives of Jewry and certainly not by satisfying the separate claims of a handful of individuals.

In 1950, at the urging of Dr. Barou, I began to occupy myself increasingly with this question. Germany's economic situation and a slightly more relaxed emotional attitude on the part of the Jews suggested that the time had come to think about a more realistic approach. Early in 1951 Israel made its first move; the government sent two notes to the four Allies, announcing a Jewish claim for restitution by the new Germany in the amount of a billion and a half dollars, one billion to be paid by West Germany and a half-billion by East Germany. The sum was calculated on the basis of Israel's having taken in approximately five hundred thousand Jewish victims at an average expense of three thousand dollars each for economic rehabilitation. Having thereby assumed a tremendous financial burden, Israel considered itself justified in making these demands in the name of the Jewish people. Of course there was no legal claim, since the state of Israel had not even existed at the time of the Nazi regime.

The reaction of the Allies was not exactly encouraging. The Soviet Union has not even answered the note to this day. Without commenting on the amount asked, the Western powers acknowledged Israel's moral justification but said they could neither force Germany to meet the claim nor mediate between Israel and Germany. They advised Israel to deal directly with

Germany. Thus the crucial question of direct contact with Germany, with all its emotional implications, became a political necessity. Israel realized it could take this momentous step only with the assent of world Jewry. It was also clear that the political and moral influence of the great Jewish organizations, especially in the Allied countries, would be indispensable if the Israeli demands were to have any chance of success.

That was how matters stood in the summer of 1951, when Israeli Foreign Minister Moshe Sharett (Schertok) approached me with the suggestion that as chairman of the Jewish Agency for Palestine, I should invite the leading Jewish organizations of the United States, the British Commonwealth, and France to a conference to support Israel's demands and create a body to execute them. I did so because I realized that Israel would not be able to negotiate with Germany alone and that a body as representative as possible of all Jews, whose authority both the Jewish public and the German Federal Republic could respect, would be required. The conference met on October 25, 1951, in New York, with twenty-two Jewish organizations from the United States, England, Canada, Australia, South Africa, France, and Argentina participating. After lengthy discussion it decided to constitute itself as the Conference on Jewish Material Claims against Germany, to endorse Israel's claims and to present supplementary ones on behalf of the Jews outside Israel. An executive committee, of which I was to be chairman, was authorized to proceed.

It was clear to me that, whatever the difficulties, the first step must be a conversation with the German chancellor to determine how sincere the German government was in its readiness to meet such claims. Until then I had had no contact with any representative of the German Federal Republic. Unofficial contacts were in the hands of Dr. Barou, who in 1950 had become acquainted with one of Chancellor Adenauer's closest associates in London, Director of the Political Department of the Foreign Ministry, Herbert Blankenhorn, later German ambassador in Rome, Paris, and London. Blankenhorn had assured him then that the chancellor was sincerely interested in a settlement and was ready and willing to engage in talks.

It had been repeatedly suggested that I should meet with Dr. Adenauer or his associates, but at this time I refused, partly because Jewish public opinion had not yet been prepared and partly on principle. I thought it essential that before making any move of my own, the chancellor should recognize, in the name of the Federal Republic, Germany's responsibility for National Socialist crimes and formally invite Israel and world Jewry to negotiate restitution. Dr. Barou and Assistant Secretary Blankenhorn presented my point of view to Adenauer, who made a statement to this effect in September, 1951. I was given the opportunity to approve the statement in advance; at the request of the chancellor it was shown to me in Paris by Jakob Altmaier, a Jewish member of the Bundestag. I made various suggestions, and on September 27 it was read with great solemnity by Adenauer to the Bundestag, which endorsed it unanimously. Indeed, the German parliament rose to its feet to pay a tribute of sympathy and respect to the Jewish victims of the Nazi regime.

This statement and other information Barou had conveyed to me about Adenauer's attitude strengthened my hope that there was some prospect of a generous response to the Jewish claims and that a meeting with the chancellor was necessary and justified. The internal Jewish situation made it impossible to announce such a meeting publicly. Even before the convening of the Claims Conference, a passionate debate had been going on in Israel and abroad about the problem of German-Jewish negotiations. Some, among them Joseph Sprinzak, the president of the Israeli Parliament, an undogmatic man, went so far as to declare that the honor of the Jewish people precluded any acceptance of restitution from Germany even if it were voluntarily and spontaneously offered. Others thought Israel and world Jewry could accept only reparations imposed by the Allies. More moderate opinion held that such payments were acceptable but that Israel should on no account deal directly with Germany. The discussion was carried on with great passion and, as I have already said, during those months I required the protection of bodyguards, both in Israel, where I spent a lot of time, and during my travels in Europe and America. At one meeting of the Claims Conference in New York, a few dozen members of an extremist Zionist youth movement forced their way into the hotel corridor, threatening to assault me, and I had to leave the building by a side door under police escort.

I continued to defend publicly the view that it was our responsibility as well as our right to accept restitution from Germany, that there was no prospect of our being able to use the Allies as mediators, that large shipments of goods from the new Germany would be of crucial importance for Israel's future, whether we liked it or not, and that it was the harsh duty of the Jewish representatives to enter into negotiations with Germany. Here I was supported to the full by the leaders of Israel, especially Prime Minister Ben-Gurion and Foreign Minister Sharett, as well as the leading members of the WJC and most of the organizations represented in the Claims Conference. All the same, I felt sure that in a plebiscite a majority of Jews would have repudiated my position. Moreover, a large section of Jewish public opinion was deeply mistrustful of the German Federal Republic and sure that it would never be prepared to meet Israel's claims.

All these reasons required my first meeting with Chancellor Adenauer to be held in secret. It also had to be held soon, because it was becoming more and more urgent for the Knesset, the Israeli parliament, and a plenary session of the Claims Conference, to make some official reply to Adenauer's invitation. A majority for acceptance could hardly be expected, especially in the Knesset, unless we had some convincing evidence that negotiations had a chance of success. Therefore I arranged with Prime Minister Ben-Gurion that I would meet Adenauer secretly outside Germany and try to persuade him to agree upon a billion dollars as a starting point for negotiations. Only after a German statement that this was acceptable would Ben-Gurion ask the Knesset to authorize negotiations. I then asked Dr. Barou to arrange a meeting through Blankenhorn. The meeting was arranged for December 6, 1951, in London.

Of all the important conversations I have had in the course of my work, this was the most difficult emotionally and perhaps the most momentous politically. I was quite aware of what it meant, after the Hitler decade and the unspeakable crimes perpetrated by the German people against the Jews, for a representative of world Jewry and of Israel—for Ben-Gurion had authorized me to act for the government—to meet with a German leader. If ever an encounter deserved to be called historic, it was this one. I was also aware of what was at stake. If I was not able to persuade Adenauer to accept the basis of Israel's claims, I could not with a clear conscience advise Ben-Gurion to go before the Knesset, any more than I could ask the Claims Conference to grant me authority to negotiate. This would mean that the internal Jewish struggle would continue for months, that the prospects of negotiations would steadily diminish, and that a great opportunity for Israel and the Jewish people would be lost. I was motivated not so much by the thought of the economic consequences for struggling Israel, as by the moral triumph of getting the Jewish claims recognized, for I saw very clearly what such a success would mean for the future.

On the other hand, I realized that the German chancellor's position was by no means an easy one. A billion dollars was a large sum for Germany at that time. The fantastic economic progress the Federal Republic was to make could not have been foreseen in 1951, and the acceptance of this figure as the basis of discussion obviously meant that a considerable proportion of it would actually have to be paid. I asked myself whether Adenauer could embark upon such a scheme without lengthy discussion with his government. The day before the meeting Blankenhorn, who showed a sincere interest in the success of the negotiations and tirelessly contributed to them throughout the difficult months of discussion, advised me not to embarrass the chancellor by a demand of this kind because it would be impossible for him to approve such an undertaking, even verbally, without first consulting with the cabinet and perhaps even with the parliamentary parties. This only strengthened my misgivings, and I told him that while I completely understood his position, I was forced to assume that the chancellor would not shrink from this reponsibility, because without such assurance the negotiations could not even begin. Blankenhorn shrugged his shoulders and said: "You must do as you think right, but don't be too optimistic."

Next morning at eleven o'clock, when I went with Dr. Barou to see the chancellor at Claridge's Hotel, taking every precaution to avoid the press, I sensed that the coming conversation was going to be a momentous one. I asked Adenauer to allow me fifteen or twenty minutes to state my case and pointed out how significant it was that for the first time since Hitler a representative of Jewry should be confronting a German chancellor. I told him of the heated, not to say passionate, controversy in the Jewish world and of the violent attacks I myself had been subjected to for months, but said that my confidence in his statement to the Bundestag had led me to arrange this conversation. I explained how important it was morally to atone for the crimes of the Nazi era, at least materially, by a great gesture of good will, and said that from the perspective of history, a contribution to the development of the Jewish state was an honor for Germany. The Jewish people would never forget what the Nazis had done to them, and no one should ever expect them to forget it, but a conspicuous symbol of atonement would show the Jews and the world that a new Germany had arisen. The form and extent of the restitution this Germany would make to the Jewish people would demonstrate, perhaps more clearly than anything else, the extent of Germany's breach with National Socialism.

At the same time I emphasized that whatever Germany did could be no more than a gesture. Nothing could call the dead to life again; nothing could obliterate those crimes; but a symbolic gesture would have a deep meaning. The coming negotiations, I said, were unique in nature. They had no legal basis; they were backed by no political power; their meaning was purely an ethical one. If there was to be any haggling, it would be better not to begin the talks at all. If the negotiations were not to be conducted on the basis of an acknowledged moral claim, if they were not to be begun and ended in a spirit of magnanimity, then I, the sponsor of this claim, would advise the chancellor and Israel not to engage in them at all. Conducted under the wrong conditions, they would only poison relations between the Jews and the Germans still more.

I told the chancellor that I understood how difficult it must be for him to accept Israel's demands as they stood as the basis for negotiation and mentioned my talk with Blankenhorn of the day before. On the other hand, I assured him that unless they were accepted neither the Israeli parliament nor the Claims Conference would authorize the opening of negotiations and postponement would jeopardize the whole undertaking. Finally, I told him that I knew I was asking something unusual, something that by conventional standards might be considered incorrect. "But this is a unique case," I concluded. "Until now, Chancellor, I did not know you, but in the twenty-five minutes I have been sitting here opposite you, you have impressed me as a man of such stature that I can expect you to override conventional regulations. I ask you to take upon yourself the responsibility of approving the undertaking I have requested, not merely verbally, as I suggested to Blankenhorn, but in the form of a letter."

Chancellor Adenauer was visibly moved and replied: "Dr. Goldmann, those who know me know that I am a man of few words and that I detest high-flown talk. But I must tell you that while you were speaking I felt the wings of world history beating in this room. My desire for restitution is sincere. I regard it as a great moral problem and a debt of honor for the new Germany. You have sized me up correctly. I am prepared to approve the undertaking you request on my own responsibility. If you will give me the draft of such a letter after our talk, I will sign it in the course of the day." As a matter of fact, I dictated a text to his secretary in his apartment and, in the afternoon, on the occasion of an address the chancellor gave at Chatham House, Dr. Barou received the letter addressed to me.

We continued to talk for a while about details and formalities of negotiation and I left him after about an hour, deeply impressed by a personality such as I have rarely encountered among the many statesmen I have met in my life. From the moment I first saw Adenauer in the lounge of Claridge's Hotel, he reminded me of a medieval Gothic figure. Austere in expression and bearing, not easy to understand or deal with but tremendously imposing in his words, gestures, and appearance, he seemed to combine deep moral convictions with an unusual political talent—a very rare combination in world statesmen. Not everybody who met him took to him, but hardly anyone could resist a feeling of the utmost respect. In all the dealings I had with him after that he showed undeviating straightforwardness and logical consistency.

I am sure he was much criticized for his letter accepting the Israeli claim as the basis of discussion, and it certainly was not easy for him to bring the negotiations to a successful conclusion. For months he was under great pressure to make less generous proposals, even at the risk of destroying all hope of an agreement. I was repeatedly warned by his opponents not to trust his word. A section of Jewish opinion and even some groups in Germany were unwilling to believe he was acting in good faith, but he fulfilled his promises to the utmost, even when this involved great personal difficulties. His moral attitude to the problem, which I sensed right at the start and which determined the success of our original conversation, and his conviction that Germany must make a genuine sacrifice to prove its good will, were demonstrated again and again and enabled the negotiations to surmount the many formidable obstacles that stood in their way. Germany fulfilled its undertakings under the Luxembourg Agreement, especially toward Israel, in full measure and beyond, and for this many elements in Germany deserve credit. But the major credit must go to the attitude, clear-mindedness, and commanding authority of Chancellor Adenauer.

I left the hotel after our first conversation much moved and gratified and telephoned Foreign Minister Moshe Sharett in Paris. While he was pleased at this unexpected success, he added, with the skepticism of the experienced diplomat, that he would not be entirely happy until the promised letter was in my hands. In the late afternoon Dr. Barou brought me the letter bearing the chancellor's signature and I immediately informed Sharett, who was now overjoyed.

In Israel a majority of the coalition parties authorized the government to negotiate, after a stormy debate in parliament accompanied by tumultuous demonstrations from outside. The Claims Conference deliberately waited for Israel's decision, but after the resolution had been passed in the Knesset, I called a meeting in New York for January 20, 1952. That produced another very heated debate, although this time it ended in endorsement of the negotiations by a much larger majority. An executive committee, of which I was elected chairman, was appointed to direct the negotiations; its members included Jacob Blaustein of the American Jewish Committee, Frank Goldman of the B'nai B'rith, Israel Goldstein of the American Jewish Congress, and Adolph Held of the Jewish Labor Committee, all of them from New York. Two European representatives were later co-opted: Barnett Janner of the British Board of Deputies and Jules Braunschvig of the Alliance Israélite Universelle.

We worked out a set of procedural directives. The main thing was to get the West German government to pass legislation applicable to all of the Federal Republic, so that claims for restitution and compensation could be handled uniformly. Up until then there had been great discrepancies in individual German states' handling of claims. Measures would also be required to make the Federal Republic responsible for enforcing this legislation, especially its financial provisions, since practice had shown how difficult it would be for several of the poorer states to meet legitimate claims. Finally, in addition to the individual claims, we demanded restitution of heirless Jewish property. A team of experts was asked to produce a detailed plan for implementing these directives and it did an excellent job.

In a joint session of the executive committee and the Israeli delegation, held in Paris on February 11, 1952, and attended by Sharett, the global claim of the Claims Conference was set at five hundred million German marks. This completed the necessary preliminaries on the Jewish side; the only thing that remained to be settled before negotiations could begin were some technical details of form and place, and I had already spoken to Adenauer in London on February 4 about these. During that talk, in which German Secretary of State for Foreign Affairs, Walter Hallstein, and Assistant Secretary Blankenhorn joined, we had agreed that the discussions should be held in Belgium or Holland in mid-March and that there should be two parallel negotiations, one between the Israeli delegation and the Germans and a second between representatives of the Claims Conference and Germany.

On March 16, 17, and 18 the executive committee of the Claims Conference held further meetings in London to appoint our team. We decided on Moses Leavitt of the American Jewish Joint Distribution Committee as leader of the delegation and Alex Easterman of the WJC, Seymour Ruben of the American Jewish Committee, and Maurice Boukstein of the Jewish Agency for Palestine as its members. They were to be assisted by a number of experts, notably Dr. Nehemiah Robinson.

On March 20, 1952, negotiations began in Wassenaar near The Hague. I deliberately took no part. I could not afford to spend months in Wassenaar and in any case I thought it better to remain in the background during the complicated and protracted discussions of detail, so that I could more effectively intervene in a crisis. It was only to be expected that difficulties would arise. In a great courageous gesture Chancellor Adenauer had accepted the Israeli claims of a billion dollars as the basis of discussions, but I knew that this gigantic sum was firmly opposed within his cabinet and by the party leaders, as well as by banking and industrial interests. I had been told by various sources that there was no hope of anything approaching that amount. I remained optimistic, trusting to the chancellor's word and his way of accomplishing what he desired, even in the face of opposition.

In the first phase of the negotiations between the Claims Conference delegation and the Germans, extensive agreement was reached on legislation for restitution and compensation. The question of the global claim of five hundred million marks was deferred by mutual consent to the second phase. The first stage of negotiations with the Israeli delegation was limited to defining the basis of Israel's claim and reaching agreement on its legitimacy. The question of what percentage Germany could meet of any Israeli claim that might be recognized as justified was postponed to the second stage. After lengthy conversations the first phase ended with a statement by the German delegation that it was prepared to recommend a sum of three billion marks (some twenty-five percent less than had been asked) as Israel's legitimate claim against the German government. This recommendation was discussed by the German cabinet during the first week of April. The German government then agreed to recognize the Israeli claim but deferred a decision on the amount and terms of payment to a time to be determined by Germany's economic capacity.

Negotiations were suspended at this point because the Germans were about to hold a conference in London with their international creditors and understandably did not wish to commit themselves to any definite obligation to Israel beforehand. From the Jewish point of view, however, such a delay was unacceptable, and the Israeli government stated that it would not begin the second phase of talks until it had received, at least unofficially, a satisfactory proposal from the German government as to the amount it was prepared to offer. Soon afterward the Claims Conference expressed its solidarity with this position.

It was clear to me that a deadlock had been reached that could be broken only by the direct intervention of Chancellor Adenauer. Apparently Adenauer shared this feeling, for he wrote inviting me to a meeting. I readily accepted, and on April 20, 1952, I had a long talk with him at his house in Rhoendorf. In the course of our discussion I expressed my deep concern over the long hiatus. "I am afraid," I told him, "that in recent weeks the so-called financial experts have dragged the negotiations down from the high moral level established by the chancellor during early meetings to the level of financial horse-trading. Nothing more injurious could have happened. Agreement is possible only if the German payments to Israel and the Jewish people are regarded as a debt of honor, and this cannot be settled by methods applicable to commercial debts." I described to him the disquiet in Israel and Jewish opinion and the widespread doubt that Germany honestly intended to rise to a truly generous action, and I asked him to arrange for a clarification of the German offer by the beginning of May, when the Zionist General Council was to meet in Israel, principally to discuss the negotiations with Germany. I explained that my position would be greatly eased if I could give the participants some idea of the German offer.

Adenauer assured me emphatically that fears that the German government might be lacking in good faith were quite unfounded. It would be easy enough for the government to assent to all the Jewish claims for the time being, only to sabotage them when the time came. Precisely because it fully recognized the ethical nature of this debt of honor, it wished to assume only such responsibilities as it could fulfill promptly and reliably. This was why its official economic advisers had to be consulted, and that naturally took time. Nevertheless, he appreciated the arguments for expediting the pace and would do all he could to give me some idea of the German offer before I left for Israel. Since essentially it was going to have to be a matter of shipping goods, he would be glad if some Jewish experts, especially Barou and Felix Shinnar, could come to Bonn to discuss technical questions with a committee of specialists appointed for the purpose. I then flew back to New York, while Barou and Shinnar spent several days negotiating in Bonn.

But my conversation with the chancellor scheduled for early May never took place. It was postponed again and again and nothing of a concrete nature happened until a meeting in London on May 19 between the German financial expert Hermann Abs, Shinnar, and Dr. Moshe Keren, chargé d'affaires at the Israeli Embassy. Abs said that he was not authorized to make any binding offer but that he would informally propose an initial annual shipment of one hundred million marks of goods that, he said, might be doubled in the event of anticipated—to us entirely uncertain—American aid. He said nothing about the total amount of the debt to be paid, and his suggestions ignored in all essential points the concrete proposals we had submitted earlier. The Israeli representatives rejected this proposal as out of court and entirely inadequate.

Informed of this, I sent a long letter to Adenauer by special carrier. In it I appealed to the spirit in which negotiations had been initiated and said that in view of the steadily increasing potential of the German economy the German proposal showed no readiness to make any real sacrifice. I also sent a copy to John J. McCloy, the American high commissioner in Bonn, a statesman who had shown great sympathy for Jewish problems and was highly respected by the chancellor and, indeed, by all in Germany. The official attitude of the United States and Britain to these negotiations was that of sympathetic support for the Jewish demands while leaving the specific terms of agreement to the two delegations. However, they did repeatedly remind the German government how desirable and important it was to bring the negotiations with Israel and the Claims Conference to a successful conclusion. Those few days, when the conversations between Abs and the Israeli representatives were taking place and my letter to the chancellor was written, were crucial, for they were to determine whether negotiations would lead to agreement. Further postponement had become impossible.

That same week two additional events occurred that went a long way toward overcoming the crisis. First, the Bundestag Committee for Foreign Affairs met to discuss the German-Jewish negotiations and unanimously adopted a resolution stressing that the claims of Israel and the Jewish people were of a moral nature and should be given precedence over the commercial claims under discussion in London. The German press generally agreed with this attitude. The other event was the resignation of one of the two German delegates to the negotiations, Dr. Otto Küster. He repudiated the German government, claiming that in his opinion it had failed to show sufficient good will in recognizing the legitimate demands of Israel and the Claims Conference. The other German delegate, Franz Boehm, also stated, though in a milder tone, that he could not countenance the attitude of the German government and was prepared to withdraw from the delegation. This stand on the part of the two chief German delegates, men of the utmost moral integrity, representatives of the German intelligentsia and German liberalism at their pre-Nazi best, was naturally of inestimable moral value. In the history of diplomatic negotiations there have been few examples of government representatives dissociating themselves so openly from the viewpoint of their government and announcing their solidarity with the other side. This took great courage, and what those two members of the German team did to avert failure through their stand should never be forgotten.

As a result of all these events, Chancellor Adenauer decided to press for a decision. He asked Boehm not to resign but instead to meet me in Paris to try and find out what our side would consider a satisfactory proposal. Professor Boehm, who was fully conversant with my ideas and those of the Israeli delegation, was able to outline them to the chancellor then and there and Adenauer authorized him to talk to me on that basis.

The climax, which in such dramatic negotiations usually occurs unexpectedly, came on May 21. That evening I received a phone call from McCloy, and he hinted mysteriously that I should hear some important news within the next few hours. After talking to him I went to the theater. When I returned home—after midnight—the telephone rang. It was Abraham Frowein in Bonn, a Foreign Ministry official concerned with Jewish matters. He asked me, at the chancellor's request, if I would be willing to see Boehm.

Professor Boehm arrived in Paris the next day and immediately came to see me. After hearing his proposals I asked Giora Josephtal, Shinnar, and Gershun Avner of the Israeli delegation, and Barou, all of whom I had invited to Paris, to participate in further talks. Essentially Boehm's position was as follows. The German government should pay in full the three billion marks it had acknowledged Israel was entitled to. Payment was to be made within eight to twelve years and for the time being it was to be exclusively in goods, since Germany had no surplus foreign currency. The amount and type of goods to be delivered in any year were to be flexible and determined by a joint committee. After a successful conclusion of the London negotiations to re-establish Germany's commercial credit, the German government would apply for a foreign loan, the full amount of which would be placed at the disposal of Israel as a payment on Germany's debt. The German government thought that it might well obtain such a loan within a few years of the conclusion of The Hague and London conferences and this would enable it to discharge its total obligation to Israel even before the stipulated date. For the first two years goods to the value of approximately two hundred million marks were to be delivered annually.

Obviously these proposals represented an enormous improvement, if not a complete reversal of attitude. This was something we could talk about. After a short consultation with my associates, I asked Boehm to inform Adenauer that we considered this offer fair and believed it could serve as a basis for renewed negotiations. I was obliged, however, to criticize three points. The time over which payment was to be spread was too long; in my opinion, the full amount should be paid in seven years at most. All payments could not be made in goods; at least one-third must be in cash. In order to shorten the time span, the yearly quotas would have to be raised.

Boehm returned to Germany with this answer. The plan was that he would immediately report to the chancellor, after which the matter would be submitted to the government for a final decision. I was to meet Chancellor Adenauer in Paris on May 27 and, assuming that we reached agreement, set negotiations going again at The Hague. After the many delays we had encountered we were all naturally somewhat apprehensive, but our patience was to be tested again. When Adenauer came to Paris on May 27, the German cabinet had not yet discussed the matter, not from lack of good will but because the Contractual Agreement between Germany and the Western powers had just been concluded, and this had naturally monopolized the attention of the government. This time, however, the delay had its positive side because it gave U.S. Secretary of State Dean Acheson and British Foreign Minister Anthony Eden an opportunity, while they were in Bonn for the signing of the Contractual Agreement, to confer with Adenauer about The Hague negotiations and emphasize the unfortunate consequences their failure would have.

On May 28 Chancellor Adenauer invited me for a talk in Paris, informed me why no cabinet decision had yet been reached, and clearly indicated that he was bent on putting into effect the proposals Professor Boehm had made with his knowledge. In order to placate excited Jewish public opinion, we issued an optimistic communiqué after this talk. I flew back to New York somewhat reassured, but I will not deny that I awaited the final decision with impatience and anxiety.

On June 8 Blankenhorn finally summoned me to Bonn by telegram. I realized a decision was imminent. My first conversation in Bonn took place on June 10 in the office of Secretary of State Hallstein. The other members of the German team were Herbert Blankenhorn, Hermann Abs, Franz Boehm, and Abraham Frowein, secretary of the German delegation at The Hague meetings. On the Jewish side Shinnar and Barou were present, besides myself. In this discussion, which lasted several hours, all major points were settled. The total payment to Israel was set at three billion marks. It was more difficult to reach agreement on the Claims Conference demand for a half-billion marks for Nazi victims living outside Israel because all the German representatives, even those who were most friendly to us, took a negative attitude to this. They had various reasons for doing so: that Germany would have fulfilled its obligation by paying three billion marks to Israel; that the German government could not on principle assume liability for the restitution of heirless property; that the Claims Conference was not a person under the law to whom the German government could obligate itself. They also asked what the Jewish organizations in other countries were to do with payment in the form of goods.

I fought tenaciously for the Claims Conference demands, which I justified on three grounds. First, it was immoral that Germany should remain in possession of Jewish property to the value of billions of dollars that had been stolen by the Nazis and incorporated in the German state treasury. Second, in his statement of September, 1951, Chancellor Adenauer had expressly invited representatives of the Jewish people and of Israel to negotiate with Germany. What would have been the point of such an invitation if it had been decided in advance not to offer anything to the representatives of world Jewry? Third, Jewish organizations had already spent hundreds of millions of dollars on Jewish victims of Naziism outside Israel and would have to raise huge additional amounts to rehabilitate them to normal life and to re-establish, insofar as this could be done, the Jewish institutions that had been destroyed. It was Germany's duty to help in this task.

I stated categorically that even if an agreement were reached with Israel, I would not sign any settlement that did not somehow satisfy the demands of the Claims Conference. It took a lot of doing to persuade Hallstein and the others to agree to a payment of about five hundred million marks to the Claims Conference, on the condition that this obligation might also be discharged in the form of goods to be delivered to Israel, which would then reimburse the Claims Conference.

Once we were more or less in accord as to the total amount, we proceeded to the next problem: the manner of payment. Abs, who was in charge of this, insisted that before the end of the London conference on German debts, Germany could not afford any payment in foreign currency. All my arguments were fruitless, and I was faced with two alternatives: to postpone a decision on this question until the London conference ended—and nobody had any idea how long it might go on or whether it would achieve anything—or to forego payment in foreign currency. In this quandary I returned to an idea we had already brought up. I said we would accept payment in goods, but the question now was how these were to be defined. If, for example, Germany were prepared to buy oil abroad and deliver it to Israel, we would be entirely satisfied with payment in goods. This solution eventually proved acceptable, with the result that for a number of years Germany paid large amounts to British oil companies for their deliveries to Israel.

Finally, there remained only the last difficult question: the schedule of payments. The German representatives all insisted on twelve years—fourteen if the Claims Conference were to get its share. Here I had to give in, though only after the Germans promised to take a foreign loan as soon as they could and place the proceeds at Israel's disposal in payment of the final installments, thus shortening the time spread by at least two years. I accepted this with the reservation that if the German economy improved, we would request a faster rate of payment.

After this exciting and very taxing discussion, the concluding conversation took place that same afternoon in the chancellor's office. Secretary of State Hallstein reported to Adenauer the results of the first talk, covering all the points on which agreement had not been reached. There followed a lengthy discussion, mainly between Adenauer, Abs, and myself. In the matter of the Claims Conference demand the chancellor immediately upheld my view and my suggestion that Germany could procure some of the goods through foreign exchange. Here the chancellor suggested, for instance, that it would be a good idea for Germany to buy surplus Danish butter and ship it to Israel, for he had read that there was a great shortage of fats in Israel. I interrupted him to remark that Israel could not accept Danish butter because for many years to come we were going to have to make do with margarine. The chancellor was very much impressed by this and turned to the German delegates and said: "Gentlemen, you see now how we must respect this courageous little nation. They won't indulge in the luxury of butter even when it's available."

Although more than an hour had passed, we had still not managed to reach complete agreement on the formulation of several points. Adenauer was called away to an urgent conference with party leaders, but before leaving he said that he must insist that full accord be reached that day. He requested us to remain in his office until we had produced a written agreement, however long it might take. Abs, who obviously did not want to get too deeply involved, said he could not stay, that his train for London left in an hour (he was the leader of the German delegation to the debts conference) and he still had to go home and pack. "That's no problem," replied the chancellor. "Give me your key and I'll send my secretary over to your apartment. While she's packing your pajamas you can come to terms with Dr. Goldmann." The chancellor left and during the next hour we dictated a memorandum in which the essential points of the Luxembourg Agreement were outlined. Just as we were initialing it, Adenauer returned. By this time it was half past seven and he was visibly pleased that we had reached agreement. He promised to recommend to the cabinet the Claims Conference demand for a half-billion marks, which was not mentioned in the memorandum.

Shinnar and I returned to the Kurhaus in Neuenahr, where I was staying. When my colleagues Josephtal, Barou, and the others heard the result they were deeply moved. We heard later that Chancellor Adenauer had attended a banquet with the premiers of the German states that evening. At the end of the proceedings he rose and said he wished to make an important announcement: He had that evening reached a fundamental agreement with me. As chancellor he regarded this accord with world Jewry as an event no less important for Germany's future than the restoration of German sovereignty. The premiers stood up and applauded. I flew back to New York the next day with Chancellor Adenauer's assurance that he would submit our agreement to the cabinet for a speedy decision. This meeting of the cabinet took place on June 17, and after a long discussion the proposals contained in the memorandum were approved, creating the basis for a resumption of negotiations at The Hague.

Although all the essential problems had been solved in Bonn, the negotiations, which were resumed at The Hague on June 22, dragged on for several months. A number of legal and political difficulties had to be resolved, affecting the stability of German currency and the eventuality of German reunification. It took a long time to work out a catastrophe clause to provide for unexpected economic collapse in Germany and similar possibilities. Many details had to be discussed in connection with the legislative program. The opposition of several ministers had to be overcome, particularly with regard to claims on behalf of Jewish victims of Naziism from non-German areas. Despite our fundamental agreement, the global payment to the Claims Conference gave rise to great difficulty because all the long refuted arguments against it were revived. Although I had hoped to leave the technical formulation of the agreements to the experts, on July 3 I was forced to return to Bonn, where I announced that I was prepared to concede to the German government the right to keep ten percent of the half-billion for distribution among non-Jewish victims of Naziism. On July 10 I had to return to Bonn again in connection with the currency-stability clause, mainly in order to allay the misgivings of Finance Minister Fritz Schaeffer. That day we finally came to terms on four hundred and fifty million marks for the Claims Conference and fifty million for non-Jewish victims. The same day I wrote a letter to Adenauer, presenting all the arguments and asking him to secure the cabinet's approval for the proposal. This he did.

After all the obstacles had been surmounted, both agreements were concluded in September, one between Israel and the German government and the other between the Claims Conference and Germany. There remained only the question of how they were to be signed. But before this could be settled, a new difficulty suddenly arose. The Arab states protested. Obviously the Arabs had not taken the negotiations very seriously at first, and as a result they were rather late in organizing their protest. But since they had a number of friends and allies in the various German parties, there was still some danger that they would succeed in delaying the signing. For this reason, and for reasons of security, the time and place of signing were to be kept strictly secret. In our final conversations in Switzerland, Adenauer had assured me that he would not allow himself to be influenced by Arab protests, particularly as it had been agreed that Germany would supply only goods to be used for peaceful development purposes. With a combination of statesmanlike skill and unshakable firmness, he warded off all last-minute Arab attempts at diplomatic intervention.

Like everything else about the negotiations, the manner of signing was unique. On the one hand, we had an agreement between Germany and Israel, two states that did not recognize each other and maintained no relations, diplomatic or otherwise. The other agreement had been concluded between the German government and the Claims Conference, a private organization with no status in international law. On the other hand, many political factors made it desirable to make the signing a ceremonial occasion. Several times Adenauer had indicated to me that in view of the importance he attributed to the agreement he would like to be present at its signing. The details and the manner of signing had to be worked out with Israel and the German government.

On August 18 I visited Chancellor Adenauer at his vacation residence on the Bürgenstock and also discussed the matter with the Israeli government. We finally arranged that the agreements would be signed on September 10, 1952, in Luxembourg and that Adenauer would sign for Germany, Foreign Minister Sharett for Israel, and I for the Claims Conference. My original idea was that the signers should each make a short speech, but unfortunately lack of time made this impracticable, especially since the Germans might have taken exception to parts of Sharett's speech. The chancellor proposed that neither Sharett nor he should speak and that I should make the only speech, but I had to decline this suggestion because of the precedence due the representative of Israel. Speeches were therefore dispensed with altogether, and at my suggestion it was arranged instead that Adenauer, Sharett, and I would withdraw for a private talk after the signing, that was to take place at 8 A.M.

At 7.45 A.M. on September 10 Sharett, the Israeli representatives, and I drove to the Luxembourg city hall, all of us quite excited. One minute later Chancellor Adenauer arrived with the German delegation. I introduced everyone and we went up to the great hall. The chancellor signed first, then Sharett. When my turn came I found that my fountain pen was dry and Professor Hallstein lent me his—the pen with which the Contractual Agreement had been signed in Mehlem. This was the only light note in the otherwise solemn, wordless ceremony. We were all glad when it was over. Chancellor Adenauer, Sharett, and I then withdrew to an adjoining room, where we had a very cordial conversation. The chancellor assured us of his happiness at the outcome and of the moral importance he attached to the agreement. Sharett, speaking, as he emphasized, in the language of Goethe, stressed its significance for Israel's future development, and then the somewhat formal and strained atmosphere of the ceremonial signing gave way to a mood of friendliness and mutual sympathy.

Sharett and I returned to Paris from Luxembourg and then went on to Israel, where the signing of the agreement was greeted with a joy that was all the greater because few people had expected the negotiations to end in success. When I went to see Prime Minister Ben-Gurion the morning after I arrived in Israel, he came up to me in a solemn mood and said: "You and I have had the good fortune to see two miracles come to pass, the creation of the State of Israel and the signing of the agreement with Germany. I was responsible for the first, you for the second. The only difference is that I always had faith in the first miracle, but I didn't believe in the second one until the very last minute."

The signing of the agreement was followed by a further chapter that was far from simple. The agreement's ratification had to be accomplished in great haste because the German government's four-year term of office was about to expire, and according to the constitution any matter not finally settled by the outgoing government would have to await its turn on the agenda of the new one. Thus it was of the utmost importance to get both agreements ratified quickly. As far as the agreement with Israel was concerned, this was relatively simple. It had plenty of opponents, to be sure, but the coalition parties were obviously not going to disavow their own government, particularly as the official Social Democratic opposition was solidly in favor of the Luxembourg Agreement. The vote resulted in a somewhat paradoxical situation in which the Social Democrats unanimously supported the agreement while several members of each of the three coalition parties abstained or voted against ratification. But in any case, the majority was overwhelmingly for it.

The law of compensation presented more difficulty. Here certain interests within the government parties as well as the Social Democratic opposition wanted to propose amendments that would have involved very complicated procedures and precluded ratification by the outgoing parliament. After the elections the whole law would have had to have been debated again, meaning a delay of at least a year or two, not to speak of the hardship to thousands of victims of Naziism. We took the view that the outgoing parliament should pass the law with all its shortcomings and leave amendment and improvement to the incoming one. This, however, required the assent of the opposition, because it could be done only if all the parties co-operated.

In a conference with the leader of the Social Democrats, Erich Ollenhauer, and his associates, I asked for them, in the interests of the beneficiaries, who had already waited so long for compensation, to forego any motions for amendment of details and approve the government bill as it stood. From the standpoint of parliamentary procedure, this meant a sacrifice on the part of the Social Democrats, but true to the perseverance they had shown throughout all these months in getting the agreements passed, their leader said he was prepared to accept the bill as it stood. This of course forced the government parties to be equally magnanimous. Nevertheless, whether it would get through all three readings required for ratification before the parliament was dissolved in a matter of hours was highly questionable. Unless everything went like clockwork, it would be an impossibility. That it was managed is one of the many improbable aspects of these negotiations, and all those concerned were greatly relieved when the third reading was completed shortly before parliament was dissolved. Yet even after this fresh proof of German good will, there were many skeptics who asked if Germany would honor the agreement.

What the Luxembourg Agreement meant to Israel is for the historians of the young state to determine. That the goods Israel received from Germany were a decisive economic factor in its development is beyond doubt. I do not know what economic dangers might have threatened Israel at critical moments if it had not been for German supplies. Railways and telephones, dock installations and irrigation plants, whole areas of industry and agriculture, would not be where they are today without the reparations from Germany. And hundreds of thousands of Jewish victims of Naziism have received considerable sums under the law of restitution.

But even more important than the financial significance of the Luxembourg Agreement is its moral significance. It established a precedent. Here for the first time a mighty nation had declared itself ready to make partial restitution for the wrong it had done a weaker people, and it had done this in response to an ethical imperative and the pressure of public opinion and out of its respect for moral law, not because of the force of a victor's military power. This agreement is one of the few great victories for moral principles in modern times.

For me there was nothing easy about it. I was exposed to violent attacks and often to personal vilification and threats. For the first few months the whole thing was like a detective novel or a story of international intrigue. Nobody was supposed to know when I went to Germany. I did not stay in Bonn or

Cologne but in little out-of-the-way places like Bad Neuenahr or Remagen on the Rhine. Rarely has an issue so divided the Jewish people as did the negotiations with Germany. From the point of view of my political career I took a great risk in sponsoring them, and I realized from the first that I would pay a high price if they ended in failure. But from the day of my first conversation with Adenauer I felt quite confident and was sure he was acting in good faith. As I look back, aware of the tremendous advantages that Israel and thousands of individuals have derived from the Luxembourg Agreement, I can say that this policy, bold and risky as it was at the outset, paid off to the full. In all the campaigns I have participated in during my lifetime, I never had such a chance to plan and lead one so definitively from its very start, nor has any other been crowned with such conspicuous, indisputable success.

This is not to deny that other people contributed to the success of these negotiations. On the German side the positive attitude displayed by a number of cabinet members and party leaders must be emphasized. Chancellor Adenauer's essential role has already been made clear, but another vital asset was the fact that his associates included several men who, besides following his instructions out of discipline, did all they could out of their own inner convictions to eliminate difficulties, avoid delays, and promote a successful conclusion. One of those cabinet members was the dynamic, resourceful Minister of Economics, later Chancellor, Ludwig Erhard, who, as one of the creators of the German "economic miracle," maintained against all opposition that the German economy was quite capable of sustaining the burden of the Luxembourg Agreement. The vice-chancellor, Franz Blücher, was always ready to throw his influence onto the scales, and even Finance Minister Schaeffer, who consistently tried—as anybody else in his position would probably have done—to reduce the total indemnity and "get off more cheaply," was scrupulous in fulfilling the terms of the agreement. Of the chancellor's immediate associates, Professor Hallstein and Herbert Blankenhorn, like the two loyal friends they were, unstintingly contributed their expertise to the success of the negotiations, overcoming one new obstacle after another.

It is only fair to recognize that nearly all the major party leaders supported the agreement as a matter of principle; at a cabinet meeting to which they were invited they declared themselves unequivocally in favor of the proposals—and that included the spokesman for the rightist Deutsche Partei. As we have seen, the attitude of the Social Democratic opposition party was inestimably helpful. Of course, the Social Democratic tradition and world outlook predisposed the party to support restitution, but it was still an impressive moral gesture for this party, which had itself suffered greatly through Nazi persecution, to forego the chance of making political capital and instead to promote the chancellor's policy even more assiduously than many of the coalition parties did. The Socialist leaders, Ollenhauer, Adolf Arndt, and the Jewish member of parliament, Jakob Altmaier, deserve tribute for what they did. It is worth noting too that the bulk of the German press, regardless of its political affiliations, fully supported the Jewish demands, especially during the critical period when there was serious danger of breaking off negotiations.

Thanks are also due to my Jewish associates. Dr. Barou deserves first mention because throughout the years, when the claim for collective compensation by Germany had almost been forgotten, he kept the idea alive with persistent tenacity. He paved the way almost singlehandedly for our first contact with the Germans. The negotiators at The Hague had at their disposal a team of first-rate experts who adroitly solved the infinitely complicated questions of detail in line with the principles agreed upon by Chancellor Adenauer and myself. Outstanding among them were the two leaders of the Israeli delegation, Josephtal and Shinnar, and the Claims Conference experts, notably Nehemiah Robinson, who was the foremost authority in the field of compensation law. The success was also due, in large measure, to the exemplary co-operation between all the participating Jewish organizations and their collaboration with the Israeli government. The Conference on Jewish Material Claims against Germany was probably the most broadly based Jewish organization of our time. It represented the bulk of world Jewry and most contemporary Jewish schools of thought. It was not always easy for me as chairman to hold together this conference comprising twenty-two organizations and maintain complete unanimity between it and the government of Israel. But both did prove possible, and in the course of these negotiations, we managed to maintain a unified Jewish front that had a tremendously important effect on Germany and on world opinion. Seldom have Jewish groups worked together so harmoniously and never was their accord crowned by such success.

It would be unfair not to pay tribute to the assistance of the Western Allies. It was not so extensive as some of us had initially hoped and at no point did they make any statement concerning our concrete claims, but I am now inclined to think that this was for the best. I have good reason to doubt that the Allies would ever have endorsed the total amount we finally obtained, and I never sought the advice of the American and British governments as to how much we should ask for. However, it was extremely helpful that they consistently stressed Germany's moral obligation and pointed out that the failure of the negotiations would be a calamity. This attitude, expressed by men like Dean Acheson and Anthony Eden and upheld by the American high commissioner for Germany, John J. McCloy, obviously gave valuable reinforcement. That success was attained is attributable to a combination of all these factors. In this remarkable chapter of history, like every other, innumerable cogs had to mesh before the individual protagonists could bring events to a favorable conclusion.

Anyone who believed that the signing of the Luxembourg Agreement meant the end of negotiations with the German Federal Republic has learned better in the sixteen years that have elapsed since then. What was signed in 1952 was no more than a basis for a body of legislation that has been steadily extended and amended during the ensuing years and that proved infinitely more complicated to put into effect than one would ever have expected, primarily because during the negotiations nobody had any idea of the extent of Nazi crimes and the great number of victims entitled to restitution.

Without going into detail, I want to quote a few figures. When the concrete negotiations began, I had a series of conver-

sations lasting several months with German Finance Minister
Fritz Schaeffer. Schaeffer thought that the total cost to the Federal Republic would be eight billion marks; on the basis of
estimates by my own experts I spoke in terms of six billion.
Now, in 1968, it seems that the final sum will amount to at least
fifty to sixty billion marks, that is, more than eight times what
we expected and almost six and one-half times the German esti-
mate. The final total may be even higher. These payments have
not of course been confined to Jews, but since the vast majority
of victims of National Socialism was Jewish, the bulk of this
astronomical sum has gone to them.

Once the basic law had been accepted by the German parliament, we proceeded during the next few years to discuss aspects
of the problem of restitution that had been overlooked, to
improve certain categories and to clear up a number of legal and
moral difficulties connected with its implementation. Administration alone posed an extraordinary problem. Two million ap-
plications had to be processed and evaluated, approved or
rejected. A rejection could be appealed. Many thousands of
people were and still are engaged in putting this law into effect,
and each state makes its own administrative arrangements. It
was often impossible to find the requisite manpower, especially
during the period of the "economic miracle." At one point the
situation grew so critical that I had to ask Chancellor Adenauer
to call a conference of German provincial premiers and finance
ministers, in which I participated, to speed up enforcement of
the law before too many of those entitled to make a claim—and
they included many old and infirm people—died.

The business of supplementary legislation and putting the law
into effect kept the Claims Conference fully occupied. Its guid-
ing spirit was Nehemiah Robinson, whose moral authority and
extraordinary expertise in all details were highly respected by
the German officials and ministers, as well as by the Claims Conference and the organizations representing the victims of persecution. Throughout these years the Claims Conference has
maintained an office in Germany, directed ably at first by Herbert S. Schoenfeldt and later by Ernst Katzenstein. It was and
still is in almost daily contact with the German authorities.

Not until 1966 did the Bundestag pass the last item of this legislation: a series of supplementary regulations that will cost another five billion marks. On that occasion I agreed, in the name of the Claims Conference, that this would be our last claim, but it will still be years before all cases have been settled and all payments made, especially where annuities are concerned. And since the significance of a law is determined by the measure and form of its execution, the Claims Conference will have to devote itself to these questions for many years to come. In addition to the billions paid in compensation or restitution to Israel and the even greater amounts paid to individual Nazi victims, we managed to get four hundred and fifty million marks awarded to the Claims Conference itself for the restoration of hundreds of Jewish schools, synagogues, and cultural organizations and to permit numerous Jewish writers, artists, and scholars to pursue their work and studies. I persuaded the Claims Conference of the need to set aside a sum of approximately ten million marks from its budget and add it to several million already appropriated for establishing a new foundation to promote Jewish culture. The Memorial Foundation for Jewish Culture thus stands as an enduring monument to this unique legislation.

A few years after the Luxembourg Agreement we tried to reach a similar one with the Austrian government. The organizations that had founded the Conference on Jewish Material Claims against Germany united with the Association of Austrian Jews in Austria and Abroad to form the Committee on Jewish Claims against Austria. What it achieved bears no comparison with the results achieved in the Federal Republic. The conditions were totally different. After the Second World War the Allies had solemnly declared that they regarded Austria as a "democratic victim of Naziism"—a somewhat premature rehabilitation of the country that, besides producing Hitler, welcomed him with even greater enthusiasm than many parts of Germany. Even Israel declared, for reasons that are still unclear to me, that it had no claim against Austria, and this seriously weakened the basis of our demands. In the course of our negotiations with successive Austrian governments and with Chancellor Raab and various ministers of finance and foreign affairs, I learned a great deal about the Austrian character. Although the sums involved were tiny by comparison, it was much more difficult to negotiate with the Austrians than with the Germans. You never knew where you stood with them. Undertakings were always hedged with reservations; terms and promises were seldom honored. Our only achievement was to get the Austrian government, which on principle denied its obligation to make restitution because it considered itself just as much a victim of Naziism as the Jews, to establish a relief fund to provide a minimal indemnity for certain pressing claims. The Austrian Jews were very upset and disappointed about the inadequacy of this appropriation and continued to demand that Germany treat them on the same footing as all other Nazi victims. This the German government refused on the grounds that Austria was at least equally guilty of the Nazi crimes, and even our best friends, such as Professor Boehm, categorically refused to support German payments to Austrian victims.

We tried to get the Austrian government to appropriate another sum for a second relief fund, but it was willing to do this only if Germany participated as well, and this was most difficult to arrange. Finally, however, we managed to override the German government's resistance and persuade it, for the sake of the victims, to contribute half of this new relief fund. The fund was established and most of the money has been disbursed. Nonetheless, as a result of their government's basic attitude, the Austrian Jews have come out worst in the matter of compensation. Our completely inadequate achievements in the negotiations with Austria are another impressive illustration of how much was achieved in the long years of negotiations with Germany.

23

Israel and the Arab World

The conclusion of the negotiations concerning German indemnification and restitution represented the closing chapter of that part of my career which dealt with my participation in the implementation of the major tasks of my generation. In the years that followed the Luxembourg Agreement I was busy with the great problems of Jewish life that remained unsolved, and are far from solution even today. I will try to analyze these problems, my approach to them, and my attempts to contribute to their solution in this and the following two chapters.

I shall begin with Israel's foreign political problems, for today, more than two decades after the founding of the Jewish state, we are, unfortunately, more justified than ever in asking whether its continued existence is assured—inasmuch as anything can be assured in this chaotic century. As long as Israel's relations with the Arab world remain unsettled, its survival is precarious. If any one basic idea deserves to be called the most fundamental conviction of my conception of Zionism it is that one, and I have held to it throughout fifty years of political activity. Soon after the Balfour Declaration, in 1917, I wrote, in what proved to be a very controversial article, that vital as this British promise was, an Arab acceptance of a Jewish homeland would be even more important. Far from changing, this conviction has only become firmer in the light of events.

The most essential factor for Israel is that as a state with a population of a few million, it must exist within an Arab world of twenty to thirty times that number. This disproportion takes on even greater significance in a century in which the political trend is toward the formation of ever larger political and economic units. The idea of a sovereign state able to conduct completely independent policies belongs to the eighteenth and nineteenth centuries and to the first half of the twentieth. Today it is largely a myth, although it will be some time before this is accepted in the theory and concepts of international law as it is already accepted in the realities of daily life. The fact that some grandiose figures such as Charles de Gaulle still cherish this essentially out-of-date idea and even personify it impressively makes no essential difference. In an era dominated by structures such as NATO and SEATO, the Organization of American States and the Eastern European Communist bloc, and by supranational organizations like the Common Market and the European Free Trade Association, the continued existence of a tiny independent Jewish state in the Near East, that can avoid being part of some larger political set-up, is inconceivable to me.

One of the great oversights in the history of Zionism is that when the Jewish homeland in Palestine was founded, sufficient attention was not paid to relations with the Arabs. Of course there were always a few Zionist speakers and thinkers who stressed them. To cite just one example, the *Freie Zionistische Blätter*, which Jacob Klatzkin and I published, was dedicated chiefly to these kinds of problems. And the ideological and political leaders of the Zionist movement always emphasized—sincerely and earnestly, it seems to me—that the Jewish national home must be established in peace and harmony with the Arabs. Unfortunately these convictions remained in the realm of theory and were not carried over, to any great extent, into actual Zionist practice. Even Theodor Herzl's brilliantly simple formulation of the Jewish question as basically a transportation problem of "moving a people without land into a land without people" is tinged with a disquieting blindness to the Arab claim to Palestine. Palestine was not a land without people even in Herzl's time; it was inhabited by hundreds of thousands of Arabs who, in the normal course of events, would sooner or later have achieved independent statehood, either alone or as a unit within a larger Arab context.

This is not to say that the Jewish people's claim to a home-land in Palestine, proclaimed by Zionism, supported by the Western Allies through the Balfour Declaration and by the League of Nations through conferring mandate status, was not legitimate. Like most Jewish matters, it is a special problem, to which regular legal and political norms do not apply. If there is in world history a case of an exception proving the rule, it is the existence of the Jewish people in all its aspects.

From the standpoint of international justice and historical ethics, it is quite justifiable that after two thousand years of suffering the Jewish people should desire a homeland as its only effective assurance of survival, and a homeland in the country with which it had been linked for thousands of years by ties of religion, emotion, and mysticism, as no other people is linked to its land. Just as it is today a recognized principle of social legis-lation that governments can make a levy on the property of rich individuals to help the less privileged, an analogous principle of international justice should provide that nations too well en-dowed with territory can be reduced in size in favor of nations that have too little. But however legitimate its claims, the Zion-ist movement should never have lost sight of the fact that it represented an exception to the universally valid rule that a territory belongs to the majority of the population that lives there. In other words, from the ideological and ethical point of view as well as from the point of view of practical politics, Zionism should have tried from the first to reach an understand-ing with the Arab world. Chaim Weizmann, the most farsighted of all Zionist statesmen in this and many other questions, made one attempt during the Versailles peace conference to get Emir Faisal's assent to the idea of a Jewish national home, but despite some initial success, this came to nothing. It is true that Zionist leaders, not only representatives of small groups such as Yehuda Magnes, the first rector of Hebrew University, but also official Zionist spokesmen like David Ben-Gurion, Moshe Sharett, and I myself during my years in Geneva, subsequently tried more than once to reach agreement with the Arabs. But in the prac-tical day-to-day reality of resettling Palestine this concern was rarely voiced.

From the very first we should have interested and involved the Palestinian Arabs directly, and not merely indirectly, in developing the country. Somehow they should have been represented in Jewish institutions and in economic and social projects. We should have sought their good will as assiduously as we sought the sympathy of the rest of the non-Jewish world. The obstacles in the way of such an effort and the total failure of the few paltry attempts that were made can be explained, like most political events, by the psychology of the two peoples concerned, and any criticism implicit in such a statement applies to me too, as one of those responsible for Zionist policy. The Arabs are cousins of the Jews, whom even the Bible describes as a stiff-necked people. The fantastic Jewish historical memory explains their survival, as well as many of their political failings and their shortsightedness in affairs of state. The same is true of the Arabs, who are slow to forget and forgive. If the Arabs were Englishmen, peace could have been concluded between them and Israel long ago.

It would not have been easy for us Jews to adopt a policy of reconciliation. Like all persecuted people, we have become egocentric and hypersensitive in our centuries of suffering. A mistrust of everybody else, a kind of permanent persecution complex, the difficulty in getting along normally with other peoples—these are inescapable results of our Diaspora history, a history of pogroms and inquisitions, massacres and expulsions, of living the segregated lives of pariahs and oppressed minorities. These characteristics of our people will disappear, I am sure, after a generation or two of normal existence—at least in the Jews who live in Israel. Nevertheless, this was the heritage with which Zionism began its evolution. The Jews who built Israel were so obsessed, in the best sense of the word, with the vision of a Jewish homeland, the idea of a new Jewish society, the burning passion to create a hitherto unknown way of life that would put an end to the humiliating existence of persecuted Diaspora Jewry, that they simply could not spare the mental energy to examine the full implications of the very complicated problem of their relations with the Arabs, to whom they were and still are invaders, and then tackle its solution.

One example of these difficulties strikingly illustrates the conflict the Jewish settlers were forced into with the Arab inhabitants. One of the most beautiful moral and social Zionist ideas was that of the *kibbush avodah,* or conquest through labor. Zionism wanted to change the Jewish people's habits and way of life radically, and one of the foremost tasks it set itself was to colonize Palestine in a way quite different from the usual pattern of importing people and capital while leaving the physical labor to the natives and exploiting them. On the contrary, Zionism, particularly the Zionist Labor Party, was fundamentally committed to establishing a Jewish communal life created from bottom to top by Jews and based on the principle that the Jews should do all the labor. If it had not been for this principle, the *kibbutzim* and *moshavim,* the collective and communal farms, which rank among Zionism's most admirable social and human achievements, could never have come into being. Yet rigorously applied, the principle was bound to conflict with the desire to absorb the Arabs into the Jewish economy. For decades a dispute was carried on within the Palestinian *yishuv* between individual settlers who employed Arab workers and the Jewish labor movement, which insisted that only Jewish manpower should be used.

During the decisive phase of the struggle for the Jewish state, there were probably a few junctures at which agreement might have been reached. The Zionist movement had conceived the creation of the Jewish State on the basis of amity and understanding with the Arabs. The memorandum I submitted to Dean Acheson on behalf of the Zionist Executive during the crucial talks in Washington, in which we presented our ideas for the solution of the Palestine problem, contained two points of principle; first, the demand for a Jewish state in *part* of Palestine; second, the participation of that state in a Near Eastern confederation of equal states. This was to be the basis of our relations with the Arab world. David Ben-Gurion, then chairman of the Zionist Executive, expressed similar ideas in a programmatic speech to the Palestine Commission of the United Nations, which finally accepted the partition plan. He spoke of a Jewish state in *part* of Palestine and an *alliance* with the Arabs.

After our great political victory, when the U.N. Assembly approved the partition of Palestine and the establishment of a Jewish state, there might still have been a chance of real understanding with the Arabs. We should not forget that both the Eastern and Western bloc voted for the resolution, so that the Arabs could not count on any serious support in their refusing to accept both the Jewish state and the partition plan. Cautious attempts (in which I played some part) were made to talk to the Arabs. President Truman had the same thing in mind when he offered to place his private airplane at the disposal of other members of the Zionist Executive and myself so that we could fly to Palestine, delay the imminent proclamation of the state, and gain time for new negotiations. An influential Egyptian diplomat suggested that he might arrange for me and some other Zionist leaders to meet with the Egyptian premier.

The possibility of an understanding with the Arabs was the principal reason why I did not vote for the resolution that President Truman's offer be declined and the state of Israel proclaimed. My unwillingness to do so was subsequently held against me, but I still think it was right. Of course I cannot prove that a meeting would have materialized or that it would have been successful, but anyone who attached the vital importance I did to Arab-Israeli relations would have been justified in briefly postponing the proclamation of independence in order to make even a problematical attempt. Yet in their ecstatic excitement the Jewish population of Palestine would probably not have accepted any postponement, and although we may regret it in retrospect, we must understand what even an hour's delay means to a people that has waited two thousand years to see an ideal realized, has prayed and suffered for it, and finally finds it within its grasp. The decision to proclaim the state rested with Ben-Gurion alone, and in pressing for immediate action he certainly reflected the mood and emotions of the *yishuv* and the bulk of the Zionist movement much more faithfully than I did, living far away in New York, where it was easier to take a much calmer view of things.

The proclamation of the state and the ensuing invasion by the Arab armies naturally ruled out reconciliation. In the opinion of some Jewish and non-Jewish politicians there might have been another chance when the Rhodes armistice agreement was reached after the Israeli victory. Of this I cannot judge, since I was not a party to those negotiations. Whether by making certain concessions we could have achieved some kind of peace treaty instead of an armistice, as some people believe, will never be known.

The basic and tragic fact is that no agreement was reached and that the state of Israel made its entrance into history with a war, albeit a defensive war, against the Arabs. How to overcome the consequences of this is the central problem of contemporary Israeli politics and will be for many years to come, for that first war and the Israeli victory produced inescapable consequences for both Israel and the Arabs. As far as the latter were concerned, the breach with Israel had been widened enormously. The defeat of the Arab armies, with their great numerical superiority, was a surprise to the non-Jewish world and particularly to the Arabs themselves, for the Arab masses, if not their leaders, had been sure that they would overrun the new state in a few days. This is the only possible explanation for the fact that the Palestinian Arabs were told to flee; it was thought to be certain that they would return shortly with the victorious armies. The unexpected defeat was a shock and a terrible blow to Arab pride. Deeply injured, they turned all their endeavors to the healing of their psychological wound: to victory and revenge.

On the other hand, success had a marked psychological effect on Israel. It seemed to show the advantages of direct action over negotiation and diplomacy. Understandably, it was a tremendous experience for Israel to see the Jews fighting as an army— and winning—for the first time in two thousand years, and this experience dominates the country's thinking and emotions till today. The victory offered such a glorious contrast to the centuries of persecution and humiliation, of adaptation and compromise, that it seemed to indicate the only direction that could possibly be taken from then on. To brook nothing, tolerate no attack, cut through Gordian knots, and shape history by creating facts seemed so simple, so compelling, so satisfying that it became Israel's policy in its conflict with the Arab world. Joy in this victory, pride in the Israeli Army and the heart-stirring experience of Jewish military superiority, still dominate the attitude of the Jewish state today and has been greatly strengthened by succeeding victories, especially after the Six Day War.

All of this was most impressively personified in one man who, insofar as any individual figure can symbolize historical events, represented the driving force behind the proclamation of the state. I refer of course to David Ben-Gurion. His role in the development of Israel was so decisive that it cannot be discussed without an understanding of the man himself and of his policies. Like all great, imposing personalities, Ben-Gurion has unconditional admirers and supporters who stand up for him blindly, as well as passionate opponents and critics. One of his most critical opponents was Chaim Weizmann, in his later years. On the personal level I was neither a supporter nor a real opponent because such extremism in human relations is not in my character. For years I collaborated closely with Ben-Gurion. I fought the battle for partition at his side; in my political conflict with Abba Hillel Silver I had his full support; in the controversy over negotiating with Germany he and I together held a common front under heavy fire. Throughout the years when he was prime minister of Israel and I was president of the WZO, we consulted one another on many questions in a completely friendly way. On many of those questions I opposed him, but I think I managed to avoid personal antagonism of the kind that might easily have involved a somewhat more sensitive man than I tend to be in politics in a personal feud. The fact that I did not succumb to this temptation may entitle me to attempt an objective character sketch of David Ben-Gurion.

His salient characteristic is his high specific gravity. Everything about him has substance and significance—whether it is positive or negative depends upon your point of view. He is anything but colorless. Strength is his outstanding trait. He is a man with a tremendous need for recognition, not in the petty, superficial sense of vanity, ambition, or desire for popularity, but in the much more profound and meaningful sense of desire for power. The older I get, the more convinced I become that

personalities are formed less by ideas than by mind and character. Ideology is nearly always secondary; the primary thing is a
man's psychology, and if we want to understand an eminent
figure, we must first determine his motivation. Men become
political leaders for very different reasons: out of what the Jews
call *yetzer ha-tov*, the impulse toward good, or *yetzer ha-ra*, the
impulse toward evil. To the former category belong motives
such as humanitarianism, sympathy, loyalty, responsibility, and
sense of duty; to the latter envy, hatred, revenge, and the desire
for power. Apart from the saints, every political or social leader
is inspired by motives of both kinds, and I suspect that the bad
impulses have been a much stronger force on history than the
good ones. Those whom we call great men, those who have
made history, have been inspired predominantly by negative
motives.

The dominant force in Ben-Gurion is his will for power, but
not in the banal sense, that is, not power for personal advantage.
In this respect he is above reproach. I mean power in the sense
of wanting to enforce what he believes to be right, of ruthlessness in pursuing his goals. The better I got to know him, the
more this seemed to be the driving force behind his personality.
There may have been one or two figures in the history of the
Zionist Labor Party whose judgment he respected even when it
contradicted his own, but in general he is not a man whose mind
can be changed, far less a man who can be led. He is the very
opposite of a figurehead manipulated by "gray eminences." His
colleagues have never been anything more than agents to his
will and responsible for putting it into effect. He does not mind
being contradicted and, as I know from personal experience,
even respects colleagues who dare to stand up to him. But while
contradiction does not provoke him, it has no effect. Ben-
Gurion ignores it. He is the most single-minded, undeviating
Zionist leader of my generation. His greatness as well as his
weakness lie in the fact that at any given moment he sees only
one goal before him and forgets everything else. In this respect
he is the very opposite of a prime minister or a chairman whose
task it is to assess and co-ordinate the over-all situation.

In a crisis, when everything is concentrated on one goal, Ben-

Gurion is unequaled in his decisiveness. He is a man possessed. But since, in addition to being possessed, in addition to being able to make decisions and accept responsibility fearlessly, he has all the talents of a shrewd, extremely adroit tactician, he has all the qualifications to make him a tremendously effective leader. In an intimate conversation with me he once said: "The difference between you and me is that I never shrank from giving orders which I knew would mean the death of hundreds of wonderful young men. You would probably have hesitated. And therefore I can lead a people in war-time. You could not." "You are right," I replied, "but maybe I could better prevent a war than you, which is still more important."

But his great qualities inevitably determine the negative side of his character too. Nothing in life is without a price and one sometimes pays a higher price for virtues than for vices. In all normal situations he is a troublemaker, because he has no balance, no sense of proportion, and is not capable of seeing individual problems in relation to the whole. As a result of his fanaticism he can lead and give orders, but he cannot cooperate. Although I am sure he considers himself a democrat in his political philosophy, he is actually the very opposite of a democratic leader. He is organically incapable of compromise; if he is forced into a compromise, he never really accepts and then forgets, but waits for an opportunity to reverse it. Yet I do not believe he dislikes his adversaries personally. His relationship to people is, with few exceptions, purely objective. As far as I know, he has never had any real friends. His associates are subordinate aides, almost servants, not because he has forced them into that position but because they have drifted into it through the dominance of his forceful personality.

However, just as he probably rarely harbors feelings of personal hatred for his adversaries, he also seems to be devoid of any sense of solidarity with or loyalty toward his colleagues and political allies. To him everything—even people—is a means for attaining his end. Since he is certain that his goals coincide with the welfare of the people he serves—and this conviction is perfectly sincere—his conscience is always clear. He lacks the profound honesty that leads to critical self-analysis and makes one skeptical of oneself, and this is of course a great advantage for a political leader. When he believes, he believes absolutely. His identification with the Zionist idea and with the State of Israel is thus completely honest, at least on those levels of honesty he is concerned with.

Taking the good with the bad, Ben-Gurion is a splendid representative of the Jewish people as it has evolved in the two thousand years of its history—the people of fantastic memory, of the God who neither forgets nor forgives even down to the thousandth generation, the people whose unique history is explained by its unbelievable stubbornness and determination to persevere, the people that, precisely because it has been persecuted, humiliated and coerced, has developed, along with its unusual qualities and strength of will, a tremendous need to be recognized, that combines an admirable faith in its God and its own history and tradition with astuteness and resourcefulness in the most desperate situations and with a mistrust of all outsiders. Ben-Gurion embodies all these and many other characteristics of the Jewish people as no other figure of our time does. He is a most imposing representative of the generation of transition, of the struggle for the state as it is now, but not of the state and its people as they should eventually be. This explains the extraordinary influence he has had upon Israel and its people.

I, who never shared and often opposed his views in foreign politics, frequently asked myself, in response to the urging of friends and supporters, whether I should not enter the political arena as his opponent. I have often been his adversary within the Zionist movement, though this has been on the periphery of Israeli life, but the reason I did not engage him politically was my certainty that such a move would have been quite ineffective. Ben-Gurion represents the Jewish people and the Israeli *yishuv* much more truly than I do.

Ben-Gurion determined the character and form of contemporary Israel to a greater extent than any other man. I once said to him: "For Israel you are rather like the Lord. Just as God created man in His own image, you created the Israeli people in yours. But I must say, when I look at people I feel a bit dubious about the Lord's success—and a lot more dubious about yours."

Quite understandably Ben-Gurion is idolized by many Israeli young people as the personification of their ideals. As a result, he intensified the psychological and spiritual effects of the war and the victory over the Arabs, and it was on the basis of this pyschological attitude that he used to deal with the Arab problem for so many years.

The defensive war of 1948 and the ensuing victory practically dictated Israel's Arab policy, and as the years went by it became more and more difficult to change it. Israel used two methods to resist the Arabs' passionate desire for revenge; it increased its armed strength in an attempt to equal and if possible surpass that of the Arabs, and it relied on the principle of military deterrence, and on the tactic of responding to any local attack with a stronger counterattack. This policy led to many dramatic episodes in which, though the Arabs were nearly always the aggressors, Israeli retaliation often far exceeded the provocation. Of course, these reprisals widened the breach between Israel and the Arabs, arousing great bitterness and forcing the Arabs to arm at an ever increasing rate. Again Israel had to keep pace, giving rise to the ominous contest we have today.

Nasser has repeatedly stated that his army staff forced him into his first great armaments deal with the Eastern bloc (a historic event because it meant the active entry of the Soviet Union into the Near East as a major power factor) because of the Israeli attack on Gaza, in which the Egyptian garrison suffered heavy losses. While I cannot judge the truth of this, there is no doubt that the policy of retaliation produced a chain reaction of incessant attacks by both sides. This policy reached its climax in Israel's Sinai campaign in 1956, which widened the breach between the Arabs and Israel still further, particularly since, as has now become clear, it was planned and executed in direct collusion with France and Great Britain. That venture definitely identified Israel in Arab eyes with the "imperialist powers." The war failed in its real purpose, which was to bring about the collapse of Nasser and force Egypt to make peace, but was a success quite apart from the lightning victory that raised Israel's military prestige to an almost legendary level. It opened the Gulf of Aqaba to Israel shipping and put a stop to Arab infiltration for several years.

Since these lines were written, another war has occurred between Israel and the Arabs. While this one was shorter, its results were more important and far-reaching than the results of the two earlier ones. In the Six Day War of 1967 the Egyptian army and air force were in effect annihilated, Jordan suffered a catastrophic defeat, Jerusalem and the non-Israeli area of Palestine were conquered, Gaza and the Sinai Peninsula occupied, and Israel's frontier extended to the eastern bank of the Suez Canal. The military triumph needs no detailed description here; even the non-Jewish experts and military authorities have paid sufficient tribute to it. How much nearer Israel's astonishing victory brought peace cannot be determined as I write this. My doubts about whether military victories can produce ultimate peace are as strong as ever, and my basic assessment of the Arab-Israeli problem has not been essentially altered.

Israel may be even farther than ever from peace with the Arab world. It is true that the possible emergence of a united Arab policy under Nasser's leadership, which seemed a realistic prospect a few years ago, is less imminent now that a historic struggle has developed between the conservative and progressive elements within the Arab world itself. That struggle will probably preoccupy the Arabs and diminish their aggressiveness against Israel for several years to come, and in terms of avoiding war, this is a positive development. But its effect on the normalization of relations between Israel and the Arab countries is more likely to be negative. Only a united Arab world will ever have the courage to recognize Israel's existence and come to terms with it, so that this temporary diversion does not affect my fundamental analysis. In the long run, the Near East will have to form some kind of union or bloc; the cardinal problem of Israeli foreign policy, upon which the future of the state depends, is still, as it always has been, its integration into some over-all Near Eastern structure.

In all these years I have never had any responsibility for Israeli policy. Twice I declined an offer to enter Israeli politics as a member of the cabinet. Since I was not prepared to accept a diplomatic post either, I had only a very minor influence on foreign policy as president of the WZO. When the state of Israel was proclaimed and David Ben-Gurion became its head, the Zionist organization was deprived of all influence on Israeli policy. In the age of sovereign states, policy could be made only by citizens.

That this principle was put into effect so quickly, both formally and in practice, and that the State of Israel was so jealously vigilant of its privileges, sometimes to the point of pettiness, is to be explained partly by the *yishuv's* exaggerated glorification of the state but also by Ben-Gurion's character, which can tolerate no interference. To cite examples would take us too far astray, but many things happened during this period that revealed a truly small-minded fear of intervention on my part. It probably stemmed from an awareness of my numerous connections with statesmen of many different countries and my frequent opportunities of discussing Israel's problems with them. While I never demanded, as many of my colleagues did, that the Zionist Executive be given a voice in Israeli politics, I still believe that insistence on absolute sovereignty for Israel, necessary as it may be formally, is anything but wise when applied to practical politics. Without the solid backing of world Jewry, Israel would never have existed and cannot survive—at least for the present. In a free, democratic world it is in the long run senseless to say to millions of Jews: You must stand by Israel through thick and thin but you can't have any say in its affairs; even the attempt is impermissible. I have upheld this point of view publicly and in countless conversations with Ben-Gurion and, although he does not in theory dispute world Jewry's right to influence Israel, in all practical instances he showed himself to be jealous and totally set against it.

This led to conflict between us, the origin of which was my fundamentally different view of the Arab problem. I never considered deterrence a really constructive method that might ultimately lead to a solution. I am not a pacifist. I realize that in this world one cannot go on passively accepting attacks and military provocation and that retaliation is sometimes unavoidable, but I regard military retaliation as an evil one should resort to only in extreme emergencies. It may be momentarily effective, but eventually it only makes any constructive solution more difficult. My criticism of Israeli policy could be summed up in the charge that it lives from hand to mouth and shows no long-range statesmanship.

One of the essential differences between Ben-Gurion and myself in our attitude to the Arab question, and one we have argued about for hours, is that at the bottom of his heart he does not believe in the possibility of peace. If he has ever allowed himself to hope for a normalization of relations, he has had only future generations in mind. He could not imagine that within the foreseeable future the Arab world would be prepared to accept Israel as a fact. As I see it, this pessimism reflects his psychology. I remember a very revealing conversation, when he tried to prove to me from his thorough study of Nasser's *The Philosophy of Revolution* that Nasser could not possibly relinquish the idea of a war of revenge and annihilation against Israel. He quoted a passage in which Nasser speaks of uniting the whole Arab world and another advocating an alliance of all Moslems. He thought that the Arab defeat in the war of liberation was a traumatic blow to Nasser and that to regain his psychological equilibrium he had to apply all his energies to healing the wound by a victory. His goal of uniting the Arab world under his leadership was attainable only if he could destroy Israel.

I replied that I had studied psychology in my younger days but had soon given it up when I realized that people judge one another essentially on the basis of their own mentalities. "My dear Ben-Gurion," I said, "I can't say whether this excellent character sketch fits Nasser because I don't know him. You don't know him either. But I know a leader whom it fits perfectly and his name is David Ben-Gurion. You are a man who wants to concentrate all the Jews of the world in Israel. You are a man who never forgets or forgives a defeat, to you a lost battle is a deep psychological wound that can only be healed by a victory. This psychology is completely valid as applied to you. But how do you know that Nasser is a second Ben-Gurion?" This half-joking answer expressed the differences between our views. Since Ben-Gurion considered it utopian to hope for understanding with the Arab world, it is only logical that he tried to guarantee Israel's safety through military superiority and pursue a policy of ruthless intimidation.

From the standpoint of short-term success Ben-Gurion's policy was right. Through his tireless efforts to increase Israel's military strength, Arab infiltration and local nuisance raids were radically reduced for a number of years. In the long run, however, this policy, far from bringing the two sides closer, has divided them more irreconcilably.

Since I had no official voice in matters of Israeli foreign politics, my position during this period was somewhat difficult. I felt the moral responsibility for Israel that I believe every Jew must feel. And I had thirty years of activity in Zionist foreign politics behind me, with all the experience and the convictions and the many connections I had accumulated over those years. It was only natural that non-Jewish statesmen should be interested in my opinion, and since I did not recognize Israel's right to exclude all non-Israeli groups or politicians from influence, I made no secret of my views. This sometimes resulted in public arguments with Ben-Gurion, for which I was occasionally reproved by him or by the Israeli Foreign Ministry.

My position was particularly difficult as long as my headquarters were in New York and my principal task was to influence American Jewry in matters of Israeli policy. I had resolved to put an end to the chaos in American Jewish life, at least as far as Israeli matters were concerned, because it was continually causing harmful complications. Despite my own dissenting position, I naturally thought it my duty to secure the support of American Jewry for Israeli policy. I had no qualms of conscience over this because it certainly would not have done any good, and could only have harmed Israel, if the great Jewish organizations of America had formally dissociated themselves from its policy. It seemed to me necessary to stand by Israel in its precarious situation but at the same time to influence its external politics.

This position became most difficult for me to maintain in the weeks following the Sinai campaign. Ben-Gurion had not informed me of it in advance—and I mean this neither as reproach nor criticism. But from the very outset I regarded this campaign as a mistake. I was confident that Israel would be victorious but felt sure that victory would not achieve the real purpose, which was to force Egypt to make peace. Even if Britain and France had occupied Cairo and put Nasser to flight, the Sinai campaign would have been doomed to failure. I knew Israel's aggression was bound to be violently opposed by Russia as well as America, and I foresaw our complete isolation in the United Nations. Nevertheless, I thought it my duty, so long as I held an official position in the Jewish world, to support Israel in this extremely difficult situation. Although their leaders were very divided in their opinions, I managed, with the help of the then Israeli Ambassador, Abba Eban, to keep the American organizations in line and obtain their support, despite the sharply critical attitude of the Eisenhower administration. In the end, the attitude of American Jewry, shared by a number of prominent non-Jews, played a considerable role in resolving the conflict.

After these criticisms I feel obliged to state my own views on the solution of the Israeli-Arab conflict. My basic starting point is that Israel cannot exist forever as a hostile island in an Arab ocean. From the realistic political viewpoint such isolation cannot be maintained in the long run; it would falsify Israel's whole way of life and make it impossible for the state to fulfill the purpose it was created for, namely, to serve as a center for the Jewish people and to be the most vital factor in Jewish survival. Granting these premises, there are only two alternatives. The first is the idea I submitted to Dean Acheson in order to persuade the American government to agree to the partition plan. This would provide for Israel's integration in a Near Eastern confederation of equal states. The Arab League as it exists, as a federation based on race, is an absurdity in the world of today. Today confederations and large-scale blocs can function only on a geopolitical basis and, since the population of the Near East is not exclusively Arab, the difference between a Near Eastern confederation and an Arab federation is obvious. In a true confederation Israel would retain autonomy in most things, including immigration, but would subscribe to common economic and world political goals. In practice this would mean that the Arabs would inevitably have the upper hand in matters of world politics. Israel would have to reach agreement with the Arab majority over its course in world politics and would not be able to conduct a policy that conflicted in any marked degree with the declared principles of the Arab world. Anyone who sees this as an infringement of Israeli sovereignty should not forget that it applies to almost all states that are part of major blocs or geopolitical structures. On the other hand, for the first time Israel would become a unit in a larger world political body, which would give it a potential influence it can never attain in its present isolation.

Among the many grievances of the Arab world, stretching practically from Morocco to Iraq, one charge is not unjustified: that Israel's central position cuts the Arab world in half. Dag Hammarskjöld told me that in a conversation about the Arab-Israeli problem Nasser once said that while under certain circumstances the Arabs might possibly accept the partition of Palestine, they would never be reconciled to the fact that Israel, as it exists today, has practically divided the Arab world. From this viewpoint too the idea of a Near Eastern confederation would have tremendous advantages. It would put an end to the state of war; it would channel Israel's great energies into purely peaceful, creative, economic and political tasks. Israel's co-operation with the Arab world would promote the rise of the Near East as nothing else could; it would mobilize not only Israel's own resources but the enormous resources of Jewry for the development of this whole area, an important part of the world that is on the brink of a renaissance.

In the last few years I have become more skeptical of this solution for two reasons. First of all, the Arab world is too divided internally. In view of the great cleavage both between the so-called progressive and the more conservative, feudal states and between Arab individualism and extremism, a long time may pass before a real confederation of Near Eastern states, including Israel, could be established. Furthermore, there is an inherent danger that Israel, being alone among so many Arab states in a confederation, would be too dependent upon and therefore inhibited by them in developing its specific Jewish character. As a result, I have recently come to favor a second possible solution.

That second solution is the neutralization of Israel. It would mean that the nations of the world would recognize Israel's unique role of providing for its Jewish and Arab citizens, offering a haven to Jewish refugees, and at the same time serving as the national and cultural center that guarantees the future of the Jewish people throughout the world. This people is unique in its history and its structure. It is the only people to have survived thousands of years of dispersal, the only one to have created a state inhabited now and for the foreseeable future by only a minority of its people. Such a state, whose mere existence requires the moral and spiritual solidarity of all the Jews of the world, must by definition be neutral if all Jews are to be able to maintain emotional and spiritual ties with it, irrespective of their nationality and political orientation. Any political alignment on the part of such a state makes it difficult and sometimes impossible for the Jewish citizens of certain other countries openly to profess their allegiance to it.

The first two decades of Israel's existence have produced a number of examples of the problems that confront certain branches of world Jewry as a result of Israeli participation in world politics. The situation of the South African Jews, who feel themselves very close to Israel, has been made difficult by Israel's stand in the United Nations against apartheid. There is also the far more serious problem of Russian Jewry, a large part of which is certainly strongly sympathetic to Israel but unable to express itself because the Soviet Union regards Israel as an ally of the Western world. As I know from many conversations with Soviet diplomats, the Soviet Union regards its own Jewish population with a certain amount of mistrust for precisely this reason, suspecting that it is no less concerned with Israel than with the Soviet Union, as one diplomat put it. If any country in the world is entitled to a unique, universally recognized neutrality of this kind, it is Israel. Such a state would set the perfect crown on Jewish history, in keeping with the unique destiny of the Jewish people. In terms of practical politics it would mean that the United Nations would have to guarantee the state's existence and integrity by methods that would be effective.

This idea is not new to me. When I think over the mistakes and sins of omission in my political career, I wonder whether I should not have tried, during my campaign for the partition plan, to stress this particular characteristic of the Jewish state— at least in principle. I did not try, because I knew how hard it was going to be merely to prepare the way for the partition of Palestine and the creation of the Jewish state. I remembered the classic admonition in the Talmud that he who tries to grasp too much grasps nothing and, in any case, I am by no means sure that it would have been practicable. It would certainly have been rejected indignantly by a large part of the Zionist movement, especially by Ben-Gurion, since the idea of full sovereignty and absolute independence is obviously not compatible with an internationally neutralized state that would have to stay out of all struggles of power politics.

With this in mind, I was against our seeking membership in the United Nations. (Switzerland, the only truly neutral state in existence, has never joined it for this very reason.) But even more difficult than winning over the majority of the Zionist movement would have been the task of getting the countries of the world to agree to neutralization. Nevertheless, I believe that under the impact of the Nazi tragedy and the nations' awareness of their obligation to guarantee an existence for the Jews after having passively watched the extermination of six million of them, it might have been possible at some point to realize this idea. Above all, I believe it is still not too late, even though it may take years for the idea to be accepted both in Israel and elsewhere.

Israeli foreign policy has not changed essentially since Ben-Gurion retired in 1952. If Sharett had been premier longer, there would probably have been a change in style and methods, because he was deeply convinced of the necessity and feasibility of a gradual normalization of relations with the Arab world and tended by nature to seek reconciliation with his opponents. But he was not in office long enough to be able to revise Ben-Gurion's policy radically.

After Ben-Gurion's second and final retirement in 1963, Levi Eshkol assumed the leadership of Israel, supported first by Golda Meir and later by Abba Eban as foreign minister. Neither of the two was a Ben-Gurionist (in fact both later found themselves in strong disagreement with him on matters of domestic policy), but the changes they made in Israeli foreign policy amounted to slight variations rather than changes of principle. Neither Eshkol, a man always ready to negotiate and compromise, nor Eban, who, more than most of his official colleagues, takes a world view of politics, was given to radical innovations. They had to pay more attention to the mood of public opinion than Ben-Gurion ever did, and, as is usually the case in democracies, allowed their foreign policy to be extensively influenced by domestic trends and party political maneuvers. Golda Meir is an outstanding woman in whom human kindness and warmth as a mother and as a friend are combined in a remarkable way with ruthless firmness, both in internal and foreign politics. While she was foreign minister, and now that after Eshkol's sudden death she became prime minister, there could be no question of a departure from Ben-Gurion's methods, since in foreign politics she was his pupil and successor.

Israeli governments have included ministers basically in favor of a more moderate policy. One of these is Pinhas Sapir, minister of finance for many years and one of Israel's most dynamic, talented, and effective personalities. Others are the leader of the Mizrachi—Moshe Shapiro, who is against extreme, bellicose attitudes of any kind—and Israel Barzilai, who strongly opposes Ben-Gurion's ideas both personally and as the representative of the Mapam Party. While these men may put their ideas into effect in specific questions, they have been unable to bring about any essential shift in foreign policy.

Moreover, a section of the Israeli press, especially the popular afternoon newspapers that are largely edited by former Revisionists and supporters of the very extreme Herut Party, encourage extremist tendencies among the people. Because of the mixed composition of Israel's population, the press is more influential there than in many other democratic countries. More than half the population consists of oriental Jews, who are given to violent emotions and extreme reactions and for whom the printed word holds more authority than it does for the more skeptical Western or Eastern European Jews. Also, the Six Day War, which was preceded by great tension and profound anxiety, tremendously strengthened the nation's self-awareness and led many people to believe that Israel can do what it pleases without having to pay much heed to world opinion or to the attitude of other countries, especially the great powers.

The result of all this is that Israeli foreign policy has reached a dead end. It has become committed to demands, both tactical and fundamental, that even the most moderate of Arabs can hardly be expected to accept. Many people in Israel believe that this situation may last for years and that the occupied areas can be held indefinitely—a belief that seems quite naïve in view of heightened passions in the Arab world and the growth of the terrorist movement.

While I cannot entirely subscribe to the basic principles of Israeli foreign policy (although my reservations apply more to its general tenor than to specific points), in my capacity as president of the World Zionist Organization I felt obliged to support it—though not, of course, without voicing my dissent from time to time. Even so and despite my close, often intimate, personal relations with men such as Eshkol, Eban, and Sapir, tensions did develop. This was one of the reasons that prompted my 1968 decision not to remain president of the World Zionist Organization. I knew that some of the principal leaders (notably Golda Meir) of the Mapai, the party I had collaborated with for decades, would welcome the resignation, while others, though they might not say so, would certainly not regret it. My resignation has allowed me greater range in dealing with the sphere of Israeli foreign politics. This is particularly important to me because I am always trying to maintain communications with statesmen, diplomats, and governments, among them also men who take a negative attitude toward Israeli foreign policy on crucial questions.

My stand on the problem of the Jewish population in Soviet Russia has caused further conflict with some of the Israeli leaders. Not that there have been differences of opinion regarding our claims on the Soviet Union which demand, in effect, that the Jewish minority be permitted to live within the Soviet constitution as an ethnic group and religious community and to preserve its identity. The differences have concerned tactics and methods to be used in fighting for these rights. I am in favor of international discussion of this question in the hope that world public opinion may influence the Soviet Union, but I have always rejected as unjustified and dangerous all extreme measures, unfounded attacks, and exaggerated charges, such as the accusation that the Soviet Union is brutally anti-Semitic and persecutes Jews as individuals and citizens. I have formulated these differences in such a way that there may be some hope of convincing the Russians that their Jewish policy, unjust and discriminatory as it is, is most harmful to themselves. Nevertheless, I do not see the slightest chance of forcing a super-power like the Soviet Union to accept our demands.

These conflicts, which were exaggerated by extravagant, vulgar attacks in the popular press, led me to withdraw somewhat from Israeli political life, though without relinquishing my deep interest in the problems of foreign policy that will determine the country's future and without ceasing to make any contribution within my power to their solution. Yet it continues to seem clear to me—even after the Six Day War and its impressive victory—that established Israeli foreign policy cannot bring about either one of the two solutions I outlined earlier. Such a policy must inevitably lead to Israel's increasing alignment, if not formal alliance, with the Western bloc. Economically Israel depends primarily on the Western countries that supply all its armaments, while the Eastern bloc steadily continues to arm the Arabs, not only intensifying the arms contest but also increasingly involving the two great world political blocs in this local conflict. With luck these developments may postpone an explosion or, at best, prevent one, but they will never lead to normalization of relations with the Arabs.

To normalize Jewish-Arab relations, one thing above all others is required: a serious attempt to produce an agreement between the Western and Eastern blocs on supplying arms and on the whole Near Eastern situation. I played a small part in bringing about the 1950 tripartite declaration by the United States, Britain, and France, which condemned the use or threat of force in the Near East. This expressed in a completely nonbinding form what might be called the West's moral interest—

"guarantee" would be too strong a word—in maintaining peace in the Near East. I suggested a declaration of this kind to Dean Acheson in a conversation and, although I am not claiming any copyright, I believe that the idea fell on fertile ground.

Much more useful would be a similar but more specific guarantee by both blocs, if not of Israel's frontiers (which is more than can be hoped for today), then at least against aggression in the Near East. This agreement would have to be accompanied by the cessation or limitation of arms shipments to Israel and to the Arabs. I know how difficult it is to obtain anything of this sort, but I do not consider it impossible, particularly if tension between the Soviet Union and the United States would relax. This would be the first and perhaps the most important step toward a solution of the Arab-Israeli problem. The Arab leaders know that alone they cannot conquer Israel. Their hope of doing so rests on the expectation that the Eastern bloc will some day be ready to help them militarily to get rid of this "Western satellite." Without practical help from the East, any Arab hope of victory over Israel, even on the part of their most extreme leaders, is illusory.

This is why I have so often stated publicly that the way to peace with the Arabs leads more through Moscow than Washington. The Western world cannot compel the Arabs to reconcile themselves to Israel's existence. The Eastern world can, because it is the source of Arab military strength. Of course, such an agreement would mean that, in any conflict between East and West, Israel would have to maintain a neutral position. This falls far short of what I mean by true international neutralization but, apart from all its other advantages, it would be a great practical step toward an ultimate settlement. In the meantime, the Soviet Union has publicly declared that it will be ready to consider participating in such a guarantee, be it with the United States, with the three Western powers, or in the more general form of a specific guarantee given by the Security Council. Until now nothing has been said in Soviet declarations about an agreement to limit or control arms shipments to the Near East, but there are many reasons to assume that once a settlement of the Arab-Israel conflict is achieved and a guarantee by the major powers has been given, the Soviet Union may accept the idea of an agreement to control arms in the area.

If and when Israel will ever be ready to adopt such an idea, I do not know. Some progress has been made. During the parliamentary elections of 1960, when I made a number of speeches advocating this concept of foreign policy on behalf of the Liberal Party (which is in a way the successor of the earlier Radical Party), Ben-Gurion outspokenly rejected it as naïve and unrealistic. After that time Levi Eshkol, and his first foreign minister, Golda Meir, repeatedly stated that Israel would welcome a guarantee from both blocs, as well as disarmament or armament control in the Near East.

But declarations alone do not make foreign policy. That would require a radical change of Israeli atmosphere and methods, which I do not need to go into here. Despite all the mistakes that have been made and the different course Israel has taken, I am sure that the day is not far when ideas of this kind will finally become a reality in Israel and in the world as a whole. As things are now, the Near East is a volcano ready to erupt, a volcano that by reason of its geopolitical location as a bridge between three continents presents a tremendous world political problem. Sooner or later the responsible world powers will have to intervene. The hope that once existed, that the Jews and Arabs might reach an understanding on their own, has become vain after the events of the last twenty years. Only the common will of the two blocs can stabilize the Near East. Failure to do this out of indolence or a shortsighted policy of self-interest can easily lead to catastrophe. Anyone who has not abandoned faith in some vestige of reason in world politics must hope for the day when the great powers will move toward a solution of the problem, if not for the sake of the peoples of the Near East, then for their own.

Although my activities in the interest of the problems of Israel were peripheral and so could not achieve practical results, except perhaps for popularizing my ideas in certain constantly widening Israeli circles, they did bring me into contact with a number of important international figures, of whom I would like to mention two. Dag Hammarskjöld, a rare synthesis of great administrator, astute politician, farsighted statesman, and devout mystic, was one of the most complex personalities I have ever encountered. To talk to him about anything but the most banal subjects demanded tremendous mental concentration. He was a master of the intricate sentence. I once said to him that in his childhood he had apparently never been taught the two words "yes" and "no." Any statement he made was hedged with clauses and provisos. His favorite expressions were "in case," "as," "if," and "possibly." He saw not two sides to every problem but a thousand sides. I once said to him: "Every political question you analyze turns into a diamond with a hundred facets." Yet behind the "buts" and "maybes," behind the whole facade of doubts and precautions, was a deep mystical faith, of which his posthumous *Markings* offers moving testimony.

For the first few years after he became secretary-general of the United Nations I avoided meeting him out of consideration for the sensitivities of the Israeli U.N. delegation, which might have taken it as unauthorized meddling. Then one day in Jerusalem he asked to see me and I was taken to his apartment in the former high commissioner's palace in neutral no man's land. His first question steered the conversation straight to the point. He told me he had read the protocol signed by Dean Acheson and me in 1947. "You were," he said, "one of the staunchest early advocates of partition and the establishment of a Jewish state in Palestine. The State Department accepted your advice for resolving the conflict between Britain and the Jews. A good many years have gone by since then and all of us are the richer for experience. Suppose I, Dag Hammarskjöld, were faced today with solving the problem of Palestine and asked for your expert opinion, would you repeat that same advice?" In reply I reminded Hammarskjöld that in that memorandum I had suggested a two-part solution, first, the creation of a Jewish state in part of the country and, second, the inclusion of this state in a Near Eastern confederation. "The second part," I said, "has not yet been realized; in fact it has not even been attempted, because the Arabs responded to the proclamation of Israel's independence with an invasion and ever since have refused to consider any such federation seriously." Hammarskjöld was satisfied with this answer and our talk turned to current problems.

I saw him frequently after that. He liked to discuss Near Eastern problems with me because he felt that our ideas were closely related. At times he was very disturbed by certain Israeli actions, expecially Israeli retaliatory raids. He knew I did not approve of this policy either, but I felt it my duty to explain the Israeli psychology behind these actions. Ben-Gurion and many other people in Israel considered Hammarskjöld their great enemy, particularly during the Sinai campaign, though I think Ben-Gurion himself later changed his mind on this. I never regarded Hammarskjöld as anti-Israel, even when he took a firm stand against Israeli policies. Since he rightly saw the maintenance of world peace as his principal task, he cannot be blamed for being angered by what he regarded as aggression. On the other hand, he had great respect for Israel's dynamism and for the idealism of its youth and, despite frequent differences of opinion, he always held Ben-Gurion in high esteem.

In fact, the problem of Israel was very close to his heart. It was one of his secret hopes that he might some day succeed in finding a way to normalize Arab-Israeli relations. I placed great hope in him, especially in his last few years in office, when his prestige was steadily increasing and he was not merely secretary-general of the United Nations but in effect its director. His sudden death was a great tragedy for the United Nations and for humanity and a blow to hopes for a solution of the Israel problem. I happened to be having lunch with Yitzhak Ben-Zvi, the president of Israel, when a radio on the table announced the crash of Hammarskjöld's airplane in the Congo. I have rarely been so saddened by the death of a statesman.

Another remarkable personality I got to know in connection with the Israeli question was Jawaharlal Nehru, with whom the American diplomat Chester Bowles arranged an interview for me at the suggestion of Eleanor Roosevelt. I was to give Nehru my views on a Near Eastern federation in the hope that he might discuss the idea with Nasser, on whom he was known to have a strong influence. Our conversation took place in London. Nehru's attitude toward Israel was well known to be ambivalent. To me he acknowledged that if he had been consulted before the U.N. decision, he would have opposed the creation of a Jewish state in a country the majority of whose people were

Arabs, even though he recognized humanity's obligation, after the Nazi tragedy, to provide the Jewish people with a secure center of existence. However, since Israel was now a *fait accompli*, everything should be done to protect it and to prevent any armed aggression, which he categorically censured. I outlined my idea of a confederation, and it made a lot of sense to him. He promised to stop in Cairo on his way home and speak to Nasser, and this he did. Nasser is said to have replied that while the idea might provide the basis for an understanding, unfortunately its sponsor did not speak for Israel—his actual English words are said to have been, "Mr. Goldmann cannot deliver the goods"—and the Arabs would in no circumstances negotiate with Ben-Gurion. The Sinai campaign occurred soon afterward and of course put an abrupt end to all prospects of negotiations on even the most modest scale.

A Talmudic proverb says that what reason cannot accomplish is often accomplished by time. Unfortunately this is not always true, but despite the perturbing events of recent decades and the continuing tension in the Near East, I am sure that time will compel Israel, long before it will compel the Arabs, to seek a constructive solution to the problem.

Let us imagine that Zionism had emerged a hundred years before Herzl founded it and had been accepted by the peoples of the world. The creation of a Jewish state in Palestine would have encountered no difficulty with the Arabs. The Arabs of the eighteenth and early nineteenth centuries were unorganized tribes and people who lacked the political and military power to resist a decision by other nations. And now let us imagine that Zionism had proclaimed the idea of a state a hundred years after it had done so. There would then have been absolutely no prospect of its realization, because by that time the Arab countries will have dominated the Near East to a point where the whole world, try as it might, could not impose a Jewish state.

These suppositions have an inner meaning. The fact that Jewish nationalism in the form of Zionism and the Arab nationalism that led to the rapid creation of a number of Arab states both occurred during the same period of history is suggestive. This parallel evolution seems to me to indicate that the two nationalisms are condemned either to live together or to destroy one another. If they are prepared to co-operate, they will not only be doing themselves a service; they will set the whole Middle Eastern region, where they are historically destined to live, on the road to unhoped-for progress. If, on the other hand, they continue to tear one another apart, as it sometimes seems that they will, they may destroy each other, and the outlook for the Near East, which is preparing to become once again the great historical center it has been several times in the past, will finally collapse.

I cannot end this chapter without saying a few words about Moshe Dayan, whom I have come to know well only fairly recently. Dayan's position in the leadership of Israel is virtually unique. In the first place he is one of the only recognized leaders who, having been born in Israel, can speak legitimately for the *sabra* generation. The inevitable difference between the mentality of Israelis, who have grown up in their own country and their own civilization since birth, and the mentality of Diaspora Jews is exemplified in him.

The sabra generation is characterized by great audacity, sometimes bordering on temerity, combined in a remarkable way with a strong sense of reality. This completely different intellectual and emotional constitution sometimes makes it very difficult for someone like myself to predict how their representatives will react to events, facts, and situations. Since ideologies and so-called principles count for much less in the sabras' thinking and reactions than is the case with the older generation of leaders, a man like Dayan, uncommitted to traditional dogma or ideas, will not hesitate to shift his position with the circumstances. Moreover, he is perhaps the only Israeli leader who possesses unmistakable charisma.

Although my basic conception of Israeli foreign policy differs from his in crucial respects, it has been valuable to me to be able to talk and argue freely with him, not merely because he is a fascinating personality but because our exchanges have enabled me to acquire a better understanding of sabra psychology. Without doubt Moshe Dayan will play an important role in the history of Israel, especially when the time comes—and it is not far off—for the sabra generation to take over leadership.

24

Israel and the Diaspora Jews

The problem of the relations between a Jewish state and the Jewish communities living outside it has interested me in theory for many years, and since the founding of Israel I have had to deal with it in practice. In order to understand it properly we must take the historical background into consideration. Diaspora has played a role in the history of different peoples but never such a central role as it has with the Jews. Most other dispersed peoples simply disappeared in the course of history, and of course a huge proportion of Diaspora Jews has been lost to Jewry. (A Jewish historian once told me that the number of Jews in the world would amount to well over two hundred million if the descendants of all those who had once been Jewish still were.) In our history Diaspora has proved to be a way of life no less enduring and no less legitimate than life in a country of our own. Our history, whether we regard it as fact or myth, begins in Diaspora: the Egyptian one. After Moses led the people into their own country, where they lived for centuries, the state was destroyed by Nebuchadnezzar and Jewish life shifted to the Babylonian exile. Yet another Jewish state arose under Cyrus and Ezra; it lasted until the Romans under Titus destroyed it. That was the beginning of a two-thousand-year Diaspora, followed in 1948 by the founding of Israel.

This alternation between dispersion and homeland, often coexistence of Diaspora and statehood, is unique in the history of mankind. The somewhat naïve Zionist idea that a normal life is possible only in a homeland and that Diaspora life is in some way abnormal is understandable in the light of the historical evolution of other peoples, but it does not hold true for us. We have probably spent far more years of our historical lifetime in the Diaspora than in our own country and it makes no sense to characterize as abnormal a way of life that accounts for more than half of a people's historical existence. Diaspora is simply a characteristic condition of our history; paradoxically it might even be said to be more characteristic than statehood, which we share with hundreds of other peoples.

Because of this historical background, Zionism never proclaimed the complete ending of the Diaspora as one of its goals. Its aim was to provide the scattered Jewish communities, living always as minorities, with a homeland to which every Jew would have the right to go if ever he wished or needed to. This particular phenomenon in Jewish history—the existence of one branch of the people in a sovereign state and another, far outnumbering the first, outside it—naturally poses one of the great challenges to Jewish self-preservation. Other peoples who live— or whose vast majority lives—in their homeland take for granted certain safeguards of national survival, such as their territory, state, language, economy, and culture. Precisely these things are a constant source of problems to a people tied up in two so radically different ways of life. These difficulties have existed as long as the Diaspora because the Jewish people has been denied the normal means of self-preservation; it is a tribute to its genius that it survived at all in such circumstances. The creation of the Jewish state did not end the problem because it did not end the Diaspora. Now it was not merely a question of uniting the many scattered communities through ties of religion, nationalism, language, or culture, but of creating a new awareness of unity that would bring together in one great community the Jews who lived "normally" in their own country and the scattered minorities in the Diaspora. From this point of view the founding of Israel actually made the Jews' position in the world more complicated, although much more meaningful.

In the joyous excitement immediately following the proclamation of the state, people lost sight of its problematical side. They began to feel—especially the young people—that all their difficulties had disappeared. Many leaders, notably Ben-Gurion, made it appear that the state could be developed and defended by the Israeli Jews alone and all that was needed from the Diaspora communities was a helping hand. I was not one of those who fostered this illusion. I knew from the outset that it is a harder task to consolidate a state than to proclaim it, and that this commonplace is doubly true of a state born under such extraordinary conditions as Israel.

It was easy to foresee that the young state would need the utmost support from world Jewry at every step. Completely isolated politically from the first and not able to rely on a single genuine ally, it was in a far more difficult position than its Arab enemies, whose numbers, geographical size, and enormous oil resources made them much more interesting to the world powers than little Israel. Israel could count on political, economic, and, possibly, military help in the fight against the Arabs only if the millions of Jews in the rest of the world exerted all the influence and economic pressure they could command. For instance, it would be hypocritical or self-deceptive to deny that in decisions of American foreign policy concerning Israel and the Arabs, the political influence of six million American Jews plays a significant role, if only because their concentration in the great urban centers makes them a factor in elections. It is undeniable that to a certain extent the American government has to consider the wishes of Jewish voters and of many non-Jewish voters who are influenced by their Jewish compatriots. This sort of thing happens in any democratic state and is true to a lesser degree of many other countries.

It is now evident that this small country Israel, very poor in natural resources, is economically dependent upon world Jewry. If not for the massive financial support it has received from abroad, amounting over the years to three and one-half billion dollars, Israel would have collapsed under the burden of quadrupling its population in two decades, admitting a million and a half destitute immigrants, and meeting its tremendous arms budget. Even today Israel has by no means solved its economic problems and struck a sound balance between expenditure and income. Since it maintains a standard of living far above that of more primitive new countries, it is clear that for decades it will not be able to do without economic assistance from world Jewry.

In the cultural development of the state, close ties with world Jewry are even more important in the long run, though perhaps less conspicuously so. Israel is in great danger of becoming a small nation in the cultural sense, of falling victim to provincialism and relinquishing everything the country stands for to Jews all over the world and to mankind as a whole. Only through psychological and spiritual closeness to world Jewry, only through the mutual enrichment of the Diaspora by Israel and of Israel by the Diaspora, which has a share in many of the cultures of the world, can Israel become what might be called a "great small nation."

Of course, such a creative exchange is no less essential to the Jewish communities outside Israel than to Israel itself. One of the most tragic consequences of the Nazi disaster was the destruction of the great bulwark of Jewish culture, religion, and tradition in Eastern and Central Europe. Practically all the great ideas the Jewish people lived by in the nineteenth and early twentieth centuries and still live by today were born in these centers. Only a Jewish state with a culture of its own can replace them and become a true source of Jewish inspiration and creative spiritual and intellectual values. This is particularly true today, when anti-Semitism is on the decline and is no longer the unifying force it used to be, and when religion has lost its significance for most Jews. Without Israel as a source of new values to nourish Jewish cultural life, Diaspora Jewry could hardly survive. It is not easy to say whether the Diaspora is more indispensable to Israel or Israel to the Diaspora, but something that has always been obvious to me is now being realized more clearly in Israel than it was during the early years of enthusiastic statehood. The continued existence of both branches of the people can be ultimately guaranteed only by their taking full advantage of a constructive reciprocal relationship.

This, however, depends upon their working out some form of

co-responsibility and acquiring a sense of common identity, which is not easy. There are no contemporary models we can learn from. Such models may perhaps have existed in historical times in, say, the mutual influence between Babylonian and Palestinian Jewry or between Palestine and the European Diaspora in its early centuries. Other peoples do not face this problem even when they live relatively dispersed, as do the Irish, Greeks, and to some extent the Italians and Germans. Among these nationalities the members who live abroad are not vital to the existence of the homeland, whose population comprises the vast majority of the people. Eighty percent of us Jews live outside the homeland and nobody can predict how this percentage is likely to change in the next few decades, when Jews may begin to go to Israel voluntarily and eagerly and not primarily as a result of political and economic oppression.

The unique sort of relationship I have in mind between these two so dissimilar branches of our people presupposes many things. It requires first and foremost a realization of how important the principle of common responsibility and effort is. Even this cannot be taken for granted. There is a tendency in Israel to turn to Diaspora Jewry as a natural helper in times of need but to permit it no voice in shaping policies, to treat it as somehow inferior and of unequal status, and to entrust the future development of the country exclusively to its citizens. If this continues, Israel will go on receiving financial, economic, and political support from Jewish communities abroad but not on the requisite scale. World Jewry's enthusiasm for Israel will not forever remain what it was in the first few years after the almost miraculous realization of an ancient dream or what it became again after the spectacular victory of the Six Day War. For the younger generation of non-Israeli Jews the existence of the state is a given fact; at best they are happy about it, but they do not necessarily feel any sense of enthusiasm or shared responsibility. What needs to be brought home to them is the precarious position Israel will be in unless they do share the responsibility. They must realize that a people that wants to ensure its continuity must, whether it wants to or not, assume responsibility for everything it has done.

Many Jews are deterred from assuming this responsibility by an exaggerated feeling of obligation toward the country they live in and a fear of being accused of dual loyalty. Immoderate worship of the state has caused much trouble in the world. It began in the nineteenth century, reached its philosophical climax in Hegel, and finally culminated into the absurdity of the "thousand year Reich," which demanded of its citizens a loyalty precluding any other human impulse. Human life and culture are the antithesis of this fanatical loyalty. The richer the life of an individual or of a whole people, the greater number of loyalties it encompasses: loyalty to one's country and religion, to church, class, family and friends, and so on. Of course these loyalties may clash, in which case every individual must decide what takes precedence. But to rule out all other loyalties just because they might conflict with loyalty to the state is to revert to a primitive, brutal barbarism. Yet Jews are always hypersensitive in their patriotism, perhaps because they are never completely confident of their equality of status. One of the great tasks of Jewish politics is to demand that the non-Jewish world grant us the unconditional right of psychological and spiritual allegiance to Israel as something in keeping with our unique history and as a right to which history entitles us.

These remarks may sound excessively pessimistic, given the great enthusiasm and unexpected solidarity with Israel demonstrated by the vast majority of Diaspora Jews before, during, and after the Six Day War. In terms of the immediate situation, they may be so. In the long run, however, and from the perspective of history, I see no reason to retract my misgivings. It would be irresponsible and self-deceptive for Israel to think that it can permanently count on the sense of solidarity that inspired Diaspora Jewry in 1967. What shocked the Jews was not merely the anxiety that Israel might be militarily defeated, but the fear that this might be followed by the destruction of the state and a great proportion of its people—and the brutal, bombastic declarations of the Arab leaders and Arab propaganda did nothing to allay these fears. After the Nazi era, Jews all over the world fortunately became much more sensitive than they had been to any threat to their Jewish existence. It is difficult to say how much solidarity world Jewry will show if the direct threat of Israel's destruction is ever removed, but in my opinion the extraordinary episode of 1967 has not basically altered the unique problem of Israel and the Diaspora. It is just as essential today as it was in Israel's first twenty years of life to find a way—for which there exists no precedent—to give Diaspora Jewry a sense of partnership and shared responsibility in Israel's future and destiny.

Ever since the moment the state was founded, I have been trying to get these ideas accepted. If I had had my way, an attempt would have been made right at the start to link Israel with the Jewish populations of all other countries in some definite structure and to provide organized Jewry at least an advisory voice in Israel's vital affairs. In this age of national sovereignty (and paradoxically, an extreme sense of sovereignty was never stronger than it is today, when the formation of supranational bodies is greatly diminishing its significance as a political factor), this voice could not be expressed in the form of franchise. But even in some more modest form, such a demand would be regarded as too radical by a large part of world Jewry, wary of any expression of double loyalty, nor would Israel, in its present state of mind, be prepared to grant Diaspora Jews such rights.

Recognizing the impasse, I have tried to achieve two things at least: to expand the existing World Zionist Organization (WZO) into a body that would encompass world Jewry and Israel, and to secure for it certain vested rights, such as direction of immigration. Even this was not easy to do. My chief opponent was Ben-Gurion. After having been chairman of the Zionist Executive for years, he lost all interest in the organization as soon as the General Council decided, at its first meeting after the proclamation of the state, to transfer all functions concerning the inhabitants of Israel to the Israeli government. I was one of the few who opposed this separation of functions, because I realized that something that was a matter of course in normal countries might be inappropriate and even dangerous for us. A majority of the General Council voted for this division of authority—the Israelis out of enthusiasm for statehood, and the non-Israelis out of fear of dual loyalty. Ben-Gurion had to resign as chairman of the Executive (although I would have liked to see him retain this position even when he was prime minister of Israel) and, self-centered as always, turned his back on the Zionist organization. Soon afterward he adopted the ideological position that now that the homeland existed, Zionism no longer stood for anything but individual immigration to Israel. Since most Zionists, including the leaders, did not go to Israel, he began a campaign against the Zionist organization, accusing it of betraying its own program and of being meaningless and even a harmful influence. I do not need to emphasize the damage such a charge did to the prestige and moral authority of the Zionist organization, coming from the premier of Israel and a man of the historic stature of Ben-Gurion.

Ben-Gurion was not interested in other ways of organizing the Jewish people to collaborate with Israel. In a great debate in the Zionist General Council he stated his position in these terms: "We, the citizens of Israel, will build the state. You, the Diaspora, can only help." To this I replied: "The creation of the State of Israel with its unprecedented type of culture must, as the greatest achievement of Jewish history, be a common task in which both branches of the people share equal rights and responsibilities. I am, however, quite ready to recognize the Israeli branch as the 'senior partner.' "

This was the background of Ben-Gurion's opposition to my demands, endorsed by the World Zionist Congress, for a privileged position for the WZO in relation to Israel and for legally establishing its right to work in Israel. I succeeded, however, in getting the political parties, including Ben-Gurion's own Mapai, to accept my ideas, and after long negotiations, the Knesset passed the Law of Status for the Zionist Movement, on the basis of which a solemn agreement, the *Amanah,* was signed between the Israeli government and the WZO Executive. This has had several beneficial results. It has enabled the WZO or the Jewish Agency, in cooperation with the government, to bring in more than a million and a half immigrants and to absorb most of them, to establish hundreds of new settlements, and to share in many areas of the country's development through the funds raised on behalf of Israel in all countries of the world.

In this struggle I acquired the vital support of Moshe Sharett.

Apart, perhaps, from Chaim Weizmann in the later years of our relationship, Sharett was my closest friend among all the Zionist leaders. Our friendship went far beyond our practical work together. I cannot call to mind any serious conflict with him, although we had occasional differences of opinion over tactical matters. His career is well known. It included all the positions of honor that Zionism and Israel had to bestow. After being in charge of the political section of the Zionist Executive for years, he became Israel's first foreign minister and, later, its prime minister. Ben-Gurion finally forced him out of the government in a most brusque and ruthless manner. Sharett was an extraordinarily gifted man, especially remarkable for his phenomenal memory and talent for languages. He knew a number of languages perfectly, and was a brilliant creator of new terms in modern Hebrew.

Sharett's political talent was chiefly analytical. He never overlooked a single aspect of a problem and backed every demand he made with logical, meticulous argumentation. He was not so much the intuitive politician, exemplified by Chaim Weizmann, as a man who depended on systematic analytical reflection. At times he carried the principle of minutely substantiating everything to the point of exaggeration. I remember Weizmann saying to him: "When you're asking something of the Colonial Office or the Foreign Office, limit yourself to two or three telling arguments and leave out the minor ones. Otherwise you run the risk that when you get through the man you're talking to will forget the important arguments and remember only the minor ones." But this was impossible for Sharett. He was afflicted with the vice of perfectionism, if I may put it that way. Everything had to be just right. Every document he drafted, every letter he wrote, was revised and polished to make sure that every word was in its right position and sparkling with just the right luster. He wasted too much time and energy on minute details, but his esthetic sense and desire for perfection required this often excessive expenditure of effort.

As the first foreign minister of Israel, Sharett created the new Israeli diplomacy. It took courage as well as knowledge of human nature to train the young diplomats to think like statesmen. For centuries the Jews had expressed their reactions purely in the form of protest and criticism. Since the Diaspora never allowed them to create a political reality of their own, they had to content themselves with reacting passively or seeking escape in dreams, illusions, and wishful thinking. This explains their tendency to extremism, bitter accusations, radical demands, and hypersensitivity, not to say persecution complexes, all of which are typical of powerless, oppressed peoples. With the establishment of a country of their own, all this has had to be fundamentally changed. The Jewish people had to be trained in realism, in accepting compromise (which in practical politics is often more important than theoretical demands), and in making the best of what cannot be helped.

The first man to recognize that this takes more strength than is required for persistently trying to do the impossible was Chaim Weizmann; as a result, he was attacked for decades as a compromiser, a weakling, and even a traitor. Sharett, like me, was a pupil of Weizmann, and he too was often criticized for the same failings. It was also one of the reasons for the clash with Ben-Gurion that led to his sudden resignation. In most conflicts between Weizmann and Ben-Gurion, Sharett had taken Weizmann's side and Ben-Gurion knew it. Sharett also rejected Ben-Gurion's ideas on many points of foreign policy, although here he did not go as far as I did. Above all, he resisted the retaliation policy that Ben-Gurion pursued for years. It was easy for Ben-Gurion to override my opposition in these matters because I was not a member of the government, but he had to pay some attention to Sharett as foreign minister and leader of a group within the Israeli government. No doubt the decision to get rid of him before the Sinai campaign is explained by this opposition. It took Sharett a long time to get over this ruthless dismissal.

In character Sharett was one of the most distinguished figures in Zionism and Israeli politics, a true aristocrat who owed his splendid career almost entirely to his own positive qualities—an extremely rare occurrence. Of course, like everybody else, he had to pay a price for his virtues. They prevented him from being a real fighter and from using the necessary ruthlessness to enforce his ideas. Goethe's saying that the man of action has no conscience did not apply to Sharett. His scrupulousness merely diminished his effectiveness from time to time. To fight a political battle with irreproachable tactics is almost impossible, and Sharett was not a man to pound the table, to mobilize his supporters for defense and attack, or to consider his choice of means justified by his ends. On the other hand, these shortcomings lent him a moral position all his own. He became, especially in the last years of his life, Israel's great ethical authority, and while he was not feared and held in awe like other leaders, he was revered and loved more than any.

His attitude toward the Zionist organization and toward relations between Israel and the Diaspora was similar to mine. He supported these ideas as long as he was an influential figure in the Israeli government, and after he resigned I tried to get him to return to a leading role in Zionism. Having become president of the WZO in 1956, I suggested more than once that he become my co-president. This he refused, but I did finally manage to persuade him to become chairman of the Zionist Executive, a position that gave him the opportunity to perform important services. His presence increased the prestige and authority of the organization, especially in Israel. Since he was also a tireless worker and took care of all the routine details in which I was not much interested, he was a much better chairman than I would ever have been and gave the Zionist movement new impetus. I had always hoped he would succeed me as president, and his unexpected death was an irreparable personal loss and a severe blow to the Zionist organization. He played a decisive part in whatever limited success was achieved in rebuilding the WZO after the founding of Israel.

Moshe Sharett's successor as chairman of the Zionist Executive, Louis Pincus, immigrated to Israel from South Africa at an early age. I had persuaded him to accept the position of treasurer when Dov Joseph resigned, and as chairman he pursued with vigor and skill the principles that Sharett and I had established for the Jewish Agency's relations with the government and with the Jewish communities of the Diaspora. He succeeded in cutting down the membership of the Executive considerably, and since I had already secured passage of a resolution providing that Zionist personalities with no party affiliation could be coopted, the influence of the parties was somewhat diminished. (There are now good prospects that an expansion of the Jewish Agency Executive through the coopting of non-Zionist organizations, especially those responsible for raising funds for the Agency's work, will be carried through, and this will bring the ideas I have outlined here considerably closer to reality.)

Yet these rebuilding achievements were not, have not been, completely satisfying. The negative attitude of Ben-Gurion and many of his government officials prevented the *Amanah* from functioning effectively; only recently, under the government of Prime Minister Eshkol, did it begin to work more productively and without friction. Nevertheless, it has proved impossible to turn the Zionist organization into the sort of institution that history would have required it to be and that would have justified its existence. Many factors have prevented this, principally the negative attitude of Ben-Gurion and of many elements in Israel, notably the young who have been trained for years not to be content with ideas and watchwords, as the Diaspora Jews were, but to concentrate on performance, practical results, and success. How exaggerated this trend has become! It has led to a realism that is sometimes carried to absurdity and to a contempt for ideologies, theories, and ideals. The whole emphasis has been on victory, on building, on achieving tangible results, and gradually the idealistic framework Israel basically owes its existence to was cast aside as useless lumber. Zionism has become a term of contempt for many young Israelis, signifying impractical, out-dated idealism.

This attitude has naturally made it difficult to strengthen the authority of the Zionist movement in the Diaspora. Its strength lay traditionally in Eastern and Central European Jewry, both of which were wiped out. Zionism was never very strong in America, except for the brief years of struggle for the Jewish state. In the period following the First World War the Zionists withdrew from the mainstream of American Jewish life because of their exaggerated orientation toward Palestine. Within the great Jewish organizations of America the Zionist movement plays no important role, although many outstanding Zionists rose to influential positions through their services to the movement. Even fund-raising for Israel has passed into the hands of non-Zionists. This has made it practically impossible for the WZO to fulfill its most important task: to become the driving force in organizing the great majority of the Jewish people to collaborate with Israel.

Israel has demonstrated no greater interest in other organizations that might possibly have served this purpose. Ben-Gurion never showed anything but indifference and lack of understanding for the WJC, perhaps because he was unconsciously against a world Jewish organization that would have been harder for him to get along with than the existing multiplicity of bodies.

The final, and perhaps most decisive, difficulty was the obsolete structure of the WZO, which was organized politically according to Israeli political parties and their offshoots in the Diaspora. This structure was unavoidable and justified before the state existed, when the Zionist organization actually had a voice in the development of the Palestine *yishuv*. The moment the state took over this function—a state jealous of its sovereignty—the continued existence of these parties in the Diaspora became ideologically meaningless and from a practical point of view dangerous. Many Jews outside Israel, who could have accepted the new Zionist program as it was formulated in Jerusalem by the first Zionist congress to meet after the proclamation of Israel's independence, were not prepared to join a specific political party simply for the sake of becoming members of the Zionist organization. The parties, on the other hand, did not want to surrender their power and used their predominant position in the Zionist organization, along with their relatively ample funds and such authority as remained to them, for party purposes. This frustrated any effective attempt to transform them to accord with a comprehensive world organization designed to link the people with the state.

Since it was impossible to organize the vast majority of Jewry inside the WZO, I had to try another way. The major difficulty was the chaotic nature of American Jewry. Nearly all the American Jewish organizations wanted to stand by Israel and took pride in being among its champions, and since the number of these organizations was very great, the chaos became more and more intolerable and the duplication of effort was endless. There was no institution that could speak in the name of American Jewry as a whole, either to Israel or to the American government. One day the director of the Near Eastern division of the State Department showed me his appointments calendar. It was just after a very violent retaliatory action by Israel that, as usual, had been sharply censured by the American government. When this sort of thing happened, the Jewish organizations would ask for interviews in Washington in an attempt to allay the negative U.S. reaction, and the calendar showed appointments for the following days with six Jewish delegations, each of which would say the same things and make the same requests. "You will agree that this is impossible in the long run," he said. "No other minority in America would permit itself to send so many spokesmen and delegations to Washington." He asked me to do something to co-ordinate this pressure, and this was just the incentive I needed.

I managed to persuade Philip Klutznick, president of the B'nai B'rith and a farsighted, astute politician, and Rabbi Maurice Eisendrath, the dynamic leader of Reform Jewry, to join me in calling a conference of the presidents of all major Jewish organizations with the object of creating at least a loosely structured forum for the discussion of all American-Israeli questions. This was not easy because each organization was concerned for its complete autonomy and would not readily relinquish its independence and the publicity that went with it, but I finally managed to bring this Presidents Conference, as it was originally called, into existence. I was its chairman for a few years and it did a lot for Israel, particularly during the Sinai campaign. I then resigned the chairmanship to Klutznick. The forum grew stronger with time and became the Conference of Presidents of Major Jewish Organizations, which in recent years has included almost all international Jewish questions in its field of activity. This is the seed from which some day there may spring a body truly representative of American Jewry, at least in international matters. One organization, the American Jewish Committee, refused to join from the first. Although programatically it is in no way different from other bodies, it insists on doing everything independently.

Next I undertook to set up a similar forum on an international scale. I knew very well that I would never succeed in getting the strong, wealthy B'nai B'rith, that had just begun to address itself to international questions, or several other organizations, into the World Jewish Congress because of the ever-present considerations of prestige and autonomy. However, I persuaded Philip Klutznick to help me in forming an international Conference of Jewish Organizations (COJO) within which all branches of the WJC, as well as the organizations I have already mentioned and a number of other Jewish groups from outside, such as the English Board of Deputies, could meet regularly and discuss international Jewish problems. This was not supposed to be a functioning corporate body but an advisory, co-ordinating one. After lengthy negotiations it finally materialized, and the COJO was founded in Rome in 1958. It too performed useful work over the years in reducing to a common denominator the viewpoints of the various organizations on important international Jewish matters and sometimes it even initiated joint action, as in the case of the International Council for Jewish Education and its intervention with the Vatican concerning the debate on the Jewish question at the Ecumenical Council. The creation of these bodies relieved the chaos in Jewish public life, although it has still not been possible to establish the comprehensive world Jewish organization so sorely needed.

In June, 1967, after the extraordinary demonstration of Jewish unity and solidarity with Israel in the Six Day War, I decided to take advantage of this mood and extend the COJO both structurally and in scope. I submitted to the executives of the Jewish Agency and the WJC, and to a meeting of the COJO, a program for enlargement that would bring in many more organizations and extend the current range of the COJO to include Jewish questions of world politics, such as safeguards for Jewish existence, civil rights, preservation of the Jewish way of life, and problems related to the development of Israel and the promotion of a sense of Jewish identity in the rising generation of Diaspora Jewry. The goal of this program was to create a kind of Jewish world parliament that, while not having the right to make binding decisions, would provide a world forum for all shades of Jewish opinion, from the Lubavicher Rabbi to committed Jewish Communists, to meet once or twice a year and more or less draw up a balance sheet of the Jewish situation in all its various aspects: political conditions, the development of Israel, problems of education, the promotion of culture, and so on. An organization of this kind would be purely consultative and co-ordinating in character. Dispersed as the Jewish communities are, no such institution can claim the right to make binding decisions, particularly as many, if not most, of the constituent organizations insist on their so-called autonomy.

But negotiations to reorganize and expand COJO into a truly active body showed the difficulties to be almost insuperable. The major obstacle was the reluctance of the constituent organizations to relinquish the least degree of autonomy. For this reason the bold idea of founding a comprehensive world Jewish organization on the basis of COJO is impractical for the present.

Fortunately, however, recent years have seen a trend relating to the World Jewish Congress that raises the hope that it might evolve into such an all-embracing representative body. During the past two years important Jewish organizations in the United States, where the WJC was weaker than in any other part of the Jewish world, have joined it or are seriously thinking of doing so. If the WJC should succeed in getting the majority of American Jews to join, it could quickly become a representative Jewish body in fact as well as in aspiration. One of the major goals of my Jewish policy would then be realized.

I have spoken of some of my WJC colleagues in earlier chapters. Here I would like to mention two more whose collaboration has been very valuable to me in recent years. One is my friend Lord Sieff, for many years vice-president of the WJC, today without doubt the most respected and beloved of the leaders of English Jewry, and a man equally esteemed by Jews

throughout the world. Israel Sieff represents a remarkable synthesis of the forces that dominate Jewish life today. The son of
an immigrant from Lithuania, he came to England as a child,
deeply rooted in Jewishness. Co-founder with his brother-in-
law, Lord Marks, of Marks and Spencer, which is often said to
be a national British institution rather than a department store,
he is a man of universal culture and one of the few contemporary Jewish leaders who is a master of the art of living. Aristocratic in appearance and manner, he is a man whose friendship
brings with it enrichment of life. His prestige and mature
understanding of Jewish problems have made his co-operation
invaluable.

A younger co-worker who has made an important contribution to the work of the WJC in recent years is Armand Kaplan
of Paris, director of the political division. Kaplan has succeeded
in bringing most of French Jewry into the World Congress—a
feat I had been inclined to consider impossible—and has also
been of great assistance in establishing relations with the socialist countries of Eastern Europe. He has managed to make contacts with representatives of these countries, Jewish and non-
Jewish, as no other member of my staff has been able to do and
has made in this way an important contribution to one of the
major tasks of the Congress—a task which, but for him, would
be badly neglected today.

If, as we now hope, we should succeed in making the World
Jewish Congress the body universally recognized as representing world Jewry (and here increasingly active cooperation with
the World Zionist Organization is of prime importance), the
problem of the bond between the Diaspora Jews and Israel
would more easily be resolved. The changes that have occurred
with regard to the appreciation of the crucial importance of the
Diaspora Jews in Israel's future are a psychological indication
that perhaps there is at last a growing awareness in Israel that
without world Jewry or, as it is often called, Israel's only absolutely reliable ally, the country will have a difficult time in the
future. On the other hand, world Jewry is also beginning to
recognize the great dangers Jewish existence faces in the second
half of the twentieth century, particularly the danger of rapid

assimilation that overshadows all others. These fears are producing a great appreciation of Israel's importance as the strongest factor in the preservation of Jewish life. Such psychological changes give me reason to hope that some means will be found to link the people with the state in such a way that they feel mutually responsible for each other's destiny. It will require all the creative energies and inventiveness that a whole generation can command to produce these ties, to constitute the state of Israel in such a way that, while maintaining its sovereignty, it will be ready to give the Jewish people a voice in decisions and to create a Jewish Diaspora that will share responsibility for Israel while participating to the full in the life of its countries of residence. Only in this way can the two so dissimilar branches of the Jewish people mutually ensure their continued survival.

25

The Future of the Jewish People

To put it metaphorically, I feel that after the long years of ascent, I have now reached the peak of my career, from where I can survey once again the singular drama of the last fifty years of Jewish history while, by turning in the other direction, I can also distinguish the landscape of the future. An outsider familiar with the major events of those last fifty years will inevitably conclude that my generation has succeeded in overcoming the tremendous dangers threatening the Jewish people. Naziism, with its diabolical assault upon humanity in general and upon the existence of the Jews in particular, has been eliminated. Practically all over the world Jews have attained full civil rights, for which they struggled in vain during the nineteenth century and the early part of the twentieth. In countries where two or even one generation ago it was unthinkable that Jews should have civil rights, they are today in full possession of them and play a political role that even a few decades ago would have seemed utopian. At the same time, and probably as part of the same development, the economic situation of the bulk of world Jewry has visibly improved. Except perhaps for the brief golden age of Spanish Jewry, there has never been an era in all the centuries of Diaspora when the Jews have been as well off as they are today. Even in the Communist countries of Eastern Europe, they are economically no worse off than non-Jews. Today hunger and deprivation are no longer pressing problems of Jewish life, although of course poverty and misery occur, as they do among all peoples. And the crowning success, for which whole generations of Jews have striven, is their establishment of a Jewish homeland.

In the light of all these facts the achievements of my generation seem extraordinary and the Jewish people's situation looks unusually favorable. But if we are not content with admiring the splendid facade and take a look inside, where the forces that will shape the future course of history are gathering, we see something quite different, and when surface characteristics differ too radically from those beneath, there is danger of an explosion. This is true of our time in general. Man has never known such prosperity, and there can hardly have been another age when technical and scientific progress has been so overwhelming. Most peoples of the world are living more comfortably than ever before. And yet not only artists and scholars but somehow our generation as a whole feels that this appearance is deceptive and that humanity is now in one of the most critical, turbulent phases of world history. Hundreds of millions of human beings have awakened from centuries of oppression. Whole peoples are demanding their independence or have already gained it. The world is in a revolutionary ferment, as well as being torn by clashes of power politics that, for the first time in history, affect all mankind. Any moment a war may break out that, considering the atomic weapons of today, could mean the end of civilization, indeed of the human race. This is not the place to describe the countless symptoms of this situation; I merely wish to characterize an atmosphere of which the contrast between the magnificent exterior of Jewish life and its anything but splendid inner reality forms a part.

What troubles me are the centrifugal forces at work behind the gleaming facade of modern Jewish life. Returning to an earlier point, when peoples vanish from the stage of history, as often happens, it is not as a result of military defeats or oppression by their conquerors but because they have abandoned hope of asserting themselves against their all-powerful enemies and maintaining their resistance. In that case the people has not been destroyed by its enemies but has perished in a kind of suicide arising out of despair for its future. This idea is borne out most impressively by the history of the Jewish people, which, according to the normal laws of history, should have been wiped out long ago. If it survived desperate periods when there were perhaps no more than two million scattered, persecuted, despised Jews left in the world, it was because Jews never abandoned faith in their future as a religion and as a nation.

The great danger constantly threatening contemporary Jewry is its rapid erosion. Jewish strength sprang from two sources. One was resistance to persecution, the need to summon the last ounce of fortitude in order to hold out and to pass on the Jewish heritage from one generation to the next. The Jews were held together by an all-embracing solidarity. Even the Nazis' cruel extermination of millions of them had the positive effect of awakening in many who had been indifferent this sense of solidarity, the determination to remain Jewish. Still more important is the other source that sustained Jewish life and indeed shaped it down to its minutest detail: religion. For centuries the Jewish religion determined the identity of the Jewish people; it dominated the individual's life from his getting up in the morning to his going to bed at night and it provided Jewish communities, however small, scattered, and hard pressed they may have been, with a spiritual and emotional security all their own. This religion is what Heine so brilliantly called "the portable fatherland of the Jews." Driven from one country to another, they took with them into exile the Jewish law, in particular the *Shulhan Arukh*—the indispensable code for their own way of life. For the majority, though certainly not all of Jews today this foundation has either collapsed or is so weakened that the vital force, once so impressive, now seems to be almost a caricature of itself and can no longer be the psychological and moral basis maintaining the Jewish identity of the individual and the community.

These two mighty pillars of Jewish life have lost their vital role. Certainly there is still anti-Semitism in the world, but it is nothing like the menace it used to be, arousing in every Jew a sense of community and identity. The great majority of Jews feels neither persecuted nor discriminated against, although social and political anti-Jewish trends still appear. Essentially the

Jews are emancipated and can participate fully in the economic, intellectual, political, and cultural life of the non-Jewish world they belong to. So the future of Diaspora Jewry depends less upon the living forces of the Jews' own ethnic world, which was the decisive factor during their centuries of ghetto life; more than ever it depends, for better or worse, upon the environment that shelters them. This in itself indicates the weakness of the inner bastions of Jewishness and makes the State of Israel incomparably more significant for the future of Jewry.

In order to explore the prospects of Jewish evolution in the Diaspora, it is first necessary to examine what effect the civilization Jews live in at present has upon their survival. I recognize certain definite characteristics of our time that may decisively influence the continuing existence of the Jewish people. In the first place there is the general nature of our turbulent century. Even if the world succeeds in avoiding war, it will be shaken for decades by convulsive social and political upheavals and the pains of redistribution of wealth. This is what gives our time its harsh, none-too-tolerant tone. The nineteenth century—in Europe at least—was liberal and forebearing by comparison; and the Jewish minorities had ample opportunities for development too. This was a time of stability in which England, France, and later Germany, secure in their possession of world power, could grant freedom to their minorities. How much less sensitive mankind is today! Compare the outrage of Europe at Turkish atrocities during the Balkan wars (which took some ten thousand lives) with the totally inadequate reaction of the democratic powers to the extermination of several million Jews during the Nazi era and one will recognize the difference between the nineteenth and the twentieth centuries.

We are living in a time of mutual mistrust in which advantages are ruthlessly seized and maintained. Millions of underprivileged people are demanding their share of the riches of the world and brutally trying to enforce their claims. A period like this has little understanding for minorities as unimportant as the Jews. In the early postwar years the impact of Nazi atrocities aroused sympathy and understanding for our claims and doubtless this played a role in attaining the Jewish state. But the reaction is growing steadily weaker, and as long as the world is in a state of tension, the Jewish minorities will not be able to count on much help from other peoples in their fight for a separate existence.

Closely linked with this is another characteristic of our century: the increasingly exclusive absolutism of the state. The modern state, which grows more and more presumptuous, which penetrates into every sphere of human life and shows less and less respect for the special life of minorities, obviously derives its support primarily from the majorities that live in it. The fact that the Jewish and other minorities have full civil rights makes no difference. In many parts of the world the modern state arrogates the right to set up conditions that seriously impede the separate existence of minorities, especially a minority as nonconformist as the Jewish one.

Consider the situation of the Jewish minority in the Soviet Union. Soviet Russia is not an anti-Semitic country in the sense that Czarist Russia or pre-Communist Poland and Rumania were. The Jews of the Soviet Union enjoy full civil rights not only constitutionally but, by and large, in actual daily life, even though they are almost totally excluded from certain "sensitive" careers, such as diplomacy or the army, at least when it comes to the higher ranks. Yet at the same time this Jewish minority, the second largest in the world, which can look back at a truly creative past, is prevented from preserving its religious, national, and cultural identity.

Outside the Soviet Union too there are countries where Jews are not allowed to profess their allegiance to Israel or proclaim their Jewishness through membership in a Jewish world organization. The extent to which even libertarian countries like the United States arrogate the right to supervise the activities of special groups can be seen from one example. The Foreign Agents Act subjects any American citizen who belongs to an international organization with its headquarters outside the United States to financial and other supervision.

This growing worship of the state and the extension of its authority and functions are a threat to all minorities, especially the Jewish one. There have been eras when minorities had to fight for recognition and equality of rights; today their task is to uphold their right to a separate existence and to defend themselves against being swallowed up by the majority.

Another characteristic of our time particularly affects the idealistic element in Jewish youth. The Jews have never been content to promote only their own ideals. Like all outstanding peoples, they have recognized the universal human meaning of their ideas and realized that in fighting for their own rights they have been upholding the rights of other minorities and oppressed groups. For centuries they have been the champions of progressive ideas: socialism, communism, pacifism, and so on. During its centuries in the Diaspora, the Jewish people has taken pride in its role among the pioneers and revolutionaries of history.

One of the fundamental reasons for this historical position—though by no means the only one, as the materialist interpretation of history would claim—has been the fact that the Jews have always been among the disfranchised, weak, persecuted peoples. In recent decades, however, this situation has been radically reversed. As a result of political emancipation and great economic progress of most Jewish communities, they are no longer economic and social "have-nots" but members of the propertied class; they belong to the "haves" and are part of the status quo.

This reversal has also produced a change in psychological and ideological outlook. Jews are no longer automatically on the side of social reform or revolution. In many countries their elite belongs to the ruling class, either as an integral part of it or as associates and followers, and the shift in position can only be extemely detrimental to the idealism of Jewish youth, the most precious reservoir for our future. Our century offers an abundance of ideals and tasks for idealistic people; indeed, those opportunities represent the obverse of its brutal struggles and wars. Rights for oppressed peoples, races, and classes, rebellion against ruthless power politics, support of a peace-promoting world system, abolition of atomic weapons—these are some of the goals of idealistic young people. There is an obvious danger that upholding Jewish rights may no longer automatically imply commitment to these human ideals, and that danger would explain the tragic fact that hundreds of thousands of idealistic young Jews are becoming more and more alienated from Judaism.

In connection with these necessarily cursory notes on the nature of our time and its effects on the Jewish way of life, I want to discuss the possibilities open to present and future generations of Jews, as I see them. What forces can be relied upon in shaping the Jewish future? The simplest, yet by no means self-evident, force is the Jewish sense of solidarity: every Jew's identification with the great Jewish community, which stems from the will to aid the underprivileged and the suffering. It is not as dynamic as it was in times of brutal persecution, but there are still plenty of political, philanthropic, and social incentives to offer the right kind of encouragement. The essential factor here is constant co-operation between Jewish organizations on an international basis. Jewish isolationism has always ended in extinction for the isolated group. Today, when religion and national tradition and race no longer have the power to reinforce a sense of identity, it is more essential than ever that all Jewish activities be internationally co-ordinated.

Another even more important source of strength, but one much harder to tap, is the Jewish way of life, which needs safeguarding and preserving. For the branch of the Jewish people that continues Orthodox tradition, this problem has essentially been solved. But Orthodox Jews are in the minority. Even if the majority could be persuaded to adopt their rituals, as the spokesmen of Orthodoxy are always advocating, little would be gained, because practice without conviction would be meaningless. This brings up the extremely difficult question of the role of religion in Jewish life today, which most people do not understand, yet upon which the Jewish future depends to a great extent.

The majority of Jews, having discarded most traditions of Jewish life, who attend synagogue only occasionally or observe a few Jewish holidays, suffer no sense of loss but a simple regret that the traditions are too antiquated to be compatible with modern life. Orthodoxy, on the other hand, knowing that it has lost its dominant position and seeing no prospect of regaining it, is engaged in a desperate and often heroic struggle for self-preservation. It lives as if within a garrisoned fortress, struggling with all the strength it can muster to prevent a breach, and with the typical psychology of a declining, defensive minority, it refuses concessions or reforms. In its heyday, when it felt sure of itself, Orthodoxy was never rigid or conservative. It was able to shape Jewish life for so long because it was creative and accommodating, because it changed laws and traditions through bold, not to say revolutionary, reinterpretations designed to make whatever was involved applicable to different conditions of life. Contemporary Jewish Orthodoxy, conscious of its own inferiority and decline, has lost most of this creative flexibility. It is stagnating, and the more it is criticized, the more fanatical and rigid it becomes.

It is time for this problem to be understood fully. If it is not tackled with statesmanlike wisdom, there is no doubt that the gulf between the non-Orthodox majority and the Orthodox minority will continue to widen. This danger is particularly threatening in Israel, the only country where Orthodoxy has governmental functions—functions it often exercises in a very unwise way, arousing a real hate-psychology among many of the non-Orthodox, particularly among young people. The problem is so vital that even laymen and non-Orthodox Jews are justified in concerning themselves with it. To paraphrase Clemenceau, one might say that religion is too important to Jewish life to be left to the rabbis.

In my opinion, two things are essential if religious questions are to be submitted to public discussion. First, a recognized body representing Orthodoxy should be established, preferably in the classic form of a Sanhedrin, as great figures like Rabbi Maimon suggested. Only a group of this kind would command the courage and authority to introduce changes, reinterpretations, and reforms in the spirit of the *Halakhah*, the rabbinic tradition. Second, such an authority would have to be prepared to enter into a dialogue with the non-Orthodox Jewish majority and to set up a sort of ecumenical council for all shades of Jewish religious opinion. In that way a minimum of common Jewish rites consonant with the spirit of Judaism could be decided upon.

This kind of arrangement is all the more necessary since a serious danger exists that fundamentals of the Jewish way of life may be falsified through the integration of Jews into the cultures of the many countries in which they live. For example, there is an obvious possibility that in America the Jewish religion may so far accommodate itself to Christian creeds as to produce a "Jewish church." Such a result would be a complete travesty of the Jewish religion, which was never limited to the religious and churchly sphere but included national and cultural tradition. A vital task of a reinterpreted Jewish religion would be to restore the universality of specifically Jewish ideals. Ways must be found to enable Jews who commit themselves to great social and political ideals to do so as Jews.

Closely allied to this concept is the exploitation of a third great force, one that most nations can call upon as a matter of course: pride in one's history and cultural achievements. Again, certain conditions will have to be fulfilled if this force is to be utilized. First and foremost, every Jew must have a knowledge of the Jewish past, without which he cannot be proud of his people's contribution to human culture. There are few nations that can look back on their history with such pride, but for it to be taught effectively requires a comprehensive system of Jewish education. It seems to me that the Jewish future now depends on this most of all. It is a hundred times more important than the tasks of Jewish philanthropy and even more important than the struggle for political rights, yet until recent times the majority of emancipated Jews did not understand its importance. Happy at having escaped from the ghetto and at their acceptance by the free nations, they thought that to demand Jewish schools and a Jewish educational system would denote a regression to self-isolation, and they opposed it vigorously. Many of them still do. But more and more Jews who are concerned for the future of their people are beginning to appreciate the necessity of a Jewish education. To make one available is an extraordinarily difficult problem. It involves great funds, an army of educators and teachers, buildings, and literature. It means the Hebraizing of Jewish youth, to give it access to the great works of the Jewish past and the new works created in Israel, and it demands as a fundamental condition a firm conviction that Jewish survival will depend on it. It also requires many Jewish representatives and organizations to rethink ideas that date back to the nineteenth century.

An interesting example of those ideas is the opposition of the majority of American Jews to government financial aid for minority educational systems. Without government aid it will be much more difficult to create a Jewish school system, and it is hard to see why a Jewish or Catholic citizen who wants his children educated in a religious school should not have the same right to government support as one who prefers the public school system. The explanation for the opposition lies in the traditional struggle for Jewish emancipation and against interference by the Christian state. The fear is unfounded. It is quite conceivable that the government should give religious schools complete autonomy while providing them with the same support as the regular schools. It is entirely unnecessary to regard this as a danger in a modern democratic state; in England, whose democratic character nobody will deny, minority schools enjoy the same right to government support as public schools, provided they meet certain minimum requirements. The fight for a comprehensive system of Jewish schools and all forms of Jewish education should be given the highest priority among the tasks facing the present generation and the next.

The last and most important source of strength is the Jewish state. Its significance as the center of new Jewish life—and not merely for the citizens of Israel—needs no elaboration. Israel is already the source of countless inspirations and incentives. Apart from the soul-stirring experience of seeing a centuries-old dream become reality, the country has given the Jewish world a new feeling of pride. For the first time in history it has offered to the non-Jewish world a new image of the Jew—a Jew who fights and wins, who no longer lives on the economic and cultural fringes of other nations but cultivates his own land, creates his own social order, and fosters his own culture. Above all, the Jewish state has given the Jews of the world a new common task—

and any individual or any nation without a task is doomed. We are only just beginning to exploit this source of strength. The share of the Diaspora communities in the founding and development of Israel up to now has been chiefly financial and political; it must be greatly deepened and expanded.

The decisive problem in the relationship between Israel and the Diaspora concerns voluntary emigration of Jews from the free world to Israel. In the implementation of the Zionist idea a great paradoxical tragedy has taken place. I once formulated it (in a slightly exaggerated way) by saying that our tragedy was that when we got the State we had lost the people for it. The annihilated Eastern and Central European Jewish communities were the natural reservoir for large-scale immigration to Israel. Today this reservoir, except for the Soviet community, has been destroyed. No one can foretell when the Soviet Union will allow its Jews to go to Israel or how many of them would be ready to do so. Therefore, it is up to the Jewish communities of Western Europe and America to provide immigrants for Israel.

The present situation, with only one fifth of the Jewish people living in their own land, is untenable. In the next decades Israel, Zionism, and the Jewish people will have to face the supreme test of the readiness of the Jewish people to secure the existence of the Jewish state by bringing about a large-scale emigration of Jews from the Western world. It is an exceedingly difficult task. There are no examples in history of large numbers of people changing their conditions of life, not out of necessity, but out of choice. Zionism will have to prove its ability to provide psychological motives for such voluntary emigration.

For the millions who will not go to Israel, it will remain essential for them to feel they have a stake in the new country and share responsibility for it. It will take time and creative talent to work out their partnership with the citizens of Israel on a basis of common responsibility. But what can be done in Israel itself to help the state to grow into its new functions?

At first it was sufficient that a Jewish national home existed, that Jews had raised an army, were winning wars, and possessed their own parliamentary democracy. But every year the existence of the Jewish state is taken a little more for granted. For the generation born after Israel came into being, Israel is no longer automatically soul-stirring, no longer the realization of a historic dream. Israel will hardly have a hold upon these Jews unless it is something more than another sovereign power structure torn by internal party warfare, indistinguishable from other small countries. If Israel is to fulfill the ideals established over hundreds of years, from the Biblical prophets to the great modern revolutionists, it will have to be something other than that: it will need, as its ideological basis, the ambition to translate the age-old Jewish ideals into the realities of a new State and a new society. It is not a matter of wanting to be better than others or pretentiously different. A Jewish state that wishes to stand symbolically for a unique people with a remarkable history must live up to its uniqueness.

These reflections lead us to the basic problem of Jewish life after emancipation and the creation of the Jewish state. Modern Jewish history and Zionism, the great renaissance movement of the Jewish people, have shown two somewhat contradictory trends. On the one hand there has been the understandable urge to put an end to the Jews' exceptional vicissitudes, the inferiority forced upon them, their lack of a country of their own, their persecution, and to give them living conditions like those of other nations, that is to say, equality of rights wherever they live as minorities and a Jewish state for those who prefer their own country. These desires found their most eloquent spokesmen in modern Zionism, above all in Theodor Herzl, who knew very little of Jewish history and was brought to Zionism by the sufferings of the Jews. On the other hand, another school of thought was emerging that regarded the new achievements of the Jewish people, their recently attained equality of rights and most of all their state, not as ends in themselves but as essential prerequisites for transforming the specific ideas and values of Jewish culture into reality. This hope was most strikingly enunciated in the ideas of Ahad Ha-Am.

The more I reflect on the Jewish past and present now, toward the end of my career, the more convinced I become that the future can only be realized in a synthesis of these two trends: to enjoy equal rights and yet to remain different; to possess a state of our own whose pre-eminent duty nevertheless must be to become the spiritual center for Jews scattered all over the world. This dilemma was unknown to earlier generations; they remained Jews whether they wanted to or not. They were persecuted; they had to live their separate lives, and they had the heroic strength to remain true to Judaism. Today the question is fundamentally different. Not only are the Jews not forced to remain Jews; on the contrary, every single one of them is confronted with a hundred temptations and incentives to become less and less Jewish. Materially inclined Jews find satisfaction in the unlimited possibilities opened to them by their economic and political progress; the idealistically minded can commit themselves to the struggle for lofty ideas in this difficult, hard, bitter era that is not without a certain splendor. Today the task is to find entirely new incentives for being Jewish. Through long experience we have learned to remain Jewish in bad times; now we must learn something harder: to remain Jewish in good times.

This applies to the State of Israel just as much as to the Jewish minorities in the Diaspora. The danger of becoming satisfied with what we have already achieved, with the glory of statehood, the impressive military victories, the role we play in the world, small as it is, with our representation on international bodies, appointing ministers, being called "Your Excellency," and exchanging ambassadors, is a very serious danger for Israel today, twenty years after the birth of the state.

Everything in history has its price. The greater the success, the higher the price and the greater the danger. My generation secured victory in the epochal struggle for civil rights, but if we are honest with ourselves and do not flinch from facts, bitter and alarming as they may be, we face a paradox. I am convinced that the existence of the Jewish people, including the Jewish state, will be in greater danger than it ever was throughout all the centuries of persecution and suffering if we rest on the laurels our successes have brought us. The great problem facing the generations of today and tomorrow is to preserve Jewish individuality in an age of conformity. Our generation laid the groundwork that enabled Jews all over the world to obtain equal rights, both as individuals and as a people, and brought to its conclusion a long, tragic, heroic chapter in Jewish history. It remains for future generations to make use of this achievement in order to preserve our people's specific identity and to reshape Jewish life so that our survival may be not merely secure but justified, and the future be worthy of the past.

INDEX